PATHS TO THE
POWER OF
MYTH

PATHS TO THE POWER OF MYTH

Joseph Campbell
and the Study of Religion

Edited by Daniel C. Noel

CROSSROAD • NEW YORK

291.13
P297
c. 2

1990

The Crossroad Publishing Company
370 Lexington Avenue, New York, N.Y. 10017

Copyright © 1990 by Daniel C. Noel

Printed in the United States of America
Typesetting output: TEXSource, Houston

Library of Congress Cataloging-in-Publication Data

Paths to the power of myth : Joseph Campbell and the study of religion
/ edited by Daniel C. Noel.
     p.   cm.
Includes bibliographical references.   ISBN 0-8245-1024-0
   1. Myth. 2. Myth—study and teaching. 3. Campbell, Joseph, 1904–
4. Religion. 5. Religion—Study and teaching. I. Noel, Daniel C.
BL311.P38 1990
291.1'3'092—dc20   90-32746
                                                          CIP

Contents

Preface   vii

Abbreviations   xiii

Part One
The Religious Heroism of Joseph Campbell:
Overviews and Critical Appreciations

1   Dancing to the Music of the Spheres: The Religion in
    Joseph Campbell's "Non-Religious" Mythography   3
    William G. Doty

2   Living by Myth: Joseph Campbell, C. G. Jung,
    and the Religious Life-Journey   13
    Richard A. Underwood

3   The Thousand and First Face   29
    Walter B. Gulick

Part Two
Aspects of the Monomyth:
Eastern, Western, and Philosophical Assessments

4   Joseph Campbell and Eastern Religions:
    The Influence of India   47
    Harold G. Coward

5   Social Factors in Mythic Knowing:
    Joseph Campbell and Christian Gnosis   68
    Karen L. King

6   Joseph Campbell the Perennial Philosopher:
    An Analysis of His Universalism   81
    Robert A. Segal

Part Three
Mythic Power: Joseph Campbell's Symbols and Stories
in Contemporary Culture

7   Masks of the Goddess: A Feminist Response   97
    Christine Downing

8   The Flight of the Wild Gander:
    The Postmodern Meaning of "Meaning"   108
    David L. Miller

9   Harney Peak Is Everywhere:
    The Place of Myth in a Planetary Future   118
    Daniel C. Noel

10 Let Talking Snakes Lie: Sacrificing Stories   134
    Lynda Sexson

Appendix
Joseph Campbell and the History of Religions —
Two Reviews

11 The Dreams of Professor Campbell: Joseph Campbell's
    The Mythic Image   157
    Charles H. Long

12 Origins of Myth-Making Man   181
    Wendy Doniger

Notes   187

Contributors   208

Index   209

Preface

The aim of this volume is threefold: to assess the intellectual achievement and popular appeal of the late Joseph Campbell, to explore major issues in the theory of myth (mythography) suggested by Professor Campbell's work, and to demonstrate the resources of the academic study of religion for addressing mythographic themes. The contributors to the collection are all scholars and teachers in the field of Religious Studies, employing one or more of its methodologies and with a particular interest in the fascinating but complex topic of myth.

This is only appropriate, since the nature of myth is inextricably tied to religious belief and practice — in their widest possible definition, to be sure — and these essayists are especially well-equipped to illuminate the connection. Here are *interpretive* paths to what Joseph Campbell's widely-acclaimed public television series (with its accompanying book) has called "the power of myth." The ten original essays and two reprinted reviews assembled in the present anthology contribute informed vantage points on what he meant by that evocative phrase while indicating implications he may have neglected.

Certainly the power he had in mind has much to do with the "religious" level of personal involvement, the passionate conviction and motivating framework of values, reflected as well as fostered by myth in our lives and culture. This is notwithstanding the fact that such shaping often operates half-consciously — or even that in modern parlance the term "myth" is taken to be synonymous with deceptive falsehood or that Professor Campbell disdained the term "religion" as indicating a narrowly orthodox dogmatism!

•

Fortunately, Joseph Campbell himself has done more than anyone to restore the positive meaning of the first term, while the contributors to this collection amply unravel the irony of his use and non-use of the second. In the opening essay by William G. Doty it is made immediately evident that although in many respects the distance Campbell maintained between his mythographic views and any *official* religious body or theology was part of his appeal, a deeper ingredient of that appeal was the unofficial religiosity, or spirituality, he both promoted and manifested.

Doty, author of the award-winning text *Mythography: The Study of Myths and Rituals*, provides us with an overview of Campbell's achievement that establishes a foundation for the discussions by the other Religious Studies scholars to follow. Professor Doty demonstrates that when Bill Moyers, as Campbell's television interviewer, characterized his mythography as "dancing to the music of the spheres" he properly implicated this self-avowed maverick in a sacred activity, a religious ritual.

Myths are also, says Richard A. Underwood, ways of understanding the passage through the stages of life as a religious journey. In his appreciative essay he focuses on the centrality of the psychological function in Professor Campbell's view of myth, showing us how C. G. Jung's notions of the mythic ramifications of personality development influenced Campbell to translate the traditional religious life-journey into terms applicable to the modern individual. For Campbell, this makes of myth something we can actually "live by" today, a guiding model for private psycho-spirituality (and thus, again, an implicitly religious phenomenon). Professor Underwood, an officer of the Society for the Arts, Religion and Contemporary Culture — of which Joseph Campbell was once president — reveals as well where Campbell departs from Jung by "re-visioning" the latter's depth-psychological version of the journey through life in what he saw as aesthetic and shamanic directions that were, in Underwood's word, "Buddhist-like."

The first section of the volume ends by examining another overarching theme in Campbell's work along with the religious quality of myth and its personal applicability: the nature of "heroism." Walter B. Gulick, convener of a Consultation on Myth for the American Academy of Religion (the major professional society of Religious Studies scholars), exploring how Joseph Campbell's activities as a thinker and writer may have exemplified their own brand of heroism, develops concepts to clarify that issue. From Gulick's perspective, "existential meaning" — which might also be called "*lived* meaning" — is an idea that addresses Campbell's oft-noted comment that myth gives us not "the meaning for life" but "the experience of being alive." What Professor Gulick refers to as the thousand and first face of the hero, then, describes Campbell himself in his attempt to make this existential meaning available through his writings.

Joseph Campbell, we know, named his central myth of the hero "the monomyth," the one pattern of meaning underlying the diversity of its expressions. This could even be said, given the thrust of his mythography, about *all* myths: each face or mask is an inflection, he claimed, of the single shared essence of myth.

But this one essential mythic meaning does contain a multiplicity of expressions, and here the special expertise of scholars in Religious Studies is pertinent in judging how successfully Professor Campbell interprets the main components of the world monomyth. Harold G. Coward, for instance, is a specialist in south Asian spirituality who has written, among several volumes, *Jung and Eastern Thought*. His assessment of Campbell's use of the themes of Hinduism and Buddhism indicates that of all the world's religious traditions those of India were the most attractive to the late mythographer. Accordingly, as Coward details, Campbell was in turn more faithful to the convictions and style of Indian spirituality than to any other religions — although even the traditions of India, like the psychological emphases of Jung, were not fully acceptable to his maverick vision.

William Doty and others have remarked on Campbell's dismissive attitude toward another primary ingredient of the worldwide monomyth: the mainstream Western religions of Judaism, Christianity, and Islam. This is the biblical tradition in which most of Professor Campbell's readers were reared — as he was — but from which many of them are no doubt somewhat disaffected: hence their positive response to his attitude. And yet there was a strand of this tradition that found favor with Campbell, and it is his relation to the Christian variants of the ancient Gnostic esotericism of "those who know" (*gnosis*), such as in the controversial Gospel of Thomas, which Karen L. King appraises. As the editor of her own recent anthology, *Images of the Feminine in Gnosticism*, Professor King gives us a discerning view of the aspects of Christian gnosis that most appealed to Campbell — especially its goal of individual enlightenment — as well as those that he failed to take into account — above all the extent to which Gnostic beliefs were shaped by the social values of their time and place.

The assessments of specific components of Joseph Campbell's monomyth in Part Two close with a philosophical analysis of an issue that touches many of the other contributors' angles of vision on his work. Robert A. Segal, a philosopher of religion whose *Joseph Campbell: An Introduction* was the first full-length critique of the popular figure, focuses his essay on the conflict between "particularists" and "universalists" in the comparative study of myths and religions. Segal refers to a debate over the nature of Jewish mysticism in making the point that Campbell was finally an arch-universalist of the "perennial philosophy" variety: those thinkers who see the core of religions as at once mystical and universally shared. Professor Segal also importantly underlines with his rigorous dissection the likelihood that those who are most in disagreement with Campbell's views are particularists, unconsciously if not deliberately.

Certainly the particularist/universalist split lurks between the lines of Part Three, where four essays try, through critical reflection as well as sympathetic extension, to "dream Campbell's mythography onward" into our cultural present and future. Christine Downing, whose work on the religious psychology of women has led to books like *The Goddess* and *Psyche's Sisters*, concentrates from a feminist perspective on Professor Campbell's handling of the goddess figures in mythology. She takes us through some of the particulars of his surprisingly affirmative reading of such figures, almost all of it produced before the most recent wave of feminism with its lively interest in women's religious experience. However, while Professor Downing is highly appreciative of Campbell's contribution in this regard, she goes on to show that an inevitably male bias blinded him to "masks" of the goddess that have psychological as well as mythic ramifications for both women and men in contemporary culture.

And this is a culture, David L. Miller hastens to remind us, that is being increasingly designated not only as "postpatriarchal" (at least in the expectations of many) but as "postmodern." The meanings of this latter term admittedly vary from avant-garde fashions to philosophical criticism in the arts; Professor Miller seeks to place Joseph Campbell's thought at the more serious end of the spectrum of postmodernisms by pursuing further the crucial issue earlier raised in essays by Underwood and Gulick. In discussing the question of how and whether myths provide "meaning" for life, Miller decides that for Campbell — preeminently in his lecture "The Symbol without Meaning" — the power of myth lies, ironically enough, in its *absence* of denotative meaning, its semantic powerlessness born of "disengagement" from all familiar reference-systems of belief. Miller, who has been mounting a mythic or "theopoetic" re-visioning of Christian theology in such works as *Christs, The Three Faces of God*, and *Hells and Holy Ghosts*, proposes a Campbell whose views, beyond echoing those of India, advance a purportedly re-emergent hunter-food gatherer spirituality appropriate to the postmodern world.

Professor Miller concludes by inferring another irony in Joseph Campbell's postmodern vision, especially when it is compared with Jung's similar perspective. My own contribution, in effect, treats this same irony: Jung worried that disengagement, the heroic ideal of Promethean freedom, could carry a psychological "shadow" of *repressed beliefs*, chaining us all the more unhealthily to the rock of unconscious compulsions. "It soars above the earth and above mankind," Jung wrote of this ideal (as Miller quotes him), "but the danger of its sudden collapse is there. . . ."

Jung's imagery suggests the version of the postmodern that is the concern of my essay: the so-called Space Age with its "whole-earth" or planetary prospects. Having become convinced in my book *Approaching Earth* that the mythic significance of the Space Age involves a "terrestrial reconnection" along with — or as an opportunity afforded by — space flight, I find Joseph Campbell's laudable attention to the moon walk and earthrise of the late sixties interacting in a most troubling fashion with his promotion of the semantic disengagement he inferred from myth. Campbell's sort of "global spirituality," I surmise, harbors dangers for the future of myth, which seems to need its *local* attachments to the planet in order to survive no less than do art and shamanism (despite his dubiously metaphysical reading of these latter).

On the other hand, as I happily acknowledge, Professor Campbell honored such attachments in the practice of his writing and storytelling if not always in his mythographic theory. This felicitous practice, in turn, spawns its own ironies, which comprise the topic of Lynda Sexson in our final original contribution. Sexson is not only a teacher of Religious Studies and the author of *Ordinarily Sacred* but also a fiction writer whose recent collection of stories, *Margaret of the Imperfections*, has won wide critical praise. She is therefore an ideal commentator on Campbell the storyteller, who helped keep the narrative core of myths alive while ignoring its theoretical implications and who dismissed the mainstream Western religions while sponsoring their fixation on heroic sacrifice in the tales he found most worth telling! Professor Sexson's concluding essay on these conundrums can leave us wondering — which is, after all, the way of stories — with questions of assessment and interpretation not fully answered, open to the onward dreaming of Joseph Campbell's mythography and of the mythic itself.

•

It will be noticed that each of these ten essays begins with an epigraph quoted from *The Power of Myth*, the book associated with Professor Campbell's public television series of 1988 (re-shown often since then). Even readers who have not followed Campbell's work over the years are likely to have seen or read these engaging conversations with Bill Moyers. Consequently it was felt that a connection to them would be an effective way to initiate the experience of reading this collection as a whole — signalled by its main title — and its individual contributions.

Nonetheless, as I have tried to sketch out here by way of a preview, these essays offer not merely access to the implications of one popular media event but also, beyond that, "paths" to the power of myth more generally — as Joseph Campbell saw that power over a long career or, in some cases, did not see it. The Appendix, with its important reprinted reviews by the noted historians of religion Charles Long and Wendy Doniger, makes it clear that the threefold aim of this volume entails serious discussion of a topic deserving that seriousness, and by scholars from a field whose formal study directly applies to such a discussion.

And yet, finally, serious examination of the power of myth, even by professors, as Professor Campbell most winningly displayed, need not be so technical as to be unengaging for interested newcomers to his concerns from in or out of academe. It is our hope that following the paths of these essays will prove to be a thought-provoking and imaginatively-empowering journey.

•

The editor should like to express his deep appreciation to all contributors and to three persons whose support has been indispensable to the success of this project: to Cathie Brettschneider, for helping to launch it; to Frank Oveis of Crossroad, for helping to bring it to completion; and to Terrie A. Murphy, for all sorts of a-muse-ments in between.

DANIEL C. NOEL

Brattleboro, Vermont
Winter Solstice 1989

Abbreviations

Joseph Campbell's principal works are cited as follows in contributors' endnotes:

Creative Mythology   *Creative Mythology*, vol. 4 of the Masks of God series (New York: Viking Press, 1968; paperback, 1970; paperback reprint: Penguin Books, 1976).

Flight   *The Flight of the Wild Gander: Explorations in the Mythological Dimension* (New York: Viking Press, 1969; paperback: Chicago: Regnery Gateway, 1972).

Hero   *The Hero with a Thousand Faces*, Bollingen Series XXVII (New York: Pantheon Books, 1949; Meridian paperback, 1956; 2d ed.: Princeton, N.J.: Princeton University Press, 1968; paperback, 1972).

Historical Atlas 1/1   *Mythologies of the Primitive Hunters and Gatherers*, part 1 of vol. 1, *The Way of the Animal Powers*, of the Historical Atlas of World Mythology (San Francisco: Alfred van der Marck/Harper & Row, 1983 [bound with *Historical Atlas 1/2*]; paperback, 1988).

Historical Atlas 1/2   *Mythologies of the Great Hunt*, part 2 of vol. 1, *The Way of the Animal Powers*, of the Historical Atlas of World Mythology (San Francisco: Alfred van der Marck/Harper & Row, 1983 [bound with *Historical Atlas 1/1*]; paperback, 1988).

Historical Atlas 2/1   *The Sacrifice*, part 1 of vol. 2, *The Way of the Seeded Earth*, of the Historical Atlas of World Mythology (New York: Alfred van der Marck/Harper & Row, 1988; paperback, 1988).

Inner Reaches   *The Inner Reaches of Outer Space: Metaphor as Myth and as Religion* (New York: Alfred van der Marck/Harper & Row, 1986; paperback, 1988).

Mythic Image   *The Mythic Image*, assisted by M. J. Abadie, Bollingen Series C (Princeton, N.J.: Princeton University Press, 1974; paperback, 1983).

Myths to Live By   *Myths to Live By* (New York: Viking Press, 1972; Bantam paperback, 1973).

Occidental Mythology   *Occidental Mythology*, vol. 3 of the Masks of God series (New York: Viking Press, 1964; paperback, 1970; paperback reprint: Penguin Books, 1976).

Open Life   *An Open Life: Joseph Campbell in Conversation with Michael Toms*, foreword by Jean Erdman Campbell, selected and ed. John M. Maher and Dennie Briggs (Burdett, N.Y.: Larson Publications, 1988).

Oriental Mythology   *Oriental Mythology*, vol. 2 of the Masks of God series (New York: Viking Press, 1962; paperback, 1970; paperback reprint: Penguin Books, 1976).

Power   *Joseph Campbell: The Power of Myth with Bill Moyers*, ed. Betty Sue Flowers (New York: Doubleday, 1988).

Primitive Mythology   *Primitive Mythology*, vol. 1 of the Masks of God series (New York: Viking Press, 1959; paperback, 1970; paperback reprint: Penguin Books, 1976).

Skeleton Key   *A Skeleton Key to Finnegans Wake*, with Henry Morton Robinson (New York: Harcourt, Brace, and World, 1944; Viking Compass paperback, 1961).

PART ONE

The Religious Heroism of Joseph Campbell: Overviews and Critical Appreciations

1

Dancing to the Music of the Spheres:
The Religion in Joseph Campbell's
"Non-Religious" Mythography

William G. Doty

In Japan for an international conference on religion, Campbell overheard another American delegate, a social philosopher from New York, say to a Shinto priest, "We've been now to a good many ceremonies and have seen quite a few of your shrines. But I don't get your ideology. I don't get your theology." The Japanese paused as though in deep thought and then slowly shook his head. "I think we don't have ideology," he said. "We don't have theology. We dance."

And so did Joseph Campbell — to the music of the spheres.[1]

You cannot reflect, as do Bill Moyers and Joseph Campbell in their popular video series, *Joseph Campbell and the Power of Myth*, upon such issues as sacrifice, the question of eternal life, the nature of goddesses and gods, ethics, and the nature of divine and human love, without engaging *religious* or even *theological* issues that one would expect to find discussed within the context of academic Religious Studies. (When I use "Religious Studies" or "the profession" in this chapter, I am referring to the academic study of religions to be encountered in university departments of "Religious Studies" or "Religion.") Hence there is a certain irony in my title when I refer to Campbell as a "non-religious" thinker, since so much of his published thought is religious, even proactively so. On the other hand, he is "religious"

3

in a way that would not ring true to many conventional expectations about a religious person in the West, and he self-consciously claimed (in the video episode called *The Hero's Adventure*) that his way of being a "maverick" was the source of much of his own creativity.[2]

As a practitioner of Religious Studies for twenty-five years, I can witness that Campbell's impact within that academic field has been "soft" indeed, even while he has disseminated mythography (the analysis and content of myths) throughout the artistic and learned world of America. His first major work, *The Hero with a Thousand Faces*, for instance, published at the start of his academic career, may well be one of the most widely-cited books used to analyze American art and literature. And recently the editor of an art journal for which I am a critic told me that the recent spate of Campbell-inspired articles they were receiving had led the staff to declare a temporary moratorium on anything utilizing Campbell's approaches!

I'm not one to argue for simple causation: there are probably several reasons for the state of affairs in which Campbell has had such an impact both within the arts and within what normally would be thought of as part of the *subject matter* of Religious Studies — the personal religiosity of his readership — even while at the same time he is not widely recognized within (and does not himself acknowledge) the field of Religious Studies itself. But surely one important explanation for the amazing popularity of this scholar's work over the long run, with books beginning in 1943, and more recently, over the short run, with the astonishingly wide acclaim for the television series and its associated printed version edited by Betty Flowers, *Joseph Campbell: The Power of Myth with Bill Moyers*, is very clear. That explanation is that Campbell provided an ostensibly "non-religious" approach to the understanding of religious experience at a time when many well-educated persons had turned away from formal participation in religious institutions. At the same time, there are ample (if sometimes ironic) reasons to see a genuinely religious core in his approach and to assess that mythography from the standpoint of Religious Studies.

Against Religious Literalizing

To begin with, such well-educated people still had many *religious* questions and a general attraction toward what is increasingly called "spirituality" — the individual quest for spiritual meaning, often pursued today by "the unchurched," or by "New Age" groups and writers. Campbell's appeal was and perhaps is by and large to just these sorts of readers, and that he has a wide readership outside more traditional religious contexts cannot be denied. I well remember obtaining first editions of his Masks of God series during the decade following 1959. They were selections of the Book Find Club, which was selling simultaneously books such as Seymour Hersh's decidedly non-religious *Chemical and Biological Warfare!* Certainly Campbell fed the anti-theological spirits by claiming that theology — by which he always meant time-hardened dogmatism — misinterpreted and reduced myth:

> Wherever myths are still living symbols, the mythologies are teeming dream worlds of such images. But wherever systematizing theologians have appeared and gained the day...the figures have become petrified into propositions.[3]

By the time of his 1986 book, *The Inner Reaches of Outer Space*, the culprit is not so much theology as *literalizing*, that is, "misreading metaphors, taking denotation for connotation...dismissing the metaphors as lies."[4]

But while Campbell's point about the literalizing of metaphors is a strong one, it is one reiterated by many philosophers, Religious Studies scholars, and even some theologians (notably Paul Tillich, Karl Barth, Owen Barfield, Robert Scharlemann). Hence it is too bad that Campbell did not find it useful to engage frontally much of this and related mid-twentieth-century scholarship: his work could have been enriched by dialogue with Mircea Eliade, the historian of religions at the University of Chicago whose works certainly *were* widely discussed within Religious Studies contexts (Campbell cites Eliade's early works a few times); with Charles Long or Wendy Doniger or Huston Smith, each of whom was working in similar research areas; or with contemporary philosophers treating myth, such as Paul Ricoeur or Hans Blumenberg,[5] or cultural anthropologists who have written widely on the topics of symbolism, metaphor, ritual, and myth such as Claude Lévi-Strauss, Clifford Geertz, or Victor Turner.

A scan of secondary studies that treat the work of Joseph Campbell, following the helpful bibliography gathered by Robert Segal for reviews and general articles, discloses a fact that will surprise no one in Religious Studies: until the present volume, his work has been reviewed and discussed primarily outside that academic field.[6] Eleven general essays on, or discussions of, Campbell appeared in publications unrelated to Religious Studies, as opposed to only five in the journals of the profession. With respect to reviews, only 14 appeared in the professional journals, as compared with 108 elsewhere. A computerized bibliographic search found nothing when queried for the combination "Joseph Campbell" + "Religious Studies." According to some of the objective standards by which we identify activity within the profession, then, it is clear that Campbell has been ignored pretty effectively up to now by the professional scholars working in the disciplinary field for his main subject-matter.

Campbell repaid the compliment by not referring to the professional journals or monographs, either. The reader seldom finds a reference to a current Religious Studies journal, and the key figures from whom Campbell drew inspiration were not contemporary but from previous generations of scholarship. Certainly these references are still of value to Religious Studies: in referring to the work of Leo Frobenius, Adolf Bastian, Heinrich Zimmer, and Carl Jung, Campbell provided a very rich revisioning and re-exploration of some important figures. In his constant recourse to Romantic philosophers such as Friedrich von Schlegel, Friedrich Nietzsche, and Arthur Schopenhauer, he likewise drew into his work concepts from important thinkers. And in terms of pointing us repeatedly toward Eastern religions, Campbell directed attention to important non-Western resources in a manner that was effective as well as comprehensive. But he often seems quite unfair in approaching Western religions,[7] and his explicit preference for Kuṇḍalinī Yoga (in *The Mythic Image*) seems of rather dubious value for contemporary Western religious life,[8] insofar as it is taken to represent advice to retreat from the clash of the competing myths of the daily world into one's own private spiritual garden. (Admittedly, some of his more narcissistically-inclined readers have no doubt found such an overemphasis on the "inner" *appealing!*)

What has seemed more appropriate and attractive to a very wide range of Americans has been the sort of direct comparative analysis featured in Campbell's televised comments upon mythical features of contemporary cultural expressions like the film *Star Wars*. The second quarter of the century witnessed a widespread movement within Christian theology and biblical interpretation known as "demythologization"; it was an attempt to recognize that the biblical materials were products of particular historical situations that were quite distant from the modern worldview. Demythologizers argued that such myths ought now to be re-interpreted and re-imagined in terms of contemporary concepts. In many ways what Campbell does with Eastern and ancient mythology (less frequently with that of the New World or Australia) could be termed a sort of demythologization in reverse: he shows the significances of contemporary materials such as *Star Wars* by reading *them* in terms of their *ancient* models.

Already in 1949, at the beginning of his career, Campbell had established in *The Hero with a Thousand Faces* this "counter-demythologizing" style that goes a long way toward explaining the popular appeal and usefulness of his work. It brought into mutually-illuminating juxtaposition contemporary and mythic events:

> The latest incarnation of Oedipus, the continued romance of Beauty and the Beast, stand this afternoon on the corner of Forty-second Street and Fifth Avenue, waiting for the traffic light to change.[9]

That same spirit of interpretation of contemporary culture was evident in the entertaining suggestion in *The Power of Myth* that religions are rather like computer programs:

> You must understand that each religion is a kind of software that has its own set of signals and will work.[10]

Or one might cite the many images from modern authors whose extensive archetypal backgrounds Campbell demonstrates; or throughout the video series, the immediacy with which he engaged Moyers' questions about contemporary social values and behaviors.

In all of his works he took very seriously indeed another way in which demythologization had a strong impact on mid-twentieth-century religion. I mean the philosophical critiques that produced the widespread acknowledgement that contemporary cultures are no longer ruled by the religious establishments, that "what we have today is a demythologized world,"[11] one in which sacred myths are relegated to the garbage dumps of a profane or secularized modernity. Campbell was writing about "The Secularization of the Sacred" (chapter 6 of *The Flight of the Wild Gander*) or "The Death of 'God'" (chapter 9 of *Creative Mythology*) right alongside the theologians debating such issues, but without using their traditional theological vocabulary.

Of course in spite of these emphases, mythophile Campbell was something of a religious *re*-mythologizer as well, since he continually sought to alert readers to the mythic dimensions of their own lives and of contemporary literature and the arts. Moreover, again and again Campbell refers to myth in such a manner that one can substitute for it the word "religion," and in spite of his animus against

Christianity and Judaism,[12] his avowedly non-religious mythography provides a helpful introduction to the study of religion as a general phenomenon, to the study of the history of religions as a whole, and to the psychology of religious behaviors and the technical subfield known as "religion and literature."

While leading a series in which an audience viewed and discussed the PBS videotapes, I found repeatedly that persons in the audience responded to the tapes by asking classical theological and metaphysical questions — a response that in itself signals the presence of religion in Campbell's mythography. While several of them resented Bill Moyers' raising what they felt were questions inappropriately derived from Judeo-Christian debates, they wondered why they'd never heard of Campbell in their churches or synagogues. The fact is that Campbell was "doing" religion all along, but in a non-religious guise, and he was encouraging readers to follow his example, as we could confirm from any number of quotations, as for example:

> The images of myth are reflections of the spiritual potentialities of every one of us. Through contemplating these we evoke their powers in our lives.[13]

Or:

> In this life-creative adventure the criterion of achievement will be, as in every one of the tales here reviewed, the courage to let go the past, with its truths, its goals, its dogmas of "meaning," and its gifts: to die to the world and to come to birth from within.[14]

For many people Campbell has been the entrée to self-exploration of the psyche or soul, involving personal journal-keeping and dreamwork as well as the long-range studies of mythico-religious resources whose significance writers for the mass media, such as *Self* and *Money*, seem never to have learned to recognize. Following group viewings of the video series, I was confronted by a wide range of intense questions: How is the path of the heroine different from that of the hero? How can you "follow your bliss" when confronting people who are suffering terribly? How can the conservative Christian movement ignore so totally the worldview that has been shaping itself since the seventeenth century? Why don't religious groups realize that the issues Campbell raises are the *real* concerns of our lives, instead of dead patriarchal issues left over from ages past? How can sacrifice be seen as anything other than as neurotic aberration? Why don't we hear in our schools about themes and mythic images such as Campbell treats? Are there ways to bridge from Campbell's individualistic perspectives to direct political changes in the public morality of this country?

The questions are not simple ones, and I had to point repeatedly to the neglect of reflection upon moral and spiritual issues that characterizes much of formal education today, as Daniel Noel pointed out in a *Chronicle of Higher Education* essay.[15] Here Campbell and Moyers — rather than the authors of recent books reflecting on American values, such as Robert Bellah, Alan Bloom, E. D. Hirsch, and William Bennett — have excited extensive popular discussion about and concern with such deeper issues, as opposed to mere listing of the canonical Great Books of the West. Following Campbell's archaic myths and newer stories and poems, we begin to ask about reforming the shallow shapings of inquiry that have set our "professional" schools so adrift that they can train broadcasters to report disasters affecting hundreds of people in the same tone that they use to report the opening of a new opera season at the Met.[16] (Some readers will remember cheering when a furious Dan Rather, reporting the 1968 Democratic Convention, let show his outrage at the way democratic dissent was being stifled.)

Religious Studies specialists have been writing recently about "stories," about narrative, the embodying of significances in the personal and social ways we recount our histories, report upon our presents, and imagine our futures.[17] But Joseph Campbell has been incarnating such en-story-ing for several decades: Bill Moyers recognizes this in his Introduction to *The Power of Myth* when he summarizes Campbell's abilities: "I never met anyone who could better tell a story."[18] In seeking to summarize his admiration for Campbell, Moyers indicated that "a story's the way to tell it. He was a man with a thousand stories," and then Moyers continues with his own story about Campbell's stories that I have used as the epigraph for this essay.

Dancing to the music of the spheres, the image-rich narrative of the universe, is an activity found in the metaphors of religious ritual and in the steps of the dancer, as well as in the narrative dance of the storyteller. The viewer of the Moyers-Campbell videos confronts a truly magical raconteur at work, and audiences stay attuned to him as storyteller even in spite of several questionable illustration sequences that the television series provided during Campbell's longer tale-spinnings.[19] What I have learned from the series for my own professional work is the importance of following-the-stories, telling them orally, as opposed to the intellectualizing abstract or summary. Following that model, Religious Studies might well restrict its broad focus somewhat, looking in more detail at fewer mythico-religious images and stories and scriptures. We professionals ought to press the in-depth probing of ethical-moral issues that our recent disciplinary specialization and professional-school careerism have eliminated in favor of courses such as that offered at my own university this semester entitled "How to Advertise to Women."

Campbell tells stories religiously, with interpretive double-sight and moral insight. He probes sources and themes for what they can contribute to a much-needed reconnection with the depths of the human experience: "Myths are clues to the spiritual potentialities of the human life."[20] And beyond the sheerly intellectual tracing of thematic meaning, Campbell remained sensitive to the embodiments of dance and the song:

> Mythology *is* the song. It is the song of the imagination, inspired by the energies of the body. Once a Zen master stood up before his students and was about to deliver a sermon. And just as he was about to open his mouth, a bird sang. And he said, "The sermon has been delivered."[21]

Thanks to Joseph Campbell, the sermon has been delivered, and the message about the importance of myth as a cultural resource has been repeated the requisite number of times in his mytho-psychology of religion:

> myth is the secret opening through which the inexhaustible energies of the cosmos pour into human cultural manifestation. Religions, philosophies, arts, the social forms of primitive and historic man, prime discoveries in science and technology, the very dreams that blister sleep, boil up from the basic, magic ring of myth.[22]

That "magic ring of myth" is loaded with much more than the "religious" in any narrow sense; it is religious, however, in being a frame for the tying-together of cultural significances, of values considered to be so important that they cannot be relinquished.[23] What is tied together is not just an orientation to the sacred and the divine as *unique* spheres separated from daily concerns, but a manner of organizing *all* the disparate spheres of life, settling them into priorities, and ascertaining that we hold the parts together in a meaningful and useful synergy. Religion is a discipline by which one interprets everything by determining values and ranking relationships.

Campbell's "follow your bliss" message was not a sort of "cheap grace" but a *disciplined* study of the rich mythic inheritance of our several cultures.[24] Asked about the sort of formal religious meditation he himself performed, Campbell responded that his own meditation consisted of underlining passages in books! There is a religious seriousness to the mythological disciplines Campbell preached throughout his books, and the quest for one's own mythic pattern was to be pursued:

> through an intelligent "making use" not of one mythology only but of all the dead and set-fast symbologies of the past, [which] will enable the individual to anticipate and activate in himself the centers of his own creative imagination, out of which his own myth and life-building... may then unfold.[25]

Anticipations of the Religion of the Next Century

The recent public reception of Campbell's sort of probing for significances has been highly favorable and voluble, and I like to think that much of it is a reflection of a mature and intelligent "making use" that is not interested in trite teledramas or vapid talkshows, but senses the need to train the imagination more satisfactorily as we move closer toward the year 2000. Campbell explored for use in our own day and culture many mythological themes and images — *religious* themes and images, despite his temperamental disavowal of that adjective — from several of our planetary brother- and sister-cultures. This exploration is possible because we are, after all, living at the beginning of a new international culture:

> the time has come when every one of the world's ethnic systems is dissolving, since there are no more locally fixed horizons within the bounds of which an ethnocentric bigotry can be honestly maintained. Dissolving, the ethnic ideas become transparent to the archetypes, those elementary ideas of which they are no more than the local masks.[26]

Perhaps we see in Campbell's search and the great contemporary interest in it some of the new shapes that twenty-first-century religion will assume. If so, it will be more symbolic and poetic in style, less parochially oriented to the historical and the particular, and more fully responsive to the archetypal themes that stem from the cultural depths shaped by the human psyche.[27] Integrating such themes in rhythms that coordinate individual and corporate applications; learning how to compare the religious traditions of different times and cultures; and recognizing the necessary balancing between the physical-material, the intellectual-rational, and the emotional-spiritual, as all these are expressed in our mythology and arts: Joseph Campbell offered an anticipation of twenty-first-century religiosity that institutional religions ought to take very seriously indeed.

Near the end of *The Power of Myth*, Bill Moyers asks Campbell what he meant by the phrase "the Christ in you," and Campbell responded:

> What I meant was that you must live not in terms of your own ego system, your own desires, but in terms of what you might call the sense of mankind — the Christ — in you.[28]

Here as at many other junctures, Campbell responded to a question faithfully, religiously, when he might have turned it aside with a glance or his puckish grin. But he didn't. Notwithstanding his avoidance of the terms "religion" and "religious," he responded instead with the sort of theological profundity that leaves us all in debt to this master "theologian": he referred symbolically to the ethical care and corporate responsibility for one another that may be evoked by the Christ figure, even if the reference was couched in more global or even cosmic terms than an orthodox Christian theologian might use.

Particularly in the final sentences of his books, Campbell leaves the reader with little doubt about the *religious* nature of the mythological path. For example he closes the collection entitled *The Flight of the Wild Gander* by stating that:

> there is, in fact, in quiet places, a great deal of deep spiritual quest and finding now in progress in this world, outside the sanctified social centers, beyond their purview and control: in small groups, here and there, and more often, more typically (as anyone who looks about may learn), by ones and twos, there entering the forest at those points which they themselves have chosen, where they see it to be most dark, and there is no beaten way or path.[29]

2

Living by Myth: Joseph Campbell, C. G. Jung, and the Religious Life-Journey

Richard A. Underwood

CAMPBELL: ...Myths grab you somewhere down inside. As a boy, you go at it one way, as I did reading my Indian stories. Later on, myths tell you more, and more, and still more. I think that anyone who has ever dealt seriously with religious or mythic ideas will tell you that we learn them as a child on one level, but then many different levels are revealed. Myths are infinite in their revelation.

MOYERS: How do I slay that dragon in me? What's the journey each of us has to make, what you call "the soul's high adventure"?

CAMPBELL: My general formula for my students is "Follow your bliss." Find where it is, and don't be afraid to follow it.[1]

The purpose of this series of reflections is to explore some of the connections between the psychiatrist C..G. Jung's ideas and Joseph Campbell's as they relate to their common concerns regarding myth, religion, and the metaphor of journey: some of the major themes, that is, relating to the concerns of the discipline of Religious Studies as well as the deeper preoccupations of contemporary human beings.

My fundamental assumption in this essay is that both Jung and Campbell participate in the long history of religious studies in its

13

most general nature, even before the nomenclature of "Religious Studies" was developed. These two thinkers are involved insofar as part of the task of the academic study of religion is to help provide a degree of rational comprehension of how and why religious phenomena have played so vast a role in the affairs of humankind. Jung and Campbell fit into this, I submit, by participating in what might be called the history of the "de-mystification" of religion. This process begins, in Western tradition at any rate, with the Hebrew break from the Ancient Near Eastern cosmological myth into the myth of history and the Greek break (through the creation of philosophical-scientific discourse) from Homeric myth (the move from *Mythos* to *Logos*).[2] It should be immediately added, however, that Jung's and Campbell's participation in this "de-mystification project" does *not* involve the debunking of religion and religious belief associated with the Modern Enlightenment and its consequent "dis-enchantment" of the world.

On the contrary, both Jung and Campbell engage in what could be called a "natural history" of religious myth, symbol, and sentiment, a *natural* history that seeks to honor the function of the religious imagination without granting it a *super*-natural authority. For Jung this approach is manifest in his career as a physician, empiricist, phenomenologist, and therapist. Indeed, at the end of his life, while composing his memoirs, Jung reiterated once again his concern to place his inquiries in the context of biology and natural history.[3] Joseph Campbell states quite explicitly in his prologue to volume 1 of the Masks of God series (*Primitive Mythology*) that he is engaged in a "natural history": the title of the prologue is "Toward a Natural History of the Gods and Heroes," with the first section being called "The Lineaments of a New Science." The allusion here is not only to Bacon and Galileo but also to the "New Science" of Giambattista Vico, who figured so prominently in the works of James Joyce, about whom Campbell wrote in his first comprehensive study of myth, *A Skeleton Key to Finnegans Wake.*

This broad context for Jung and Campbell in relation to the discipline (or "inter-discipline") of Religious Studies is important: "de-mystification without dis-enchantment." It is important in the first place because it helps the academic study of religion guard against excesses in the direction of an Apollonian rationalism to which the critical intellect is so often prone. It is important also because it provides an antidote to those who would turn Jung and Campbell into New Age prophets exclusively, tending to see in them justification for any amalgam of subjective, pseudo-mystical, occultish spirituality that simply feels good. Within this general framework of "natural history" and "demystification," the fundamental starting point for both Jung and Campbell was the psychology of the unconscious, and both began their researches by dealing with the myth of the hero-journey: Jung in the work that marked his break with Freud in 1913 (*Symbols of Transformation*) and Campbell with his *Hero with a Thousand Faces*, published some thirty-five years later. In the preface, written in June of 1948, Campbell begins with a statement from Freud's *Future of an Illusion* and then observes that a key to learning the grammar of symbols has to do with the psychology of the unconscious:

> I know of no better tool than modern psychoanalysis. Without regarding this as the last word on the subject, one can nevertheless permit it to serve as an approach.[4]

Campbell's use of Freud was balanced by his growing interest in Jung — an interest that was evident already in *Hero* when it came out a year later. But Campbell (as was the case with Jung himself) never left Freud behind and at several crucial points in the development of his work he returns to the insights of Freud and Freudian-influenced anthropology. I am not sure, therefore, that the label of "Jungian" so often applied to Campbell is appropriate. Admittedly, Campbell's search for correspondences and even unity underlying the various forms of world mythologies throughout diverse cultural locales and historical epochs made Jung's hypothesis of the archetypes of the collective unconscious a useful interpretive tool. But Campbell is equally indebted, as far as the sources of his critical understanding are concerned, to Vico, Kant, Schopenhauer, Nietzsche, James Joyce, Thomas Mann, and Robinson Jeffers — not to mention Einstein, Planck, and Heisenberg. Furthermore, it was not necessary for Campbell to read Jung in order to inspire his quest for the underlying unity of the world's mythologies. He had already discovered this in Joyce's *Finnegans Wake*, as is so beautifully stated in the conclusion to *A Skeleton Key to Finnegans Wake*:

> Besides being a Dream Confessional, *Finnegans Wake* is also a Treasury of Myth. Myths, like dreams, are an upworking of the unconscious mind — and western scholarship has recently become aware of their essential homogeneity throughout the world.... Other writers — Dante, Bunyan, Goethe — employed

mythological symbolism, but their images were drawn from the reservoirs of the West. *Finnegans Wake* has tapped the universal sea.

> The complexity of Joyce's imagery — as distinguished from that of his language — results from his titanic fusion of all mythologies.... [5]

Jung's works, therefore, helped Campbell find a theoretical framework for what he had already discovered in Joyce.

From the retrospective of the seventy-five years since Jung's *Symbols of Transformation* was published and the forty years since Campbell's *Hero with a Thousand Faces*, we can see that the joining together of depth-psychological method with the theme of the hero-myth unites the two authors in another common concern: namely, the theme of transformation of consciousness and the ways in which participation in myth and ritual facilitates this.

The dynamics of transformation in Jung's psychology are the equivalent of what in Freudian terminology is called "sublimation," though there are some important, even radical, differences that have to do with the theories of dream and repression and the nature of libido. The importance of these differences lies in the fact that, from the beginning marked by *Symbols of Transformation*, Jung was profoundly concerned with the processes of wholeness and the coincidence of opposites, processes that the theory of sublimation could not take into account since it depended, at least in part, on a mind-body dualism inimical to any theory of holistic processes.

Campbell's concern with transformation of consciousness was developed in his *Hero* book, though the term he used ("monomyth") to describe the basic stages of the hero-journey was derived from Joyce. Campbell both builds upon and goes beyond the work of Jung. He builds upon it insofar as he shows how the hero-journey parallels what Jung later came to call the individuation process, including the reconciliation of opposites by a journey of descent into the "lower round" of the unconscious. He goes beyond Jung by showing, even more explicitly than Jung had, how the dynamics of myth and dream are identical. Campbell also succeeds, at least in my opinion, in placing the whole moment of twentieth-century depth psychology in the context of the scientific revolution of the seventeenth century and its elaboration in the nineteenth century. He does this by way of describing what he calls "the descent of the Occidental sciences"

from the heavens to the earth (from seventeenth-century astronomy to nineteenth-century biology), and their concentration today [Campbell writes this in 1949], at last, on man himself (in twentieth-century anthropology and psychology)....
[Thus the descent of the Occidental sciences] marks the path of a prodigious transfer of the focal point of human wonder. Not the animal world, not the plant world, not the miracle of the spheres, but man himself is now the crucial mystery.[6]

This formulation by Campbell, incidentally, is reminiscent of what Freud calls the "three narcissistic wounds" inflicted by the "researches of science": the cosmological wound inflicted by Galileo, the biological wound inflicted by Darwin, and the psychological wound inflicted by Freud himself. They can also be seen as three ordeals besetting the modern hero-journey.

The themes of "hero" and "transformation" are inseparable from the theme or image of "journey" in both Jung and Campbell. This, of course, is due to no idiosyncrasy on their part. "Journey" is a theme of archetypal significance in the history of Western religious consciousness, as is evident when one thinks of the *Exodus*, the *Odyssey*, the *Aeneid*, and Dante's *Comedy*.

In the works of Jung and Campbell, as in contemporary psychological theory generally, the theme of "journey" has been transmuted into that of "stages of life" — where "stage" should be understood not only as that "place" where the drama of life is played out, but also as the "vehicle" of time (the developing body) that carries the player through the journey of life. Each stage, in both senses of the word, has its own psychological-spiritual task, where the "task" is cooperatively defined by the intersection of biological potential and societal custom.

The most direct statement by Jung on the stages of life, and thus, implicitly, on the metaphor of journey and its relation to the religious quest, is an essay entitled just that: "The Stages of Life." It is of more than passing interest to note that Campbell's edition of selected works of Jung begins with this essay.[7] The basic thrust of Jung's essay is the principle of *enantiodromia:* the reversal of values that begins in the "healthy" life ("healthy" understood as *wholeness*) at its mid-point. This reversal involves a transition from the energies and strivings devoted, in the first half of life, to the building of a viable and strong ego-identity to a different sort of task during the second half: a task that becomes more "interior" in the sense that the awareness of finitude and death becomes more pressing, revealing at the same time that the values strived for in the first half of life must be let go now in the second half. Thus Jung:

> A human being would certainly not grow to be seventy or eighty years old if this longevity had no meaning for the species. The afternoon of human life must also have a significance of its own and cannot be merely a pitiful appendage to life's morning. The significance of the morning undoubtedly lies in the development of the individual, our entrenchment in the outer world, the propagation of our kind, and the care of our children. This is the obvious purpose of nature. But when this purpose has been attained... shall the earning of money, the extension of conquests, and the expansion of life go steadily on beyond the bounds of all reason and sense? Whoever carries over into the afternoon the law of the morning, or the natural aim, must pay for it with damage to his soul, just as surely as a growing youth who tries to carry over his childish egoism into adult life must pay for this mistake with social failure.[8]

This illuminates, in a sense, what Jung means when he says on occasion that Freud's psychology, with its emphasis on the Oedipal conflict (that is, the struggle to gain self-identity and self-sufficiency in the face of parental power and the establishment-institutional forms of that power vested in education, law, and religion), is relevant to the first half of life, whereas his own psychology is appropriate to the second half of life.

It is not clear whether Campbell is indebted to Jung at this point — indebted, that is, in terms of specific, concrete influence — or whether he arrives at something of the same view independently. What is clear is that Campbell cites Jung to support his own view. But Campbell does amplify Jung's thesis regarding the stages of life by giving it a different twist, and this different twist issues, eventually, in Campbell's famous formulation of the fourfold myth-function.

Part of this "new twist" is Campbell's attempt to provide a biological basis for myth and its various functions. This is, of course, already implied in Jung's distinction between the first half of life being directed by nature, while the second half "belongs to culture." Campbell adduces, at this point, the biological fact that human beings are born too soon, born incomplete, thus remaining in a stage of dependency for a considerably longer period, proportionately, than other mammals. (This is an insight derived, at least in part, from the work of the German biologist Adolf Portmann.) Culture, then, in Campbell's view, becomes a "second womb," the "organism" that supports, protects, sustains, and guides human life into its precarious post-natal, life-long, neo-nate situation of fragility and dependency.

Campbell's critique can be seen in rough analogy to Freud's "civilization and its discontents." What Campbell does here, however (and Jung, too, though with a somewhat different inflection), goes beyond Freud's basic stoicism and sees in the myths, rituals, and symbolisms of culture (including its specifically religious forms) dynamics of transformation that provide the possibility not only of coping with but of going beyond the dangers posed to human being by the "superior powers of nature." So Campbell (in both the "Bios and Mythos" and "Mythogenesis" essays in *The Flight of the Wild Gander*) distinguishes two general aspects of mythology in the "marsupial pouch" called culture: there is an *adaptive* aspect and there is a *transcendental* aspect. Furthermore, these can be seen in relation to the fourfold function of mythology spelled out by Campbell at the end of volume 3 and the beginning of volume 4 of the Masks of God: the mystical-metaphysical, the cosmological, the sociological, and the psychological-spiritual.

The adaptive aspect, appropriate to the first half of life, is manifest in the cosmological and sociological functions: namely, the processes of acculturation whereby the individual is taught (if everything is working "right") the fundamental rules of both the cosmic order and the social order. Campbell compares this adaptive-pedagogical feature of mythology, in both its cosmological and its sociological functions, to the first two stages of life as specified in classical Hinduism: the student and the householder. The adaptive aspect of mythology, however, is to be superseded by the transcendental function, if indeed humans are to recognize and affirm their destiny beyond mere conformity to the authority of social teachings regarding the moral law and the cosmic order. The function of the social teaching is the development of a self-sufficient adult ego-consciousness in accord with the cultural definitions of the *cosmos* and the *socius*. What lies beyond this requirement of adaptation? Campbell raises the question this way:

> ...[humans have] not only to be led by myth from the infantile attitude of dependency to an adult assumption of responsibility in terms of the system of sentiments of [their] tribe, but also, in adulthood, to be prepared to face the mystery of death: to absorb the *mysterium tremendum* of being: for [humans], like no other animal,...[know] that [they] too will

die. . . . Furthermore, even in the period of childhood, and certainly throughout one's adult years, the wonder of death — the awesome, dreadful transformations that immediately follow death — strike the mind with an impact not to be dismissed. . . . [9]

So, beyond the function of the "imprinting of a sociology," myth has a *transcendental* aspect, an aspect that is to help initiate one into the great mystery of Being and Death, an aspect manifest in the other two of the four myth-functions specified above: (1) the metaphysical-mystical and (4) the psychological-spiritual.

These two functions are rooted in the religious vision of the culture and are thus still a function of the society and its transmission of the tradition through its foundational myths. But this transcendent feature is, in Campbell's view, a means of "seeing-through" the lessons and symbols of the adaptive stage. He uses the image of "second birth" (and extends this image in a comparative way to various religious traditions) to describe this second set of functions (the mystical and the psychological): that is, just as the organism must be delivered from the first, biological womb at the "right time" or suffer consequences of malformation and maladaption, so it must be delivered from the "second womb" of culture at the "right" time or the journey of life will not be appropriately consummated. And the "obstetric device" by which this second birth is to be facilitated is myth in its mystical and psychological functions.

In clarifying what he means by this, Campbell appeals to the third and fourth stages of life in Hinduism: the stage of the Forest Dweller and the stage of the *Sunyassin:* leaving the adaptive-pedagogical dharma which has been fulfilled in order to live in the forest and seek the metaphysical bliss of the true self — which bliss is ultimately enlightening beyond the power of the adaptive aspect ever to achieve. It is important that this be understood in light of what Campbell reiterated on the PBS *Power of Myth* series with Bill Moyers: the injunction, namely, to "follow your bliss." The possibility of "following your bliss" presupposes, if I read Campbell correctly, one's having experienced already the painful discipline of the adaptive aspect of mythology in order to discover that this "dharmic necessity" does not constitute fulfillment of the psychological-spiritual function of mythology's transcendental aspect: initiation into the authentic and mysterious depths of one's own being. If this is not understood, then "follow your bliss" can become a mindless principle, an example of the most vacuous and hedonistic dimensions of the worst aspects of "New Ageism."

Up to this point there has been a certain congruence between Jung and Campbell. This congruence includes also a concern by both that the transformational journey of life, in its various stages, issue in an experience of one's own individuality, one's special uniqueness. What this involves for both Jung and Campbell is a deliverance from unconscious identification with or participation in the collective, be it the archetypal dimensions of the collective unconscious, which the adaptive function of mythology is to help one differentiate from in growing into a self-conscious ego identity, or the collective of the social group itself, identification with which can prevent the "second birth" and thus inhibit the journey toward realization of one's authentic being. Jung's name for this process is "individuation" — the journey toward wholeness and completion. Campbell's vision of the heroic journey is analogous with Jung's understanding of the process of individuation, but Campbell does, I think, begin to articulate the nature of this journey in significantly different ways. It is in the specifying of these "different ways" that we come to what I think is Campbell's own unique "re-visioning" of the religious life-journey.

I want to state my "thesis" here in at least two ways.

(1) Jung remains a Christian — a *Gnostic* Christian, to be sure, but a Christian nevertheless. Campbell, on the other hand, breaks through the Christic mandala to a Buddhist-like experience of the No-thing in the Every-thing.

(2) Jung's de-mystification of mythology issues in a re-enchantment of the symbol, which continues to assume an uncanny archaic sacredness of the unconscious that we must both journey from and return to.

In *Memories, Dreams, Reflections*, recalling his break with Freud and his "confrontation with the unconscious," Jung asks what myth *he* lives by. He wonders if it is the Christian myth, but says to be honest he must admit it is not. Then he raises a more general question: " 'Do we any longer have any myth?' 'No, evidently we no longer have any myth.' "[10] The myth Jung eventually found, announced to him in a 1926 dream as a task he would have to pursue, was the myth of alchemy; he lived by the myth of alchemy throughout his entire life from 1926 until his death in 1961. That was thirty-five years, the traditional length of the second half of life, even though he surpassed the traditional three-score-and-ten by some sixteen years (roughly the number of years, interestingly enough, he lived mythlessly in search of his own myth).

The myth of alchemy, as interpreted and experienced by Jung, was not only a disguised Christianity but also a disguised-symbolic prefiguration of his own analytical psychology of the unconscious. Thus Jung could say (without it being a contradiction) in a talk before a group of Anglican clergy in London in 1939 that the Catholic Church still had a symbolic life as expressed in the living mystery of the Mass and that "it works!":

> ...when I say a "living mystery," I mean nothing mysterious, I mean mystery in the sense which the word has always had — a *mysterium tremendum*. And the mass is by no means the only mystery in the Catholic Church.... So you see, if I treat a real Christian, a real Catholic, I say "you stick to it!"... [11]

Jung, the scion of a long line of Swiss Protestants, discovers, through the myth of alchemy, the mysterious, mandalic meaning of the Roman Catholic Mass and becomes a twentieth-century mystagogue of the symbolic life.

Campbell, on the other hand, raised in the tradition of Roman Catholicism and its mysteries, is delivered into another vision. He says somewhere that the myth should be a bow and not a snare: it should be that which catapults one forward into a new experience of being and self, not a trap that inhibits the movement through and out of the mandala.

Given the importance of mandalic symbolism in Jung's psychology (see the entry on "mandala" in the Glossary to Jung's *Memories, Dreams, Reflections*), Campbell poses a series of questions that strikes at the very heart of Jungian theory: is the mandala an archetype of the collective unconscious? Or is it, rather, a form that appears at a specific time for a specific function under specific societal-cultural conditions? To be sure, Jung does not interpret the mandala as a vehicle revelatory of the gods, unless the "gods" are seen themselves as being born out of the unconscious. Nevertheless, Jung seems constantly to insist that the mandala represents an archetypal pattern of psychic order, and it is this which Campbell is calling into question (although he continues to cite Jung's analyses of the mandalic construction as late as the appearance of his own *Mythic Image* in 1974).

But let me return now to Campbell's response to his question: is the mandala something "eternal" and archetypal or is it to be seen in a different light? Basically, Campbell suggests that the mandalic symbol arose as a result of the shift from the hunting age to the agricultural age and that its highly differentiated geometric design can be seen as a way to express the increasingly complex division of labor associated with village-agricultural life. In contrast to this new and relatively complex division of labor, Campbell suggests (referring to the researches of Geza Roheim), for the pre-agricultural hunting group "the community was constituted by a group of practically equivalent individuals, each in adequate control of the whole inheritance."[12] The "sacred" geometric form of the mandala, Campbell therefore argues, appeared "suddenly" at a specific time in history, an appearance that can be explained only by the new conditions imposed by the shift into a community where one felt himself or herself to be only a fraction of a larger whole. Thus:

> The problem of existing as a mere fraction instead of as a whole imposes certain stresses on the psyche which no primitive hunter ever had to endure, and consequently the symbols giving structure and support to the development of the primitive hunter's psychological balance were radically different from those that arose in the settled villages, in the Basal and High Neolithic, and which have been inherited from that age and continued into the present by all the high civilizations of the world.[13]

"...continued into the present by all the high civilizations of the world": the dominance of the sacred form of the mandala (in a variety of ways) as the inheritance of the psychological stress of the archaic agriculturalist persisted for some 6,500 years, continuing into our own modern age. It remained, and in some instances still remains, as the symbolic code designed to express the spiritual relationship between the microcosmic psyche, the mesocosmic society, and the macrocosmic universe. In this code there is a radical tension between the shaman and the priest, where the shaman represents the "titanic individual" seeking on his or her own. The priest, on the other hand, represents the acquiescent group subservient to the authority of the divine as represented in the traditional mandalic closures and their symbolic-dogmatic formulations.

Campbell's fundamental challenge is to the continuing authority of this symbol over our contemporary religious life-journey, a challenge that is spelled out tentatively in the important 1957 lecture "The Symbol without Meaning" and then in profuse and profound detail in *Creative Mythology* appearing in 1968. *Creative Mythology* is the fruition of an intuition that, in my opinion, first came to Campbell in his experience of and critical reading of James Joyce, especially in *A Skeleton Key to Finnegans Wake*, published in 1944. The term "creative mythology" itself indicates a return to the way of art. This would be a return to the role of the artist, understood by Campbell to be identical with that of the shaman, as first revealed in the hunting culture of the cave paintings, the pre-geometric, pre-mandalic figuration of the mysterious presence of *That Which Is*, Being, in its immediate, mysterious, overwhelming Presence.

In the area of twentieth-century philosophy, Martin Heidegger has argued that Plato's "turn" from the concern for Being in the pre-Socratic philosophers was the beginning of a 2500-year detour, a history of the metaphysical forgetting of Being. Similarly, one might say, the mandalic structure originating with the "turn" from hunting to agriculture, with its corresponding hierarchies in architecture, city planning, temples, cathedrals, dogmas, and organizations of priestly personnel, was the beginning of another detour, beginning a history of the forgetting of the sacred (a necessary detour and history, to be sure, in order to concentrate the prodigious, Promethean energies of early humankind on "world-building" and "psyche-making"). However, in wondering, in *Creative Mythology*, if the historical-psychological-spiritual function of the once-sacred mandala has outlived its "usefulness," Campbell is posing the possibility of the individual now becoming his or her own shaman-artist, following the creative way through the mandalic form to a renewed experience of the mystery of Being.

Just as the historical event that marked the appearance of the mandala was the shift from one cultural experience to another, new one, so the historical events that signal the "emergent new symbol" can be precisely dated: 1492, "when Columbus sailed the Ocean Blue," and 1609–1611, when Galileo spotted, with his telescope, the imperfections on the surface of the moon and the system of moons orbiting the planet Jupiter, thus confirming the Copernican hypothesis of a heliocentric solar system.

Columbus and Galileo figure prominently in both "Symbol without Meaning" and *Creative Mythology*. They are the shamanic-visionaries who paint new images on the cave walls of our imagination. Both break, not only figuratively, but literally, the prevailing mandalic structures: Columbus breaks the mesocosmic medieval Christian geography, stretching the bounds of the then-known world to discover a new world beyond the European mandala, and Galileo breaks the mandala of the Ptolemaic universe, rooted in Plato's *Timaeus*, with its concentric circles from the sub-lunar sphere of miserable earth — the realm of birth, life, suffering, and death — to the Heavenly Empyrean, the Abode of God and of all the Angels and the Elect.

To the dates of the fracturing represented by Columbus and Galileo should be added, as Campbell does most emphatically and poetically, the date of July 20, 1969, the occasion of the first moon walk.[14] Now the mandala of Mother Earth herself had been left, and we saw her floating there against the blackness of space from the perspective of the moonscape, the logical extension of the voyages of Columbus and the viewings of Galileo.

In Campbell's view, the new age emergent requires a joining together of the way of science and the way of art: both are "ways" to be seen under the paradigm of the shaman, not the mandala:

Let us...recognize...that what is intended by art, metaphysics, magical hocus-pocus, and mystical religion, is not the knowledge of anything, not truth, or goodness, or beauty, but an evocation of a sense of the absolutely unknowable. Science, on the other hand, will take care of what can be known.

Art and science...constitute a "pair of aspects" system. The function of art is to render a *sense of existence*, not an *assurance of some meaning:* so that those who require an assurance of meaning, or who feel unsure of themselves and unsettled when they learn that the system of meaning that would support them in their living has been shattered, must surely be those who have not yet experienced profoundly, continuously, or convincingly enough, that sense of existence — of spontaneous and willing arising — which is the first and deepest characteristic of being, and which it is the province of art to waken.[15]

Here we have, I suggest, the fundamental "re-visioning" by Campbell of Jung's perception of the religious life-journey: a journey that moves from the quest for meaning as expressed in the quaternal-mandalic representation of the psychic structure to an experience of Being, which renders all specific mythological forms as something to be seen through, as vehicles, so to speak, to assist in that journey, as the "bow" to catapult us into that experience.

And it is here, too, that we see Campbell the Buddhist, if by Buddhist we mean the Zen variety, as revealed in the following story Campbell re-tells in another context. Some five hundred monks were gathered together in a contest to see "who could summarize best in a single stanza the essence of Buddhist teaching." The one expected to win was the "extraordinarily gifted" Shen-hsiu. And indeed, they were *his* four lines that were selected and formally inscribed on the wall by the door of the refectory:

> The Body is the Bodhi-tree
> The mind, a mirror bright,
> Take care to wipe them always clean,
> Lest dust on them alight.

The idea here being that the essence of the Buddhist way is diligent purification.

[An] illiterate kitchen boy, however, having learned of the competition, asked a friend that night to read to him the poem inscribed there on the wall; and when he had heard, begged to have the following set beside it:

> The body is no Bodhi-tree,
> The mind no mirror bright,
> Since nothing at the root exists,
> On what should what dust alight?

The abbot, next morning, hearing the excited talk of his monks, came down, stood a while before the anonymous poem, took his slipper and angrily erased it. But he had correctly guessed the author and, sending that night for the kitchen boy, presented him with the robe and bowl. "Here my son," he said: "here are the insignia of this office. Now depart! Run away! Disappear!"[16]

It is the way of art and the artist that Campbell opens up for us in his "creative mythology" as the response to the fracturing of the mandala and that leads, in the end, to his Buddhist-like vision. The earliest, apparently most powerful visionary artist who revealed to Campbell the lineaments of his own new science was James Joyce. Joyce's *Ulysses* and *Finnegans Wake* were, it could be said, the *koan* that opened up Campbell's vision.

One of the shortcomings of most criticism of Joseph Campbell — whether from the side of the history of religion, psychology, anthropology, theology, and/or literary criticism — is that his view of the way of art and its power is not sufficiently taken into account. Consider for example the following passages: one from *Skeleton Key* in 1944 and the other from *The Inner Reaches of Outer Space* in 1986, just a year before Campbell's death:

> ...Joyce actually plunges into a region where myth and dream coalesce to form the amniotic fluid of *Finnegans Wake*. Joyce well

knew that this deepest level of creation could not be tapped by the siphons of conventional literature. He believed also that somewhere in the noncerebral part of man dwells an intelligence which is the most important organ of human wisdom. He knew further that it operated most typically during the mysterious process of sleep. And for these reasons, he chose night logic, expressed in dream language, as his method of communication.[17]

And:

James Joyce, in *A Portrait of the Artist as a Young Man*, like every one of those young artists of his time who, during the century that has now run its course became the masters of the period, put his mind to the problem of reawakening the eye and heart to wonder. With the profound sense of a call, a vocation, he turned his mind (like the ancient Greek master craftsman Daedalus, when he found himself entrapped in a labyrinth of his own fashioning) to the invention of a hitherto unknown science of escape from bondage on "wings of art."[18]

Jung began as a clinician with a clinician's interest in myth and dream as clues to unconscious processes — clues which, if read in the context of the mythological tradition, might help restore lost meaning to a patient's life. Jung became a physician, and he transformed the physician's craft into the alchemical art of the therapy of soul. He was also sage, philosopher, mystic, and visionary. He opened up new worlds within. In the end, his understanding of the religious life-journey involved the expansion of consciousness so as to include these "worlds."

Campbell, even though he found useful the theoretical framework provided by Jung, began at a different place. He began with myth as a work of art as presented in the creative mythology of James Joyce. Following the directions suggested by Joyce, the lineaments of Campbell's own new science of mythology led him to see the ultimate function of mythology as one of providing "Wings": Wings of liberation and releasement from bondage to the traditional mandalic forms now in the process of dissolution. The conventional and exoteric use of mythology is to maintain control of the religious imagination. In Campbell's viewing, however, the true power of myth lies in its capacity to move one through and beyond so as to experience the mysterious Presence of Being. In the end, then, Campbell's understanding of the religious life-journey was an understanding that enables one to live *by* myth, not *in* myth.

3

The Thousand and First Face

Walter B. Gulick

The courage to face the trials and to bring a whole new body
of possibilities into the field of interpreted experience for other
people to experience — that is the hero's deed.[1]

"Criticizing Campbell could get me in a lot more trouble than
denying the existence of God!" So wrote a friend of mine, a minister
of a liberal mainline church. While written mostly in jest, these words
contain a truth that is important to comprehend by all who would
hope to decipher the power of Joseph Campbell's thought. Campbell is taken by many with the seriousness that generally is accorded
the prophet, the priest, or the guru — in contrast to the literature
professor. That is, the impact of his thought is most plausibly interpreted as *religious* in character, rather than simply as academic or
expository.

Yet if Professor Campbell is seen by many as a religious spokes-
person, he is certainly an unusual example of such. He is not an
ordained member of any denomination, nor does he claim any prophetic insight or priestly knowledge. He doesn't even usually claim
to be addressing religious issues; his avowed focus is the literature
of myth. Who, then, are his admirers, the persons who have helped
make him such an influential religious figure in our time?

I know of no survey that details the characteristics of Campbell's
audience, yet if one is to interpret the significance of his thought,
surely it is important to have some conception of who has been
affected by it and to what end. Based on personal observation and discussion with other students of the Campbell phenomenon, I will ten-

tatively characterize two sorts of Campbell enthusiasts from among the many attracted to his work. The cogency of my argument is not dependent on the accuracy with which I delineate the views of members of these two groups; my point is to try to explain why Campbell's impact is best seen as religious in nature.

For those in the first group, institutional religion is not a live personal option. Some people in this group have long had a distaste for organized religion, often because of unfortunate personal experience with it. Others in this group have had little direct contact with institutional religion, but have gradually been disaffected from it because of the way it has been portrayed in the media in recent years. After all, what religious figures have garnered the greatest public attention? Jimmy and Tammy Bakker, Robert Schuller, Oral Roberts, Jimmy Swaggart, and Shirley MacLaine will do for a start. To countless Americans this is an unappetizing cast of characters through which to conceive the religious enterprise, and they therefore wish to have nothing to do with religion if such are its representatives. And yet the appetite for religious insight and discipline does not thereby disappear. Campbell attends to this otherwise unsatisfied hunger.

There is a second group to whom Joseph Campbell's ideas appeal. Members of this second group still belong to churches, often mainline churches, and sometimes they remain active in these churches. Yet many of these people are looking for greater spiritual nourishment than they find in traditional services or religious activities. Moreover, members of this second group tend to be sophisticated and aware of the many different religious and social traditions in the world. They are made uneasy by religious provincialism in any of its guises. They are interested in knowing what the great thinkers and saints of many traditions have to say about the spiritual journey and the ultimate issues.

Campbell's thought is attractive to members of both of these groups. Indeed, the impact of Campbell on these groups is comparable to the effect Friedrich Schleiermacher's lectures on religion had on the cultured despisers of religion of two centuries ago.[2] Just as Schleiermacher's emphasis on the broad scope of spiritual feeling disarmed those used to thinking of religious feeling in terms of narrow pietism, so Campbell's focus on myth and story appeals to those who have considered religion to be limited to dogma and creed. Similarly, just as Schleiermacher's emphasis on the experiential aspects of religion attracted educated individuals unmoved by Enlightenment deism or rationalism, so Campbell's exposition of the existential meaning of many religious traditions excites those who have only experienced religion as a narrowly theological discipline or as a sort of glorified social action.

Campbell as a Hero

For a significant number of Americans, then, Joseph Campbell has become a modern religious hero. They see him as heroic because he confronts the great issues that religions have traditionally dealt with. He speaks about how to live zestfully, overcome desire, become more compassionate, conquer the fear of death. By providing viewers and readers with stories attuned to the ultimate things, and by articulating his perceptions of the meaning of what he describes, Campbell is able to balance affective attractiveness and intellectual insight in a way not characteristic of the prevalent contemporary view of religion as featuring either emotional bombast or arid ritual and vapid head trips.

Professor Campbell's contemporary heroism is nicely highlighted by his own analysis of the hero. Actually, Campbell's attention to the hero is essential to the foundational mythic form he has so effectively promulgated. He describes the monomyth — the standard path followed in the mythological adventure — as being structured by the patterned activities of the hero: "A hero ventures forth from the world of common day into a region of supernatural wonder: fabulous forces are there encountered and a decisive victory is won: the hero comes back from this mysterious adventure with the power to bestow boons on his fellow man."[3] This is the monomyth in its starkest form, but Campbell assures us that countless changes may be rung on this archetypal pattern.[4] The heroes of myths flesh out the heroic archetype with a thousand different faces. Campbell's incarnation of the heroic form has some things in common with the thousand other faces, but in some ways he has discovered a new face of the hero, a thousand and first face. He represents not the hero in the story but the storyteller as the hero. Campbell is a heroic storyteller who has brought "a whole new body of possibilities into the field of interpreted experience for other people."[5] He has ventured into a region of supernatural wonders (the field of myth and other religious phenomena), confronted the mysteries of many traditions, and returned to the multitudes with hard won interpretive insights he freely shares.

What makes Campbell heroic in our age is that he is able to convey to ordinary citizens a sense of the meaning he has found in the myths, rituals, and practices of diverse peoples. He makes insights accessible without simply popularizing them in a reductive way. This is a heroic achievement because in our age of irony, rhetoric, and specialization few are willing to speak directly from the heart about important things. Fewer still have the insights or communication skills to say anything of interest when they try to speak from the heart. Campbell states the current situation well: "The hero is today running up against a hard world that is in no way responsive to his spiritual need."[6] Recognizing that spiritual hunger, Joseph Campbell made it his life work to provide spiritual food for others.

Campbell acknowledged the heroism of not only the creator but also the restorer of tradition. "There is a kind of secondary hero to revitalize the tradition. This hero reinterprets the tradition and makes it valid as a living experience today."[7] Is Campbell's thousand and first face that of the secondary hero, the revitalizer of traditions?

Campbell's work transcends provincialism by attending to many traditions within the compass of a single book or television interview. But, it must be asked with all seriousness, can traditions remain intact when selected stories and activities are pulled out of their native contexts and juxtaposed with stories and activities from quite different traditions? Is not the thousand and first face something more than simply a secondary hero? Do not his novel juxtapositions represent more the accomplishments of a creator than those of a restorer?[8] What sort of elixir is delivered by one who is a purveyor of the most diverse cultural wares? When the mask is removed, does Campbell stand forth as the prophet of a new transcultural culture? Or is he one who reduces transcultural diversity to a hidden Western (and androcentric) intellectual vision? Or, after all the analysis and appreciation is over, is his work merely a sort of intellectual entertainment that fulfills the needs of a special type of elitist consumer, the public television viewer?

Perhaps none of these alternatives quite captures Professor Campbell's elusive accomplishments, but certain it is that he is more than simply a restorer of traditions. His vantage point upon stories and ceremonies is informed by a definite set of views, not all of which are necessarily consistent or complementary. Psychological categories are chief among his interpretive criteria, and they are buttressed by an array of assumptions and value judgments. These include the priority of experience over doctrine, the mysterious transcendent referent of "god talk," the spiritual necessity of turning within, the superiority of intuition to explanation, a preference for the mystical to the ethical, and so on. Thus his use of myths is guided by the values he honors and the assumptions he presupposes. His stories are snatched from their cultural contexts, and in the process their meaning is frequently transformed rather than simply restored.

Some scholars may wish to see Campbell as a representative in myth studies of the postmodern phenomenon of uncentered eclecticism. He certainly says things that would support such an interpretation: "This is the mythological way of being an individual. You are the central mountain, and the central mountain is everywhere."[9] Yet to understand him as a scholar lost in a maze of myths misses what he achieves with his stories: he deploys them according to his interpretive criteria, and they also serve to support *his* vision of things. Campbell artfully [uses] stories to support a personal point of view that he otherwise argues little for.

The boon that Campbell delivers to his followers thus is double layered: it contains a level at which a specific story is told and its meaning interpreted, but the many meanings jointly contribute to a deeper level expressive of his personal vision. Because the details of his personal vision are often not made thematic, readers do not always appreciate that they are subtly being urged toward Campbell's own distinctive worldview. Campbell believes that myths and rituals, supported by symbols and metaphors, give humans access to a dimension of experience that underlies the normal, perceptual world. Thereby we enjoy entry to an otherwise unconscious stratum of our own being, a stratum that may in turn connect us with cosmic energies. By dwelling in the mythical worldview we gain the power to adjust to the demands of life in general and to pass safely through the special thresholds of life established by our society in particular. Ultimately, myths encourage us to see beyond the limits of this dualistic world of thought and perception.

The power in Professor Campbell's use of myth, which leads people to return again and again to his presentations as if to a prophet or a sage, is thus multidimensional. However, the religious attractiveness of his thought is of a peculiar, ungrounded sort. Raised as a Catholic, Campbell in his maturity seems more attuned to Vedantic Hinduism than to Christianity.[10] Yet he also borrows generously from American Indian traditions, Tantric and Zen Buddhisms, Arabic legends, medieval romanticism, and numerous other traditions. The result is not a unique syncretistic religion, however. Because Campbell uses the traditional stories to illustrate his own often tacit vision of things, the stories themselves are not integrated into some new whole with an integrity of its own, but remain in uneasy juxtaposition as illustrations. Consequently, Campbell at times seems like a prophet without a religion. No rituals, traditions, or practices support his vision (unless one counts turning on and being attentive to the television set as a ritual). The heterogeneity and even incongruity of his sources plus the thinness of his theory make his work appear closer to myth than mythography, more the stuff of dreams than the construction of a scholar. His writing assumes a shape that itself has features which are similar to the characteristics he finds in the myth and poetry that he interprets: "Mythology is very fluid. Most of the myths are self-contradictory. You may even find four or five myths in a given culture, all giving different versions of the same mystery. Then theology comes along and says it has got to be just this way. Mythology is poetry, and the poetic language is very flexible."[11] Campbell's underlying vision of things seems pretty stable throughout his writings, but the way he communicates his vision is in style far closer to poetry and art than to systematic theology.

Because his work depends so heavily upon images and stories, it has not encouraged widespread theoretical criticism. That is putting the point a bit kindly; scholars in Religious Studies have tended to ignore his work because it has been regarded as facile, pontificating, derivative, or confused. Campbell, it is often thought, has helped stimulate popular interest in myth, but he has done little to further the understanding of myth.

I would agree with Campbell's critics that there is a limited amount to be gleaned from his theoretical study of mythic structure, but I learn much from another dimension of his thought, one we have circled warily about for some time now. Let me repeat my claim: Joseph Campbell is heroic to many because he concentrates again and again on the meaning of a wide variety of stories and traditions and the meaning of life found by those who live according to the lessons of the stories. He consistently attends to issues of existential meaning without bringing the nature of this meaning to thematic focus.

Actually, he does mention the issue of meaning in life, but by way of denying his interest in this topic. "People say that what we're all seeking is a meaning for life. I don't think that's what we're really seeking. I think that what we're seeking is an experience of being alive, so that our life experiences on the purely physical plane will have resonances within our own innermost being and reality, so that we actually feel the rapture of being alive."[12] It will soon become apparent that there really is no inconsistency between my claim that he promotes issues of existential meaning and his claim that he is more interested in intensity of living than in meaning. Our subsequent analysis will show that experiences of existential meaning involve the rapturous living Campbell stresses.

If Campbell's great gift is to help people to experiences of existential meaning, but he is inarticulate about what this meaning is, one of the best ways to extend Campbell's positive impact in our time is to delineate the nature and dynamics of existential meaning. In order to do this, however, we will have to turn from the warmth and charm of stories to the coolness and rigor of theory. That is, we will take steps Campbell largely eschews; we will develop conceptuality in the service of theoretical insight. Entry to the requisite theory is obtained by way of an analysis of Campbell's understanding of the power of myth.

Rethinking the Power of Myth

Does Campbell provide us with theoretical resources to comprehend the undeniable power of myth? In fact, it is difficult to know just what he is talking about when he refers to myth, so diffuse is his usage, so varied are his claims. He loosely holds his understanding of mythology together through his oft-repeated claim that traditional mythology has functions relating to four realms of being: the mystical, cosmological, sociological, and psychological. The mystical and the psychological functions, rooted in human ontology and biology, have remained relatively constant through the ages and across cultures. "The spheres of the two that in the course of time have most radically changed are the second and third, the cosmological and the social; for with every new advance in technology, man's knowledge and control of the powers of earth and nature alter, old cosmologies lose their hold and new come into being."[13] Thus his claims about the consistent, archetypal quality of myths tend to refer to the mystical and psychological functions, while his comments about the protean, fluid nature of myths tend to refer to the cosmological and sociological functions.

Because his notions of the myth are so fluid, internal contradictions crop up. For instance, he can say, "When a person becomes a model for other people's lives, he has moved into the sphere of being mythologized."[14] This makes it sound as if we dwell easily and constantly in the mythic realm, for we continually model our behavior on the actions of others. Yet then he states, "We can't have a mythology for a long, long time to come. Things are changing too fast to become mythologized."[15] Campbell is also inclined to advance exaggerated universal propositions. For example, he asserts that there exists a "basic theme of all mythology — that there is an invisible plane supporting the visible one." Again, "what all the myths have to deal with is transformations of consciousness of one kind or another."[16] We shall attempt later to assess these confusing or extreme claims.

To be sure, it is no easy task to define the nature and scope of so complex a notion as myth.[17] Joseph Campbell opens up a useful approach to the study of myth with his analysis of its four functions. Now I wish to extend his analysis by suggesting that myth's mystical, cosmological, sociological, and psychological functions — the source of myth's power — are themselves the products of human intentionality. When a person seeks and finds within a story self-involving clues as to why life is as it is or directions concerning how it should be lived, that person approaches the story through a mythical intentionality.

Actually, all our life experiences unfold out of some framework of intentionality. In our age, many people seem to be stuck in a pragmatic intentionality attuned to achieving everyday goals. But we also interact with and shape our experiences through other frameworks of interpretation. Religious, aesthetic, ethical, playful, or problem-solving frameworks may define our intentionality at given moments. Indeed, components from several different domains may simultaneously influence the way a person engages the world. These subjective frameworks of interpretation represent various ways of "seeing as," to use Wittgenstein's term.

What is distinctive about mythical intentionality?

(1) A person engages a story with *mythical intentionality* when a self-involving normative meaning is sought in and through the narrative.

If the self-involving meaning sought deals with how one's being relates to the reality beyond language and perception, then the mystical dimension of the story is engaged through mythical intentionality. Similarly, if the nature of one's relation to the cosmos or society is comprehended through myth, one's mythical intentionality is attuned to cosmological or sociological norms. When stories are read as sources of advice about how to live well under any circumstances, the psychological function of myth predominates.[18]

Mythical intentionality can be utilized by a person not identifying with any religious tradition. Yet the concerns manifest within mythical intentionality are often similar to those expressed through religious intentionality. A person engages the world through *reli-*

gious intentionality when events are interpreted through a framework shaped by the religious tradition with which one identifies.[19] For a liberal Protestant, sensitivity to the issues of social ethics is highly significant in shaping religious intentionality. In the religious intentionality of many evangelical Protestants, it is difficult to distinguish mythical from religious elements. Campbell's approach to myth is largely devoid of either ethical or religious elements.[20] Yet because he involves his readers in concerns commonly dealt with by the world's religions, it is useful to speak of Campbell's impact as religious in character.

The intentionality within which one dwells at a given time is crucial in governing the nature of one's experience. For example, consider several possible types of intentional approaches to a myth Campbell often refers to, the story of the Garden of Eden in Genesis 2–3. This account may be taken simply as a story, as a sequence of entertaining interactions between God, the woman, the man, and the serpent. Biblical scholars often view the story through an analytical intentionality — for instance, when they scrutinize its form or vocabulary and search for Sumerian antecedents. It becomes a myth only when the items and events in the story are seen via mythical intentionality as revealing a deeper message; they must be seen as existentially meaningful items, as having an allegorical, analogical, or metaphorical weight. It is seen as a *religious* myth when the metaphors are interpreted in religious terms — for instance, as revealing human capability for evil and sin through willful disobedience of God.

My insistence that acquaintance with myths as myths requires a mythical intentionality will seem overly subjective to many people. They will claim that the story of the Garden of Eden or Hesiod's *Theogony* are myths whether or not they are regarded with mythical intentionality. But if they do not go beyond this claim, they may not fully understand the power of myth, nor may they be clear about the difference between myth and mythology. Only if a story has the power to evoke in the reader or listener an emotional interest bearing upon meaning in life does it function as a myth. If our linguistic habits permitted it, it would be desirable to regard "myth" as a verb in order to emphasize that the power of myth resides in an activity it induces in its readers or auditors. A story entertains one's mind and fills one's time; a myth touches one's heart and enriches one's life. For young children, the Garden of Eden can only be a story, never a myth.

It is a convenient shorthand, however, to refer to stories like the Garden of Eden as myths because they have proven to have the power to evoke mythical intentionality among a critical mass of people. Myths can lose that power and become only stories. In ancient Greece, the stories about Zeus and the Olympian gods had the power of myth in Homeric times, but by the time of Plato and Aristotle they had ceased to evoke concern among the majority of people; they had become mythology rather than myth.

Campbell is consistent with many scholars of myth in insisting that myth is a social rather than an individual phenomenon. Thus he states that "a myth is the society's dream. The myth is the public dream and the dream is the private myth."[21] The analysis of myth in terms of mythical intentionality should serve as a caution against seeing myth as an exclusively social phenomenon. One may utilize mythical intentionality in reviewing the important events of one's own life and assessing what they reveal about the direction and purpose of that life. When one tells the story of one's life in harmony with that assessment, one will be in essence the hero of one's *personal myth*. A personal myth is much more than a dream. It links together one's past insights, present activities, and future aspirations into a coherent whole. One may also attempt to view ordinary stories or events with mythical intentionality, but there are shortcomings in such an attempt. Not every story when viewed with mythical intentionality can yield a satisfying or helpful assessment of meaning in life — actually, rather few stories have that capacity. Those stories that prove over time to have the power of myth for social groups or religious bodies can be properly analyzed as social phenomena. Social and religious myths are stories endorsed by social consensus.[22] Hence it is useful to distinguish three major types of myth: personal (individual in nature), social, and religious.

To understand better the benefits and burdens associated with the use of mythical or religious intentionality, it is useful to examine the notions of existential symbols and religious symbols, each produced through an intentionality concerned to find meaning in life.

(2) *Existential symbols* are words, objects, images, or events that represent something of personal significance beyond what they literally seem to mean in everyday existence.

An important type of existential symbol is the *religious symbol*, which gains its meaning from a religious tradition.[23] A seer or diviner typically perceives the world through religious intentionality, and the arrangement of sheep entrails, the flight of birds, or the pattern of clouds may be taken as religious symbols indicating what is to occur.

Likewise, animism may be seen as a disposition to perceive various objects in terms of religious symbols. And yet animistic perception is not an act far distant from reading people's body language in order to assess their state of mind. Thus perceiving the world through existential symbols is not an exotic but a common occurrence as one interprets the meaning of events. Typically existential symbols are organized in inner narratives of significance — surely as much a source of myth as dreams or the unconscious, Campbell's favored founts of myth.

Existential symbols may be vehicles whereby a person is involved in life as a deeply meaningful drama. But they may overwhelm people also, and when a firm anchorage in signals and empirical symbols is undercut, paranoia, schizophrenia, and other dysfunctional states of mind may take over. Writer A. Alvarez gives classical voice to the way that a person contemplating suicide may overdetermine life with existential symbols:

> Once a man decides to take his own life he enters a shut-off, impregnable but wholly convincing world where every detail fits and each incident reinforces his decision. An argument with a stranger in a bar, an expected letter which doesn't arrive, the wrong voice on the telephone, the wrong knock at the door, even a change in the weather — all seem charged with special meaning; they all contribute. The world of the suicide is superstitious, full of omens.[24]

There is no clear line separating religious from other types of existential symbols. One might best ask the interpreter whether he or she considered the symbolic significance of an interpretation religious or not. Does it deal with ultimate issues? The tendency to perceive the world through religious symbols (and existential symbols in general) increases as a person is led to try to deal with uncertainties, for religious intentionality is a strategy employed to find acceptable order in the world. When life is as uncertain as it is in a concentration camp, the tendency is magnified. Thus Simon Wiesenthal talks about such tendencies among fellow Jewish prisoners.

> At that time we were ready to see symbols in everything. It was a time rife for mysticism and superstition. Often my fellow prisoners in the camp told ghost stories. Everything for us was unreal and insubstantial: the earth was peopled with mystical shapes; God was on leave, and in His absence others had taken

over, to give us signs and hints.... We often clung to completely nonsensical interpretations if only they gave us a ray of hope for better times.[25]

Now we are in a position to attempt to clarify some of Campbell's confusing comments about myth mentioned near the beginning of this section. When he claims that we mythologize a person by making that individual a model, he is referring to an action whereby some qualities of an individual are regarded as normative, as existentially meaningful. Modeling is better seen as analogous to the act of forming an existential symbol than as associated with creating a myth (although the model may eventually be incorporated in a personal myth).

What of Campbell's claim that things are changing too fast in American society to become mythologized? Well, the forces leading to increased rapidity of change — primarily the great technological advances in communication and transportation — also allow for an increased pace in the forming of social consensus (and therefore the development of myth). Indeed, the heroic status of Campbell (a religious model for our time) is based upon a consensus formed through the technology of speedy book and video distribution. My concern is not that a mythic vision will fail to develop, but that the many visions that are being constantly projected via the media appeal on the basis of superficial consumer values. They are rooted in desire satisfaction rather than in a holistic vision that includes Campbell's four mythic functions.

Is there any sense to Campbell's claim that all mythology has as a basic theme the support of the visible plane by an invisible one? At the very least, it can be seen that in appreciating a story through mythical intentionality one must look beyond the literal (visible) meaning of the story to its deeper (invisible) existential meaning. Similarly, we can agree with Campbell that all myths have to deal with transformations of consciousness in the sense that a transformation to mythical intentionality from everyday pragmatic consciousness is required if the story is to be appreciated as myth.

The Heroic Communication of Existential Meaning

Another excessive claim frequently creeps into Campbell's discussion of myths. "The main motifs of the myth," he says, "are the same, and they have always been the same."[26] Joseph Campbell has long been influenced by C. G. Jung's thesis that embedded in the consciousness of all humans are certain psychological archetypes that reappear time and again in dreams and myths in different culturally-influenced manifestations. The debate about whether there are such psychic archetypes is difficult to bring to conclusive closure.[27] But I will insist that there is one indisputable constant feature associated with persons experiencing the power of myth. They will inevitably experience existential meaning (and sometimes religious meaning).

(3) A person experiences *existential meaning* when basic interests or concerns of that individual are brought into significant cognitive relation with their aims or validating contexts (whether a purpose, value, community, or sense of the sacred) in a way that over a period of time is felt to matter.

Notice that existential meaning is something experienced. It is based on experiences that are deeply satisfying, and when the satisfactions are experienced frequently and with enough intensity, a person is led to testify that life is worth living. Our everyday experience provides many possibilities for experiencing existential meaning: falling in love with an attractive person, feeling in harmony with nature while hiking through the woods, being engrossed in the middle of a challenging game of chess, being energetically involved in closing an important business deal, finding that a friend understands and accepts our shortcomings, and the like. Each of these experiences involves both feeling and cognition, for both are necessary to experience existential meaning. Our felt interests are satisfied by cognitively-mediated occurrences.

Consequently, experiences of existential meaning *connect* us as caring people to persons, places, projects, and objects in a way that produces feelings of satisfaction. They may connect us to the sacred realm in a way that produces experiences of religious meaning.

(4) The experience of *religious meaning* may be defined to have occurred when important elements of a person's selfhood (especially those of deepest affective significance) are integrated with that person's notion of what is ultimately most real, valuable, and/or powerful through a myth, symbol, ritual, creed, or experience interpreted as religious.

As a variety of existential meaning, religious meaning is an experience involving the fulfillment of a person's basic interest(s). The basic interest might concern such issues as the fear of death, the need for moral guidance, or a quest for ultimate purpose. The satisfaction of that interest would be supplied through religious means — for instance, through a consoling myth religiously intended, or through a type of meditation authorized by a scripture or teacher regarded as authoritative.

Religious meaning is experienced in three rather different modes. The modes differ in the type of power and authority they exhibit. The first mode, originative religious meaning, awakens a person to previously unrecognized sacred dimensions of reality and incidentally contributes to a transformed notion of oneself and life's possibilities. Experiences of originative religious meaning are not consistent with what a person expects, but in their novelty and power force that individual to reconceive what is of religious importance in life. The second mode of religious meaning occurs because the harmony, orientation, purpose, or satisfaction experienced during the originative event fades with time. Thus secondary religious meaning, the second mode, is experienced as a return to the originative source of power and insight via a religious ritual, discipline, or symbolic structure. Often the vehicle used to return is drawn from features of the originative event. The third mode of religious meaning is conventional in nature. When people are socialized into the religious symbolism and belief of a society without concomitant emotional involvement, they experience tertiary religious meaning, an attenuated form that has to do with speaking a language rather than sharing an ecstasy.

Now we are in a better position to understand why Joseph Campbell has been so often seen as a sort of modern religious hero. His skill in communicating the meaning of myths, which we earlier applauded, can now be seen to rest on an exceptional ability to illuminate how images, objects, and ideas can function as existential symbols and allow people to experience existential meaning. He makes numerous connections between different cultures by showing how apparently different religious symbols contribute to similar experiences of religious meaning. This appeals to those seeking to overcome provincialism. Yet it is his quasi-confessional pleasure in revealing the nature of the existential symbols that is especially infectious; the readers or viewers soon begin sharing first the interest and then the emotional involvement in the subject matter, which can in turn become the occasion for them experiencing existential meaning themselves. Rare is the person whose speaking or writing has such power to produce experiences of existential meaning.

The stories, rituals, and occasions Campbell recounts, if merely told and not interpreted, would likely function as a form of entertainment. But Campbell is masterful in the way he pushes beyond the literal meaning of a slogan or a story to entice the viewer into thinking about the slogan's or story's deeper meaning, a meaning that may link up with the viewer's own interests or story. He focuses on key images or ideas — the tree, the circle, the monster, the mother, the serpent — and deepens them into existential symbols by suggesting how they represent more than their literal meanings. He teaches people how to attend to stories with mythical intentionality rather than as forgettable occasions for entertainment. That is, he has the ability to make a myth a myth and not just a story.

For that group of people alienated from institutional religion, Campbell shows how traditional mythic and religious materials have existential meaning. For those at least marginally within a religious tradition, Campbell may suggest how traditional materials taken for granted — and even materials outside one's tradition — manifest religious meaning. That is, he can take material that functions at the tertiary level of religious meaning and enliven it so that for some people it may even gain the power of an originative experience of religious meaning. Probably that is atypical. More likely he refurbishes myths, symbols, and perhaps rituals so that they may be appropriated by others as worthy symbolic expressions for their own interests and concerns. This would result in a move from tertiary to secondary religious meaning.

Myths die. As the great theologian Paul Tillich made clear, social conditions may change so that a story loses its power to interpret the conditions of life in the new situation.[28] Or a myth may be repeated so often that its deeper insights become too obvious and therefore lose their evocative power. That is, myths follow the same course of development that metaphors follow. When fresh, they lure the imagination and sponsor creative synthesis. When old, they become clichés and die as myths. Theology and ritual are subject to similar laws of cultural evolution. Yet the most profound theological insights and ritualized activities — those grounded in a strong living tradition — will be returned to again and again when a certain stylized interpretation has worn out.

For most people Campbell's interpretations have the enormous advantage of being fresh. He therefore appeals to the despisers of religion as well as the group of people who remain in churches yet are uninspired by the usual religious activities. The intrinsically interesting quality of the material he recites attracts those distanced from institutional religion. But lacking any institutional or traditional support, Campbell's thought would seem exceptionally vulnerable to shifting social conditions and changing fads. The thousand and first face of the hero, the storyteller-scholar who interprets the religious literature of the world, may be more subject to the laws of the television market than in harmony with the perennial philosophy. But if in the process of being consumed, so to speak, Campbell enriches the lives of numerous people — and he has — one suspects that he would not mind that his day passes. Or rather one suspects he might be double-minded about his heroic status. One part of him (his more egoistic aspect) would like to see his memory persevere, but a higher level knows that this is neither possible nor desirable. Thus he says that for a limited view

> the desired end is normally a victory of the hero, of the higher, saving and releasing power over the lower, binding and limiting.... But on the other hand, when the aim is to dissolve and surpass the limitations even of the highest names, forms, and modes of understanding of the dream-bound will, the desired end becomes the opposite, namely the sacrifice of the hero-form itself, as itself limiting and binding.[29]

Joseph Campbell would be a most profound hero if he led his followers to experiences of religious meaning that made any dependence upon further guidance dispensable.

One speculates — is the all-too-vulnerable thousand and first face but a prelude to the thousand and second face? And what might that succeeding face bring us — an accounting of the meaning of the world's religions backed by a global mythology, a world theology, and institutional support that would sustain the insights? Might it even ensure that mythically grounded existential meaning is also ethically sensitive? Perhaps, but for now there is much to learn from the deeds of the thousand and first face.

PART TWO

Aspects of the Monomyth:
Eastern, Western, and
Philosophical Assessments

4

Joseph Campbell and Eastern Religions: The Influence of India

Harold Coward

MOYERS: And your life comes from where?

CAMPBELL: From the ultimate energy that is the life of the Universe. And then do you say, "Well, there must be somebody generating that energy"? Why do you have to say that? Why can't the ultimate mystery be impersonal?

MOYERS: Can men and women live with an impersonality?

CAMPBELL: Yes, they do all over the place. Just go east of Suez.[1]

Joseph Campbell searched the world for the common themes in world myths and religions. In these he found not so much the meaning of life as the source of that meaning in the fundamental *experience* of being alive.[2] While he used all traditions as grist for his mill, Campbell was particularly attracted to the life experience embodied in the Indian religions — especially Hinduism and Buddhism. Much of the Indian perspective was parallel to his own perception of life, although there were points where he drew the line. For example, basic Indian teachings such as individual rebirth he rejected.

This essay will chart the course of Campbell's spiritual odyssey with the great religions of India. It is not too much to say that the Indian melodies of the "music of the spheres" (Campbell's definition of

47

mythology) had an abiding influence on his life and thought. Indeed it was in the Indian "melodies" of the Upanisads and Bodhisattvas that Campbell found the only mythology that is valid for today and for the future.[3] In the Indian religions he found the template for fitting together the future myth of our planet.

Joseph Campbell was greatly influenced by the Indologist Heinrich Zimmer. Campbell remembers as a young man hearing Zimmer lecture: "He was the first man I know of to speak about myths as though they had messages that were valid for life, not just interesting things for scholars to fool around with. And that confirmed me in a feeling I had had ever since boyhood."[4] The confirmation that Campbell found in the Indian stories Zimmer recounted paralleled the earlier experience of Carl Jung. For Jung the Indian texts, especially those on yoga, provided independent confirmation for his own developing insights.[5] The stories Campbell encountered in Hinduism seemed to be the same stories nuns had taught him as a young Roman Catholic boy and that were also present in Native American mythology. Later he was to find them repeated in Western medieval materials.[6] But it was their formulations in the Indian religions that seemed foundational for Campbell. This drew him to learn Sanskrit and to edit four of Zimmer's books: *Philosophies of India, Myths and Symbols in Indian Art and Civilization, The King and the Corpse* and *The Art of Indian Asia: Its Mythology and Transformations*.[7] He was also strongly influenced in his understanding of Indian yoga by Mircea Eliade's *Yoga: Immortality and Freedom*,[8] and by the writings of Jung, whose views on India Campbell frequently quotes. Although he did not have a comprehensive grounding in Hinduism and Indian Buddhism, Campbell often successfully highlighted their essentials. On occasion he does misrepresent the Indian viewpoint and at places, as noted, he rejects the Eastern teachings, so that it is necessary to examine the points of confirmation Campbell found for his view of mythology in Indian religions, and then identify where he stops short in his acceptance of the East.

Confirming Parallels in Indian Religions

In a recent lecture Campbell defined "religion" as "misunderstood mythology."[9] The misunderstanding is the interpretation of mythic metaphors as references to hard fact: for example, the Virgin Birth seen as a biological anomaly or "God" as denoting "an actual although invisible, masculine personality, who created the universe and is now resident in an invisible, though actual, heaven to which the 'justified' will go when they die, there to be joined at the end of time by their resurrected bodies."[10] It is the tendency of religion, says Campbell, toward such factual interpretations of metaphors that leads to problems of narrowness. From early in life religious dogmatism of this kind seemed to Campbell to be nonsense. Such metaphors were not literal fact but productions of the human imagination from the perceptions provided by the world around and by the contents arising from the deeper levels of our inner psyches. These are organized into mythic patterns by the ancestral forms or archetypes, inherent in our unconscious.[11] Whereas our dreams give us individual expressions of these archetypes, the contents of religions at their height reveal universal manifestations. Campbell found this to be more evident in Eastern as opposed to Western religions. While Eastern religions focused on the primordial patterns of truth, Western religions (Judaism, Christianity, and Islam) are seen as relating persons to their particular society rather than to universal forms.[12] Instead of concentrating on individual or tribal experience, the Indian religions have the genius of seeing that inherent in the natural world are the same universal patterns that organize our personalities (body, mind, and spirit). Campbell quotes the *Chandogya Upanisad:* "Just as those who do not know the spot might pass, time and time again, over a hidden treasure of gold without discovering it, so do all creatures of this world pass daily into that Brahma-world [in deep sleep] without discovering it, distracted as they are by false ideas."[13] The role of religion, in the Indian view, is to awaken one from false ideas so that the true reality (the treasure of gold that has been there all the while) is revealed. This is also Campbell's understanding of how myth functions. This traditional wisdom from the past has the power to awaken us from our ignorance so that we can truly experience life.

The story of the Hindu god Indra is one of Campbell's favorite illustrations of this point.

> Now, it happened at this time that a great monster had enclosed all the waters of the earth, so there was a terrible drought, and the world was in a very bad condition. It took Indra quite a while to realize that he had a box of thunderbolts and that all he had to do was drop a thunderbolt on the monster and blow him up. When he did that, the waters flowed, and the world was refreshed, and Indra said, "What a great boy am I."
>
> So, thinking, "What a great boy am I," Indra goes up to the cosmic mountain, which is the central mountain of the world,

and decides to build a palace worthy of such as he. The main carpenter of the gods [Vishvakarman] goes to work on it, and in very quick order he gets the palace into pretty good condition. But every time Indra comes to inspect it, he has bigger ideas about how splendid and grandiose the palace should be. Finally, the carpenter says, "My god, we are both immortal, and there is no end to his desires. I am caught for eternity." So he decides to go to Brahma, the creator god, and complain.

Brahma sits on a lotus, the symbol of divine energy and divine grace. The lotus grows from the navel of Vishnu, who is the sleeping god, whose dream is the universe. So the carpenter comes to the edge of the great lotus pond of the universe and tells his story to Brahma. Brahma says, "You go home. I will fix this up." Brahma gets off his lotus and kneels down to address sleeping Vishnu. Vishnu just makes a gesture and says something like, "Listen, fly, something is going to happen."

Next morning, at the gate of the palace that is being built, there appears a beautiful blue-black boy with a lot of children around him, just admiring his beauty. The porter at the gate of the new palace goes running to Indra, and Indra says, "Well, bring in the boy." The boy is brought in, and Indra, the king god, sitting on his throne, says, "Young man, welcome. And what brings you to my palace?"

"Well," says the boy with a voice like thunder rolling on the horizon, "I have been told that you are building such a palace as no Indra before you ever built."

And Indra says, "Indras before me, young man — what are you talking about?"

The boy says, "Indras before you. I have seen them come and go, come and go. Just think, Vishnu sleeps in the cosmic ocean, and the lotus of the universe grows from his navel. On the lotus sits Brahma, the creator. Brahma opens his eyes, and a world comes into being, governed by an Indra. Brahma closes his eyes, and a world goes out of being. The life of a Brahma is four hundred and thirty-two thousand years. When he dies, the lotus goes back, and another lotus is formed, and another Brahma. Then think of the galaxies beyond galaxies in infinite space, each a lotus, with a Brahma sitting on it, opening his eyes, closing his eyes. And Indras? There may be wise men in your court who would volunteer to count the drops of water in the oceans of the world or the grains of sand on the beaches, but no one would count those Brahmin, let alone those Indras."

While the boy is talking, an army of ants parades across the floor. The boy laughs when he sees them, and Indra's hair stands on end, and he says to the boy, "Why do you laugh?" The boy answers, "Don't ask unless you are willing to be hurt." Indra says, "I ask. Teach." (That, by the way, is a good Oriental idea: you don't teach until you are asked. You don't force your mission down people's throats.) And so the boy points to the ants and says, "Former Indras all. Through many lifetimes they rise from the lowest conditions to highest illumination. And then they drop their thunderbolt on a monster, and they think, 'What a good boy am I.' And down they go again."

While the boy is talking, a crotchety old yogi comes into the palace with a banana leaf parasol. He is naked except for a loincloth, and on his chest is a little disk of hair, and half the hairs in the middle have all dropped out.

The boy greets him and asks him just what Indra was about to ask. "Old man, what is your name? Where do you come from? Where is your family? Where is your house? And what is the meaning of this curious constellation of hair on your chest?"

"Well," says the old fella, "my name is Hairy. I don't have a house. Life is too short for that. I just have this parasol. I don't have a family. I just meditate on Vishnu's feet, and think of eternity, and how passing time is. You know, every time an Indra dies, a world disappears — these things just flash by like that. Every time an Indra dies, one hair drops out of this circle on my chest. Half the hairs are gone now. Pretty soon they will all be gone. Life is short. Why build a house?"

Then the two disappear. The boy was Vishnu, the Lord Protector, and the old yogi was Shiva, the creator and destroyer of the world, who had just come for the instruction of Indra, who is simply a god of history but thinks he is the whole show.

Indra is sitting there on the throne, and he is completely disillusioned, completely shot. He calls the carpenter and says, "I'm quitting the building of this palace. You are dismissed." So the carpenter got his intention. He is dismissed from the job, and there is no more house building going on.

Indra decides to go out and be a yogi and just meditate on the lotus feet of Vishnu. But he has a beautiful queen named Indrani. And when Indrani hears of Indra's plan, she goes to the priest of the gods and says, "Now he has got the idea in his head of going out to become a yogi."

"Well," says the priest, "come in with me, darling, and we will sit down, and I will fix this up."

So they sit down before the king's throne, and the priest says, "Now, I wrote a book for you many years ago on the art of politics. You are in the position of the king of the gods. You are a manifestation of the mystery of Brahma in the field of time. This is a high privilege. Appreciate it, honor it, and deal with life as though you were what you really are. And besides, now I am going to write you a book on the art of love so that you and your wife will know that in the wonderful mystery of the two that are one, the Brahma is radiantly present also."

And with this set of instructions, Indra gives up his idea of going out and becoming a yogi and finds that, in life, he can represent the eternal as a symbol, you might say, of the Brahma.

So each of us is, in a way, the Indra of his own life. You can make a choice, either to throw it all off and go into the forest to meditate, or to stay in the world, both in the life of your job, which is the kingly job of politics and achievement, and in the love life with your wife and family. Now, this is a very nice myth, it seems to me.[14]

Campbell's fondness for this Hindu scripture is easily understood. The Indra story displays all of the key characteristics Campbell finds in myths: surface ego-centered ignorance that, when removed, reveals an eternal truth; an eternal truth that manifests itself over and over in human experience; human experience which repeats an eternal pattern that, when understood, allows one to choose well and live life to the full; the hero as the one who makes the right choice by sacrificing his own desires to live in conformity with the divine pattern.

If we are attentive, the scripture or the myth provides us with the clue about how to live our own lives. This is its metaphorical function. It relates our own psychological experience to a pattern/truth/reality that is transcendent and has the power of transforming us.[15] In passing we might observe that Campbell especially likes the Indra passage because of its refusal option that tempts Indra, namely, to go off from the responsibilities of this life and live as a world-denying yogi. The final section of this essay will show that this is one of the points where Campbell, like most Westerners, rejects the apparently world-negating yogic path of the Indian religions.

The Stages of Life and the Hero

Indian religion also presents a fully developed understanding of the stages each of us must go through in realizing the experience of Indra in our own lives. These four stages of life are manifested in the great heroes of the Indian tradition (e.g., Indra, Buddha, and Ramakrishna) and are found by Campbell to parallel and confirm his theory of the stages to be traversed by the heroes in *The Hero with a Thousand Faces*.[16] His favorite example is Buddha because the Buddha, perhaps more clearly than anyone else, saw that playing the game of life, and going through the various stages of transformation, does not release from pain and frustration but, to the contrary, makes us see the unending suffering of life more clearly. We don't escape life's suffering but our attitude toward it gets transformed and therein lies our peace. This, according to Campbell, parallels what happens in the departure and return of the transformed hero.

In Heinrich Zimmer's *Philosophies of India*, which Campbell edited, the four stages of life (*asrama*) are described as follows.[17] First, there is the student stage characterized by obedience and submission to one's teacher from whom one learns the basics of one's tradition. The external forms of one's myth or religion are absorbed into consciousness and begin to resonate to the archetypal patterns already present in the unconscious. The remainder of one's life is spent in actualizing the rote learnings of the student stage.

Second is the householder stage — the stage Indra was in in Campbell's favorite story. One gets married (the partner being chosen by one's parents), produces children, materially supports the family by engaging in trade and commerce, and fulfills one's *dharma* or social duty in terms of community responsibilities that in Indra's case included being king. In this stage one is fully identified with one's biological and social personality. The trick is not to become so totally caught up in these worldly activities that the transcendent reality behind such everyday events is lost to sight. This is exactly what happened to Indra and what Campbell says happens to us. Our egos get carried away with our apparent power and success. Just as occurred with Indra, the role of story/scripture/myth is to awaken us from our ego-encapsulation in worldly life, to put it in perspective, and to prepare the way for the spiritual transformation of the final two stages.

When the hair turns gray, and wrinkles and grandchildren appear, it is time to give up one's material goods and worldly concerns, take a new name, and go into the third, or forest, stage. One's children now must shoulder the responsibility of bearing the joys and burdens of the world. Our essence, which transcends our identification with the householder world, begins to clamor for actualization. This is what Jung referred to as the individuation of the Self, the God archetype, a task that could not usually be taken up until one was over forty and entering the second half of life.[18] For Campbell, the myths guide us through this same process. When asked by Bill Moyers what myth helped him through the transition of moving into the last years of his life, Campbell replied,

> The tradition in India, for instance, of actually changing your name as you pass from one stage to another. When I retired from teaching, I knew that I had to create a new way of life, and I changed my manner of thinking about my life, just in terms of that notion — moving out of the sphere of achievement into the sphere of enjoyment and appreciation and relaxing to the wonder of it all....
>
> The problem in middle life, when the body has reached its climax of power and begins to decline, is to identify yourself not with the body, which is falling away, but with the consciousness of which it is a vehicle.[19]

In the Indian view, this process requires the leaving behind of one's worldly pleasures and possessions, joining oneself again to a teacher (*guru*) and devoting the remainder of one's days to the quest for the spiritual Self submerged under the worldly concerns of the householder stage. Husband and wife can enter this forest stage together, but they must both be dedicated to the same spiritual aim. Thus, activities appropriate to the worldly aims of the householder stage, such as engaging in sexual intercourse, must be left behind. Their love relationship continues but now suffused with spiritual rather than worldly concerns.

The fourth and final stage is that of the wandering holy beggar — no longer linked to any teacher, place, or discipline. Now fully identified with one's essential Self, one returns to the world as the guide and teacher for others. It is in this guise that Śiva appeared as the wandering hermit with no need for a house before

Indra. It was to fulfill this stage that Buddha after his enlightenment did not go off into his private *nirvāṇa* but, in conformity with the essential nature of his enlightenment consciousness, returned to his fellow hermits and to worldly society, spending the remaining thirty or so years of his life in teaching, healing, stopping wars, and helping others.[20]

The struggle and achievement of the spiritual transformation through these four stages of life is effectively evoked in Hermann Hesse's novel, *Siddhartha*.[21] The fourth stage is the discovery of what a human being is behind all the marks, clothes, achievements, possessions, and activities that mark his or her worldly status. In the Indian view not only are the markings of the family and social life transcended, but also those of religious ritual and institution. One is fully identified with the reality that underlies, supports, and animates all social action and all of nature. In the Indian tradition this final release is the work of yoga or self-discovery. Zimmer describes the proper end of the last two stages of life as "...the time for wiping off the actor's paint that one wore on the universal stage, the time for the recollection and release of the unaffected and uninvolved, yet all-sustaining and exacting, living Person who was always there."[22] In Campbell's analysis, this is also the goal of the Hero myths — *Apotheosis*, the release of the potential within each of us as a result of our own divinization. After that, as was the case with the Buddha, there is the return of the hero carrying the boon that will restore the world.[23]

The Indian notion of "the Four Stages of Life" and Campbell's analysis of the stages of the Hero's adventure are meant to teach us to change what we identify ourselves with. In the earlier stages, under the influence of the strong thrust of our biological drives, we tend to identify with our bodies and our capacity for external achievements. In the later stages when the body has reached its climax of power and begins to decline, the focus of the adventure turns inward to the conquest of the psyche and the spirit. While many of the Western myths, especially those from classical Greece, tend to highlight beautiful youth, the myths and religions of India constantly lead on past the ephemeral beauty and pleasure of youth to the challenge that sickness, old age, and death represent. As roadmaps for our own self-discovery, the Indian teachings lead us to discover the underlying reality behind the passing stages of life. Campbell frequently quotes the teaching of the *Bhagavad Gita* in this regard:

Finite are these our bodies indwelt by an eternal embodied self....

As a man casts off his worn-out clothes and takes on other new ones, so does the embodied self cast off its worn-out bodies and enter new ones.[24]

The function of Indian religions, and of the world myths, is to help us recognize the passing stages of life as ephemera and to identify ourselves instead with the continuing reality of the Self. Like the myths, said Campbell, the Indian religions offer *margas*, or pathways back to ourselves.[25] We learn to identify not with the body, which is falling away, but with the consciousness of which it is a vehicle — not with the bulb that carries the light but the light of which the bulb is a vehicle.[26] In conformity with both Hinduism and Buddhism Campbell conceived of this eternal inner Self in terms of universal consciousness.[27] The superiority of Eastern religion, said Campbell, is that it allows for a direct identification of the individual searcher with the divine consciousness. The gods of the various religions are understood to be simply masks by which the universal consciousness manifests itself in different times and places.

The problem with the Western religions of Judaism, Christianity, and Islam, Campbell believed, is that they take their masks of God too seriously. Instead of seeing them as metaphors of God they are taken to be literally true. This mistaken focus on the outer image as the reality, on the denotation rather than the connotation of the symbol, gets in the way of one's identification with the divine. "We cannot identify with Jesus, we have to imitate Jesus."[28] To identify oneself with God in Jesus or Yahweh or Allah is blasphemy in the West. In Campbell's view, this Western stance is a serious obstacle to the transformation of our surface selves into our true selves by direct identification with the divine. He seems to completely embrace the Indian position that, for example, "We are all manifestations of Buddha consciousness or Christ consciousness, only we don't know it."[29] Unlike Western religion, neither Buddha nor the Hindu Veda is the truth. Both, however, are metaphors that show the way to truth. In India Campbell found that the metaphoric nature of the divine images and the mythic stories is well understood, as is the need for a direct identification with the divine if the "waking-up" or transformation of the devotee is to take place. Indeed, that is exactly the role played by Indian Yoga in the latter two stages of life, and, as such, it held a great fascination for Campbell.

Yoga and Transformation

In discussing the nature of the ultimate illumination Campbell quoted the words of William Blake, "If the doors of perception were cleansed man would see everything as it is, infinite."[30] This he found to be the exact function of Eastern yoga — the removing of obstacles from the psyche so that one's sense organs and consciousness would be cleansed and reality, both external and internal, clearly perceived. While the Indra story provided a mythic guide to the earlier stages of life, especially that of the householder, for the last two stages and the ultimate transformation of consciousness Campbell repeatedly turned to Indian Yoga for guidance. Yoga, especially Kuṇḍalinī Yoga, functioned as Campbell's key to understanding the myths of transformation he found in other traditions.[31] In Kuṇḍalinī Yoga Campbell found a pictographic lexicon of the stages of transformation of one's vital energy and consciousness. These various stages are represented as being controlled from spinal centers known as *chakras*. The *chakras* are pictured as a system of seven psychological centers up the spine. They are arranged in ascending order along an invisible nerve or spinal channel.

The *chakras*, or lotus centers, represent psychological spiritual stages in the transformation of consciousness. Campbell follows Tantric theory in his understanding of these centers. In this he differs from Carl Jung, who interpreted Kuṇḍalinī Yoga through the eyes of his own psychology and as a result concluded that the last two *chakras* cannot be assimilated into our Western experience. In Jung's view the two highest *chakras* proposed transformations into states of consciousness that simply did not exist.[32] As a result Jung dismissed the last two stages of Kuṇḍalinī Yoga as "superfluous speculations with no practical value."[33] By contrast Campbell faithfully follows the Kuṇḍalinī model right through to the complete identity experience of the *sahasrara chakra*. In this respect Campbell accepts much more influence from Kuṇḍalinī Yoga than does Jung. Let us now briefly examine Campbell's description and analysis of the ascending *chakras*.

Campbell's most extended discussion of the *chakras* occurs in chapter 3, "Metaphors of Psychological Transformation," of *The Inner Reaches of Outer Space*. The first and lowest *chakra*, the *mūlādhāra* (*mula* meaning "root"), is located at the base of the spine between the anus and the genitals. It is identified as the motivating center of the primal holding-to-life of infancy and early childhood. Its concern is with the simplest and most basic life-sustaining functions such as

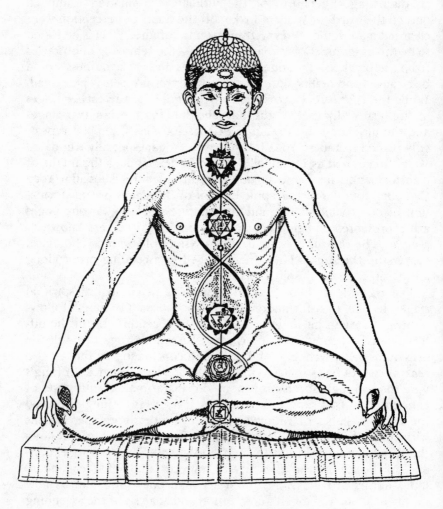

eating. Materialistic concern is ascendent and spiritual energy is at its lowest ebb. As Campbell puts it, "The world view is of uninspired materialism governed by 'hard facts'; the art, sentimental naturalism; and the psychology, adequately described in behavioristic terms, is reactive, not active."[35] On this plane life is a lethargic hanging on to existence, a blockage that must be broken through so that the flow of spiritual energy may be freed to expand. This blockage is symbolically portrayed in the form of a *linga* with the *Kuṇḍalinī* (translated as "serpent") coiled eight times around it and blocking the opening of the *linga* with its mouth. Thus *Kuṇḍalinī* blocks the awakening and manifestation of the "root power" of the *mūlādhāra chakra*. Campbell likens the *Kuṇḍalinī* on this level to the mythic dragon, "for dragons, we are told by those who know, have a propensity to hoard and guard things...."[36] Their blocking effect, however, makes them unable to use things; they simply hang on, as did King Midas, until the values in their treasury are lost to themselves and the world. The first task of the yogi, then, is to break the cold grip of spiritual lethargy and release the creative powers of his own spiritual energy for ascent to higher levels where bliss awaits when one is awakened from dull sleep. In mythology Campbell relates this first *chakra* to Cadmus fighting the dragon, St. George killing the dragon, and Sigurd defeating the monster Fafnir.

The next higher *chakra*, or, as Campbell terms it, "bioenergetic station," is called the *svādhiṣṭhāna* and located at the level of the genitals — the center of the urge to procreate. It is pictured as a vermillion lotus of six petals in the center of which is a white half-moon upon which is written a seed (*bija*) *mantra*, or sound. When the *Kuṇḍalinī* energy and consciousness break free of the *mūlādhāra* and rise to this level the whole aim of life is in sex. Every action or thought is either explicitly directed toward sexual ends or, as Freud taught, is sublimated into other activities due to sexual frustration at the conscious or unconscious levels. Myths and religious rituals are understood and experienced in sexual terms. Here Campbell thinks of fertility rites, marriage rites, and orgiastic festivals. He cites Dionysos, Eros and Psyche, Venus and Cupid as mythic examples of this stage of psychological transformation. It relates to the sexual awakening of adolescence and the Householder stage of life. Unlike the Freudian reading, which tends to get stuck here, Kuṇḍalinī Yoga "recognizes affirmatively the force and importance of this center and lets the energies pass on *through* it, to become naturally transformed to other aims at the higher centers of the 'rich in happiness' *sushumna* [the highest *chakra*]."[37]

The third *chakra* at the level of the navel is called *maṇipūra* and is pictured as a blue-black lotus of ten petals in the middle of which is a red triangle upon which a god and goddess sit mounted on a bull. Here the rising *kuṇḍalinī* actualizes the will to power, mastery, and control. In its positive aspect it is a sense of pride in responsibility and achievement, but its negative manifestation is as an insatiable will to conquer, plunder, and subjugate, making the world over into a likeness of oneself. Here Campbell adduces the Western parallel of the Adlerian "will to power" under which the *Kuṇḍalinī* energy is frequently transformed into violence with its aim of consuming and mastering for oneself. Even sex now becomes an occasion not of erotic experience, but of achievement, conquest, self-reassurance, and sometimes even revenge. In terms of mythology Campbell relates this *chakra* to the Hindu goddess Lakini, who presides over rites of human sacrifice and over wars, the Great Hunt of King Ashurbanipal, and religious persecutions such as St. Dominic burning books or the Inquisition. One thinks of Dostoyevsky's story "The Grand Inquisitor," the struggles Siddhartha had with his son in Hesse's novel of the same name, or, at its most horrific, the Holocaust of the Nazi death camps in Eli Wiesel's *Night*.

These first three *chakras* govern the lives of most people and a large portion of human history. They represent human experience up to the Householder stage of life. Symbolically located in the pelvic basin, these three levels of energy transformation remain close to the levels of animal instinct: namely, (1) to survive by eating and securing material resources, (2) to generate offspring, and (3) to conquer and subdue. Unrestrained, these manifestations of our basic life energy (*Kuṇḍalinī*) can become very destructive. So Indian society developed its own set of controlling rules in the *Arthaśāstras*.[38] Freud in his *Future of an Illusion*[39] and *Civilization and Its Discontents*[40] argued that this was the role religion had played in society up to the present but that now should be taken over by reason and science. Unlike Freud, however, Campbell, following Kuṇḍalinī Yoga, sees the role of religion as mythic spirituality and the potential of human transformation as having much more to offer than just negative control. These more positive transformations of psychic energy and consciousness are symbolically represented in the final four *chakras*. While the biological urges that remain predominant in the first three *chakras* characterize human development during the first half of life, the final four *chakras* portray inward spiritual transformations that can be realized through heroic struggles during the second half of life. In India this would correspond to the forest and holy wanderer stages.

The beginnings of this spiritual awakening occur with the rising of the *Kuṇḍalinī* energy from the level of the pelvis (the first three *chakras*) to the heart, the level of the fourth *chakra*.[41] Like Jung, Campbell warns against the reductionistic mistake (the mistake of Freud) of interpreting the imagery, powers, and values of the higher *chakras* in terms of the pelvic *chakras*. To do this, says Campbell, is to lose contact with oneself and "with the whole history and heritage of mankind's life in the spirit."[42] Both Campbell and Jung feel that this is the trap in which modern Western society finds itself caught. The importance of Eastern teaching, such as Kuṇḍalinī Yoga, is that it can resensitize contemporary persons to the fact that their pelvic region is not the sum total of their personality and its potentialities — that higher levels of psychological/spiritual transformation await them.

The *anāhata*, or fourth, *chakra*, found at the level of the heart, is colored red with a twelve-petaled golden lotus in the middle of which are two intersecting triangles. In this *chakra* spiritual awakening is said to occur as the Lord awakens the devotee by the sound OM or by touch. This awakening is the beginning of new life — the taking of a new name as one enters the forest stage or goes through some kind of initiation ceremony that opens one to compassion. "Here," says Campbell, "you move out of the field of animal action into a field that is properly human and spiritual."[43] Although the *lingam* and *yoni* (the male and female organs) reappear from the first *chakra*, they are now represented in gold, symbolic of the birth of the spiritual human out of the animal human. In this Campbell finds the key to understanding the myth of the Virgin Birth, which appears in both the birth of Jesus and the birth of the Buddha. The Virgin Birth, Campbell says, symbolizes a spiritual rather than a physical birth. "Heroes and demigods are born that way as beings motivated by compassion and not mastery, sexuality, or self-preservation."[44] The second birth occurs when you transcend, not refute, your lower three centers, and they become servants to the heart center. This is Campbell's interpretation of the significance of the myth that Buddha was born from his mother's side — from the level of the heart *chakra*. It is also the moment when Dante at the opening of *La Vita Nuova* first beheld in Beatrice the spirit of life that dwells in the secret chamber of the heart. The awakening to his higher spirit causes the natural spirit (of the lower *chakras*) "to weep, and, weeping, [say] these words: 'Woe is me, wretched! because often from this time forth shall I be hindered.'"[45] The ascendance of the higher centers over the lower has commenced. From here on the transformation of character required is that of the mind pursuing ends beyond the range of the physical senses.

The fifth *chakra*, the *viśuddha*, is centered in the throat and is symbolized by a lotus of sixteen petals of smoky purple hue. In the middle is a white circle containing an elephant representing complete purity. What is required is a complete cleansing of the doors of perception by a turning in upon oneself of the energy expressing itself as malice and aggression. Rather than being focused outward upon the world as a criticism of others (as in *chakra* three) one's critical energies are turned inward. Here Campbell quotes the thought of Jesus: do not attempt to remove the speck from your brother's eye until you have first removed the plank from your own (Matthew 7:3–5). This represents the overcoming of the Freudian defense mechanism of projection by which we seek to deal with our own weaknesses by projecting them on to another and then ruthlessly criticizing the other. Tantra yoga texts refer to this *chakra* as the gateway of the Great Liberation and pictorially represent it as a wrathful deity in demonic form cutting off heads, arms, and legs (one's own aggressive impulses) and trampling human forms (one's own aggression, recognized for what it is and turned back upon itself). In myths, says Campbell, this corresponds to the thresholds "where the frightening Gate Guardians stand, the Sirens sing, the Clashing Rocks come together, and a ferry sets forth to the Land of No Return, the Land Below Waves, the Land of Eternal Youth."[46] The *Katha Upaniṣad* adds that it is like the edge of a sharpened razor, very hard to traverse (*Katha Upaniṣad* 3.14). In art Campbell references "The Temptation of St. Anthony" by Martin Schongauer and William Blake's "To Annihilate the Self-hood of Deceit and False Forgiveness." In India various Yoga techniques have been devised to turn one's temptations to power or sex against oneself. There is even a dream yoga that parallels the modern Western techniques of dream analysis (e.g., Freud and Jung). Such techniques enable one to come to awareness of the contents of one's unconscious and purge them. When purified, when the *Kuṇḍalini* energy is transformed to this level, then, said the modern Indian saint Ramakrishna, "the devotee longs to talk and hear only of God."[47]

The last two *chakras* deal with a direct mystical experience of reality or the divine by becoming one with it either through a finite form (the yogic *savikalpa samādhi*), *chakra* six, or without finite form (the yogic *nirvikalpa samādhi*), *chakra* seven. Here Campbell goes beyond Carl Jung in his willingness to accept these last two *chakras* as real psychological states. Jung, in his 1932 analysis of Kuṇḍalini Yoga, discards these last two *chakras* as non-existing products of the over-heated Indian imagination.[48] For Campbell, however, the last two *chakras* are clear descriptions of the experiences of great saints such as Ramakrishna and Meister Eckhart. Indeed, they represent the final goal of identity with the divine that we each have to realize.[49]

The sixth, or *ājñā*, *chakra* is located between the eyebrows. It is pictured as a white lotus of two petals in the middle of which is a white triangle pointing downward and containing a white *linga*. It is said to be the locus of the cognitive faculties, mind (*buddhi*), ego-sense (*ahāmkāra*), and the sense organs (*indriyas*), but purified so completely as to be free of all normal limitations. There, one is said to experience a direct intuition of the essence of reality (e.g., as the *Rishis'* "seeing" of the Vedas, or the devotee's vision of the Lord). In theistic religions, the form intuited is of one's ultimate vision of God. For Campbell the form one's ultimate vision takes is both a function of one's own state of mind and a product of one's culture:

> Catholic nuns do not have visions of the Buddha, nor do Buddhist nuns have visions of Christ. Ineluctably, the image of any god beheld — whether interpreted as beheld in heaven or as beheld at Chakra 6 — will be of a local ethnic idea historically conditioned, a metaphor, therefore, and thus to be recognized as transparent to transcendence.[50]

Within this historically-bound appearance Campbell includes such examples as Dante's view of the Beatific Vision of God, the *Mandala* of the Admantine Bolt, and the *yin-yang* — the last two symbolizing the pairs of opposites in balance. This is as high as one can go in the experience of form. Hinduism refers to it as the level of *saguna Brahman* — Brahman with qualities. At this point Campbell quotes the Hindu saint Ramakrishna. Having seen the form of God the devotee "becomes mad with joy and wishes to be one with the all-pervading Divine, but cannot do so. It is like the light of a lamp inside a glass case. One feels one could touch the light, but the glass intervenes and prevents it."[51] Moving beyond *chakra* six requires the removal of the glass-like barrier so that the ultimate aim of the yogic transformation, namely, the experience of identity, can be realized.

Sahasrāra, the final *chakra*, is described as beyond all duality and located at the top of the head. It is represented as a many-colored thousand-petaled lotus, facing downward. The petals bear all the possible articulations of the Sanskrit alphabet and therefore of all sound. In the center of the lotus is the full moon enclosing a triangle.

It is here, says Eliade, that the final union of Śiva and Śakti, the male and female powers, is realized.[52] Here the *Kuṇḍalinī* energy (the *Śakti*, or female, power) ends its journey after having passed through the various *chakras* and, in passing, awakening each lotus to full blossom. In the union of the serpent power (*Śakti*) with the Lord (*Śiva*), the level of the body, mind, and worldly experience has been transformed, purified, and completely transcended. Thus, this final *chakra* is simultaneously a complete union of all the opposites of experience (e.g., male and female) and an ultimate transcending of them. Again Campbell cites Ramakrishna along with Eckhart:

> If we remove that glasslike barrier of which Ramakrishna spoke, both our God and ourselves will explode then into light, sheer light, one light, beyond names and forms, beyond thought and experience, beyond even the concepts "being" and "non-being." "The soul in God," Eckhart has said, "has naught in common with naught and is naught to aught." And again: "There is something in the soul so nearly kin to God that it is one and not united."[53]

To this *chakra* refers the Hindu term *nirguṇa Brahman* — Brahman transcendent of all forms and qualities — and the Buddhist term *śuñya* — the Buddha-nature empty of all forms and qualities. At this stage both visions of God vanish and the separate identity, the I of the knowing consciousness, is no more. This, Jung felt, was psychologically impossible and so he rejected it as an example of Eastern intuition overreaching itself.[54] However, Campbell seems to have had no difficulty in fully embracing Eastern Yoga even at this most rarefied level. Thus it is clear that Campbell accepted much more direct influence from Kuṇḍalinī Yoga than did Jung.

Where Campbell Draws the Line in His Acceptance of Indian Influence

Although Campbell fully accepted the claims of Indian Yoga and used them as a template to organize his interpretation of other Eastern and Western myths, his understanding of Indian Yoga was at times confused. For example, he uncritically lumped together Patanjali's *Yoga Sūtras* with Kuṇḍalinī Yoga. This is especially true in his book *The Mythic Image*. Although it does not cause serious problems for his interpretation, since he assumes the Kuṇḍalinī position throughout, he might well confuse others by presenting Patanjali's

Yoga as being virtually identical with Kuṇḍalinī. This is simply not true. In contrast to the Sankhya-Yoga system of Patanjali, in which the aim is to circumvent and crush the passions within, the Kuṇḍalinī hero goes directly *through* the sphere of the passions to the spiritual goal. Rather than being puritanically avoided (the approach of Patanjali's Yoga), the energy of the passions is transformed and used as the very means (*sadhana*) by which the goal of self-realization is achieved. Rather than attempting to repress their personal biological impulses through the ascetic rigors of classical Jain and Hindu Yoga, the Kuṇḍalinī Tantric practitioner was world-affirmative. The Tantric hero triumphs by way of the passions themselves, riding them the way a cowboy rides a wild bronco to obedience. Heinrich Zimmer states the philosophy clearly: "It is an essential principle of the Tantric idea that man, in general, must rise through and by means of nature, not by the rejection of nature."[55] It is this Tantric version of Indian Yoga, and not Patanjali's Yoga, that Campbell assumes throughout his writings.

Although Campbell was strongly influenced by Indian thought, there are a few specific points where he rejects the Eastern teachings. Reincarnation or rebirth is a basic presupposition of all Indian thought, and it is taken quite literally. Each individual has had an infinite number of births previously and will continue to be reborn in future lives until release from rebirth is achieved. The various Indian religions — Hinduism, Jainism, and Buddhism — prescribe different paths by which release may be obtained, but all accept the reality of rebirth. Campbell interprets the idea of rebirth as a metaphor that should not be taken literally.[56] For him the end of this life will be a return of his vital energy to the cosmic energy pool of the universe with no notion of an individual rebirth. The Indian metaphor of a reincarnating monad that puts on various personalities life after life Campbell interprets as merely an indication that you are more than you think you are. The rebirth metaphor, he suggests, teaches that each of us has potentials and dimensions of being that are not included in our current concept of ourselves. "Your life is much deeper and broader than you conceive it to be here. What you are living is but a fractional inkling of what is really within you, what gives you life, breadth, and depth."[57] In this regard Campbell agrees with Jung, who also rejected the Indian idea of individual rebirth.[58]

Campbell also seemed to share in the Western caricature of the Indian yogi as one who selfishly glories in his own release by going off to identify himself with the Light and never returning.[59] This Campbell rejects as an unacceptable self-aggrandizement on the part of the hero. The true hero, said Campbell, would never permit himself such an escape into personal ecstasy but would return to use his wisdom and power to serve others. While one might be able to find individual yogis who practice their yoga for their own selfish ecstasy, the major Indian examples all demonstrate that the above interpretation is merely a Western caricature. The Buddha, for example, does not go off selfishly into his own *nirvāṇa*, although that is a temptation he had to face. Instead he turns back into the everyday world and devotes the remainder of his long life to teaching, healing, and serving others. Patanjali's *Yoga Sūtras* require that the yogi, while practicing various kinds of *samādhi* or mystical trance, must at the same time follow a full range of social virtues in the *yamas* and *niyamas*.[60] The example of the great *rishis* and yogis of India is that they did *not* go off into private ecstasy but devoted their post-enlightenment lives to the teaching of others; otherwise how would we have their teachings?

This social responsibility of teaching others is fully institutionalized in the Indian ideal of the Four Stages of Life. After an individual reaches the final goal and becomes a wandering holy beggar, the social role of that individual is not to wander through India selfishly enjoying ecstasy but to go from village to village sharing one's enlightenment as a wise teacher and staying in each village for as long as the teaching is required. This model of service to society for the yogi would actually fulfill Campbell's requirements that the return of the hero must benefit society with the hero's new-found power and wisdom.

While Campbell recognizes the value of the Eastern extended family, its tradition of arranged marriage, and the possibility of deep love developing within such marriages, he gives special place to the Western troubadours of the twelfth century for developing for the first time our modern notion of person-to-person love.[61] The *amor*, or personal love, of the troubadours is different from *eros*, rooted in our biological urge, or *agape*, "love thy neighbor as thyself," a spiritual love without regard to who the neighbor is. The high achievement of the Indian yogi would be to manifest a universal love of the *agape* type. But this is impersonal in nature and Campbell finds a particular virtue, missing in India, manifested in the troubadour tradition of freely chosen individual love. Although individual, it is in no way selfish, for, like the *agape* of the yogi, *amor* is compassion — but a compassion individuated in a relationship with one person. As such the *amor* of the troubadours was not only an opening of the heart; it was also the highest spiritual experience.[62]

In Campbell's view this is a special contribution of the West that is not found in India. The *amor* of the troubadours was especially important in that it established the validity of personal individual experience over and against the tradition of the Church. This gave to the West an accent on the individual not found in India: "It stresses the validity of the individual's experience of what humanity is, what life is, what values are, against the monolithic system."[63] All this is seen as essential not so much for the confrontation of the church by the individual as for the basis it establishes for the individual to stand against the monolithic ideologies and technologies of the twentieth century. Here Campbell evokes the romance of Tristan and Isolde as the archetype of *amor*, or spiritual love. Although he argues it in a different way, Campbell's point here would seem to support a criticism Jung offered of India — namely, that its spirituality was still essentially collective and impersonal, and had not yet reached the higher, more fully evolved, psychological individuation of the West. In the troubadours' individuated experience of *amor* Campbell found a spiritual peak that he felt was absent in the East.

Joseph Campbell went much further than other sympathetic Westerners like Carl Jung in his acceptance of Indian influence. Although he rejected the notion of individual reincarnation and saw something special in the Western ideal of individual romantic love, Campbell fully embraced the Indian understanding of the Stages of Life and the Yoga transformation of consciousness required in order to move through the four stages (*āśramas*). This Indian approach not only shaped his personal approach to life but also provided a theoretical model that he used to interpret the myths and religions of the world. To a great extent Campbell's "mono" or "master" myth is the myth of India.

5

Social Factors in Mythic Knowing: Joseph Campbell and Christian Gnosis

Karen L. King

The symbolic field is based on the experiences of people in a particular community, at that particular time and place. Myths are so intimately bound to the culture, time, and place that unless the symbols, the metaphors, are kept alive by constant recreation through the arts, the life just slips away from them.[1]

In his conversations with Bill Moyers, recorded in the book and television series *The Power of Myth*, Joseph Campbell succeeds in bringing the study of religion to the attention of a wide public audience. For scholars and teachers, his lesson of engagement with the concerns of the contemporary world is pedagogically useful. The refusal or inability of "specialists," as he calls them, to write for and communicate with the public has left a gap between the public and the academy, and a void in academic research. Campbell has sought in his own writing and in his teaching to bridge this gap.

I believe Campbell has succeeded in reaching a large audience because his direct engagement with many issues of contemporary concern and his wonderful storytelling make his a compelling voice for many people. His books present in a sense "one man's view of things." In the production of this view, he has consumed a major portion of the world's religious literature. For Campbell, the study of religion is very much the practice of religion; reading myth will help one to experience life, or, as he puts it, to find one's own "rapture."[2] Drawing on this human richness, Campbell adds his personal engagement with these traditions, his animated oral style, and his love of sampling the smorgasbord of myth.

One attractive aspect of his thinking may also be that he shares certain values and perspectives that are popular in America: individualism[3] (including a dislike for institutions and authority), American democracy, romantic love, an admiration for the selfless hero, a certain disdain for intellectualism, and an emphasis upon experiencing life. Part of his popularity is certainly due to the fact that the way those questions are formulated and the answers he suggests are quite culturally reflective of late twentieth-century America.

In considering the violence in Northern Ireland or the Middle East, for example,[4] Campbell states that human beings can transcend differences in culture and values and achieve peace by appealing to a higher set of principles common to humanity. In his own writings, however, those higher principles are largely expressions of American individualism[5] and democracy, principles that are particular to American culture rather than transcendent and universal. In the end, then, he does not himself rise above the particularity of his own culture to a "higher plane of common humanity" and in not doing so provides a good example of the difficulties of the project he insists we must achieve. This naiveté is a serious limitation throughout to the value of his work as a comparativist.

It is also a limitation to his work in terms of social responsibility. As will be discussed below, his denigration of the value of the sociological function of myth means that Campbell's treatment takes an uncritical "universal" stance that ignores the social and political contexts of particular myths. Though he wishes to eschew violence, such a stance has its own dangers.

However personally voiced, it is not difficult to locate Campbell's position within a particular historical/cultural tradition, which, for these purposes, we might call American Romanticism. This is one particular tradition of American religion, one whose primary symbol, ironically, is "universality." Campbell frequently appeals to this and other doctrines of the Romantic tradition, such as the claim that truth lies in the authentic experience of the inner self, a self that is not only sacred but divine. His interest in Gnostic traditions lies precisely in the congruences he sees between these myths and aspects of his own (American) Romantic perspective; for example: the affirmation of the self as divine, the practices of asceticism and libertinism as rejection of ethical laws that block authentic experience, and the

Gnostic rejection of the world as an affirmation of the interiority and transcendent quality of religious experience.

In the following consideration of Campbell's treatment of Gnosticism, I want to discuss each of these topics in turn from the perspective of a historian and student of ancient Gnostic myth. As a historian, a "specialist,"[6] my own perspective differs from Campbell's "generalist" approach[7] in rejoicing in the multiplicity of things, in the vitality of differences and change more than in the discovery of similarities. And in contrast to Campbell's consuming interest in myths as keys to human psychology and metaphysics,[8] historians are notoriously interested in society, culture, and politics since they tend to believe implicitly that the "genuinely human" is encountered only in the "specifically cultural."[9] More particularly, there are moral issues involved in academic work, especially regarding standards of accuracy and comprehensiveness, and regarding social responsibility. In my opinion, there are serious problems with Campbell's work in these regards.

The Divine Self

According to Joseph Campbell, in the realm of myth "God does not become Man; but man, the world itself, is known as divine, a field of inexhaustible spiritual depth."[10] Discovering this divinity within is the basis for authentic experience of life, for "finding one's rapture." Again and again Campbell turns to Gnostic sources to support his belief in the divinity of the self.[11] But what, we might ask, is this self?

Study in the "deep structure of Western theological traditions" has shown that even in the private search of the Gnostic for spiritual experience, there was an implicit political perspective, one that is mirrored in much of Campbell's writing — he calls it "the voice of reason."

MOYERS: The voice of reason — is that the philosophical way suggested by these mythological symbols?

CAMPBELL: That's right. Here you have the important transition that took place about 500 B.C. This is the date of the Buddha and of Pythagoras and Confucius and Lao-tzu, if there was a Lao-tzu. This is the awakening of man's reason. No longer is he informed and governed by the animal powers. No longer is he guided by the analogy of the planted earth, no longer by the courses of the planets — but by reason.

MOYERS: The way of —

CAMPBELL: — the way of man. And of course what destroys reason is passion.[12]

This pattern of dualistic thinking in Western philosophy — reason versus passion — can be seen already in Plato's doctrine of the self. Karen Torjesen has traced the Western version of that pattern to the political model of the state conceived by Plato:

> Convinced that democratic political institutions had failed to create a just society, Plato envisioned a return to an elite oligarchy where truly just rulers arose through a revolutionary educational program aimed at the formation of justice in the soul.... Plato's political philosophy, as well as his epistemology and metaphysics are all organized around a doctrine of the self, which fundamentally set the direction for Western thought for the next 2500 years.... Plato's doctrine of the self [constructs] a higher self and a lower self, which are in conflict with each other. The higher self is constituted by the reasoning or rational faculty; the lower self Plato designates as the irrational part of the self, the passions and the body.

This self is modeled on the sphere of social and political relations:

> A similar or related phenomenon is visible within the patriarchal household in that the relations of dominance (master and mistress over slaves, parents over children and husbands over wives) were maintained primarily through the use of physical violence. This was accepted as a necessary and legitimate means of social control. The consequences of all of this, i.e., both physical and sexual domination, is that the values placed on body and sexuality were subverted by their being primarily seen as the instruments through which social dominance was exercised. As a consequence of this social function, the values of body and sexuality became symbols for weakness (or irrationality) rather than strength (or rationality), and thus in Plato's construction of the complex self, body, sexuality and passions represent the lower self, while ruling dominance and reason represent the higher self.[13]

Given that the female was identified with the earth, body, and reproduction, and the male was identified with mind and reason, the social relations of dominance of male over female become the primary analogy for describing the self. By projecting these social relations onto the level of philosophical abstraction, the association of male with rationality and female with sexuality become part of the deep structure of the Western intellectual tradition, both philosophical and theological.[14]

One might also add: the Western mythological tradition.

At this point, readers of Campbell might point out his very positive, even pivotal, valuation of *amor*[15] and the feminine principle, of body, sex, and nature. It is true — but contradictory — that Campbell does oppose the devaluation of the body and the world implied in the dualistic type of thought he supports:

> The human woman gives birth just as the earth gives birth to the plants. She gives nourishment, as the plants do. To woman magic and earth magic are the same. They are related. And the personification of the energy that gives birth to forms and nourishes forms is properly female.... And when you have a Goddess as creator, it's her own body that is the universe. She is identical with the universe.[16]

Or again:

> The true marriage is the marriage that springs from the recognition of identity in the other, and the physical union is simply the sacrament in which that is confirmed. It doesn't start the other way around, with the physical interest that then becomes spiritualized. It starts from the spiritual impact of love — Amor.[17]

Campbell's admonition to return to harmony with nature[18] will not succeed, however, because he has hung on to the view of the self (a higher, spiritual self of reason over a lower, physical self of passion) that is the basis for the rejection of nature, body, and sex in Western myths and because he continues to identify the feminine with earth (the universe), body, and reproduction, a position that is repeatedly taken by Campbell in his consideration of the Goddess.[19]

Torjesen goes on to draw out some implications for religious thought that are particularly applicable to Campbell's thought. She notes that "the disparity between the higher and lower self, when projected as a metaphysical framework, creates a nearly unspannable chasm between the concrete, particular and material on the one hand and eternal, unchangeable and universal on the other."[20] This chasm appears in Campbell's statement that the ultimate is beyond human expression, but not human knowledge:

MOYERS: But people ask, isn't a myth a lie?

CAMPBELL: No, mythology is not a lie, mythology is poetry, it is metaphorical. It has been well said that mythology is the penultimate truth — penultimate because the ultimate cannot be put into words. It is beyond words, beyond images, beyond that bounding rim of the Buddhist Wheel of Becoming. Mythology pitches the mind beyond that rim, to what can be known but not told. So this is the penultimate truth.[21]

All these factors are easily illustrated from Gnostic texts: the view of the self as divine, the need for the mind to transcend the body in order to achieve enlightenment and attain knowledge of the divine, and the connection between self and metaphysics.

A good example is *Allogenes*. In this Sethian Gnostic text, the writer, Allogenes (literally, the Stranger or Foreigner), gives an account of several revelations and visions, followed by an extrabodily ascent to a direct vision of the Unknowable One. His journey begins within with his discovery of his own divinity.[22] After preparing himself for a hundred years, he receives a vision of the divine hierarchy and is transported out of his bodily garment, relying upon his own self-knowledge. Ascending from the lower to the higher realms, he reaches the pinnacle of mystical experience: a primary revelation of the Unknowable One — "that one who, when you know it, you must be ignorant of it" (59.30–32). Unlike a verbal revelation communicated through a mediator, this experience is metaphorically expressed as a direct vision and the knowledge that results is "an unknowing knowledge."[23] This vision is then complemented with a description of the Unknowable primarily in terms of negative theology, i.e., a denial that the Ultimate can be known or described in any positive terms, even those of Goodness or Being.[24]

I am reminded here of Campbell's statement quoted above that "mythology is the penultimate truth — penultimate because the ultimate cannot be put into words.... Mythology pitches the mind beyond that rim, to what can be known but not told."[25] The narrative and the revelations prepare the soul for that journey, but each seeker must follow himself or herself. And the journey in this case is a tour of the metaphysical structure of the cosmos; the hero[26] of the story brings back the secret knowledge and writes it in a book preserving it for those who are worthy.

The entire schema of *Allogenes* — the identification of the self with an inner divine principle, the need to transcend the lower self in order to gain higher knowledge and experience the ultimate, and the organization of everything in an ascending hierarchical order — all these notions belong to the cultural sphere of antiquity out of which the mystical traditions of Christianity and Judaism arose. Joseph Campbell finds himself in agreement with modern versions of the first two points, but wishes to keep them while replacing the notion of an ontological hierarchy with democratic principles. The question is whether it is possible — or even desirable — to do so since the whole metaphysical schema he presupposes is based on a social-political pattern of hierarchy not acceptable to modern Americans.

The psychological effects of this divided self are also apparent in Gnostic myth. A particularly poignant example is the rape of Eve in *The Hypostasis of the Archons*.[27] When the wicked world-rulers (the Archons) attempt to rape her, she divides into two figures: The Female Spiritual Principle (Eve's higher self) abandons the merely physically (lower) Eve to the brutality of gang rape while She stands back laughing at their folly. Similar to the practice of extreme asceticism, this technique of psychic dissociation from the body successfully protects the self from the pain and suffering associated with life in the world, but at tremendous cost.

Ethical Laws

Robert Bellah writes in *Habits of the Heart* that Americans

> believe in the dignity, indeed the sacredness, of the individual. Anything that would violate our right to think for ourselves, judge for ourselves, make our own decisions, live our lives as we see fit, is not only morally wrong, it is sacrilegious.[28]

This attitude in some cases is accompanied by a rejection of conventional ethics and the social institutions that promote them. In a modified form, Campbell's treatment of myth illustrates a deep mistrust of just such "sociological" aspects of culture, one of the four functions he ascribes to myth:

CAMPBELL: The third function is the sociological one — supporting and validating a certain social order. And here's where the myths vary enormously from place to place.... It is this sociological function of myth that has taken over in our world — and it is out of date.

MOYERS: What do you mean?

CAMPBELL: Ethical laws. The laws of life as it should be in the good society. All of Yahweh's pages and pages and pages of what kind of clothes to wear, how to behave to each other, and so forth, in the first millennium B.C.[29]

In addition to illustrating his dislike for what he regards as "particularistic" ethical laws, this sentiment expresses a real misunderstanding of Israelite and Jewish tradition. The care taken — in what one eats, what one wears, how one prepares food, how one behaves toward others — to express and experience the presence of the divine in the everyday illustrates beautifully Campbell's own view of the deepest desire of the human heart:

> I think what we are looking for is a way of experiencing the world that will open to us the transcendent that informs it, and at the same time forms ourselves within it. That is what people want. That is what the soul asks for.[30]

The practice of classical Judaism is precisely this opening to the transcendent and the formation of one's life within it. It is regrettable that Campbell chooses as his example a common stock of Christian anti-Judaism, the charge of legalism. It is all the more regrettable considering its association with the violence of anti-Semitism in our own century. I believe Campbell sincerely regrets the violence related to religion, but he also illustrates the necessity of critically comprehending the "sociological" dimensions of myth in order to avoid political polemic and cultural misunderstanding. In terms of their current influence in world affairs, such sociological functions and ethical laws are certainly not "out of date." Attitudes of individualism make it hard at times for persons who share those views to appreciate the richness of traditional communities, but this misunderstanding can be extremely dangerous and therefore must be acknowledged and addressed.

Campbell's suspicion that conventional ethics can block authentic experience is also quite apparent in his treatment of Gnostic ethics.

The context for his discussion of Gnostic ethics is drawn at the beginning of *Creative Mythology*, the final volume in his Masks of God series. There Campbell states that he wishes to describe mythology that springs from authentic individual experience in contrast to the stultifying communal faith of "dogma, learning, political interests, or programs for the renovation of society."[31] He begins by acknowledging the enormous influences of social and cultural formation upon the individual,[32] but he believes that experience is possible outside of moral and linguistic boundaries[33] — indeed this experience is the basis of authentic individual faith, "faith in one's own experience, whether of feeling, fact, reason, or vision."[34] Myths have served as "guides to the silence of the Word behind words and as the means to communicate its rapture."[35]

Joseph Campbell rightly notes that Gnostic Christian views differed from those of other Christians whose views became "orthodoxy" in that Gnostic Christians believed that the world was created, not by the good God of love, but by an ignorant and wicked lower divinity, the Demiurge. Most Gnostics considered the world to be corrupt, describing life as imprisonment, drunkenness, and death. Salvation meant escape from the fetters of materiality to the spiritual perfection of the place of light, the Pleroma. According to Campbell, Gnostics sought "release from corruption through a systematic disobedience of those laws (of God the Creator) in either of two ways, through asceticism or its opposite, the orgy."[36] For Campbell, this disobedience is an affirmation that the individual needs to mark out his or her own path based on personal experience, not social mores, in order to have true faith and live authentically. Clearing away the debris of social convention is necessary in order to set out on the path toward one's own rapture.

As noted by Campbell himself,[37] our understanding of Gnostic beliefs and practices was limited until relatively recently because essentially what we knew about them had to be gleaned from descriptions written by other Christians who opposed them. In the late nineteenth and twentieth centuries, however, discoveries of original writings by Gnostics themselves have become available to us. Because Campbell's work was based more on descriptions of Gnostics written by the Church Fathers intending to *refute* and *repudiate* Gnostic beliefs and practices rather than the newly available Gnostic texts, his descriptions tend to reflect the polemical attitudes of their detractors, as do all but the most recent studies.[38]

Closer study of the new texts themselves, seen especially in the work of Michael Williams,[39] has put the widely-held position that

Gnostics were either ascetics or libertines into considerable doubt. It appears that the charges of libertinism were based, not on good evidence of Gnostic practices, but on the polemical interests of Church Fathers who were ill-informed and may have misunderstood the sources they did have[40] — much the same way as Christians were charged with cannibalism by hostile Romans who already disliked Christians and happily misinterpreted their ritual language about eating and drinking the body and blood of Christ. On the other hand, the texts we possess from the Gnostics themselves are unremittingly of an ascetic bent — a moral position much more difficult for the Church Fathers to attack than supposed libertine behavior.[41] The ascetic practices of the Gnostic spiritual athletes, rather than opposing social values, expressed the moral values of the Graeco-Roman world to a considerable degree, differing more in intensity than in kind. The supposition that asceticism and libertinism were "two sides of the coin" of Gnostic dualism is not the case.

But my question here is whether Gnostics may have understood their ascetic practice as a way to "authentic existence," to following their own "rapture." It is clear from *The Book of Thomas the Contender* that at least some of them did. There Jesus distinguishes fools from the wise on the basis of their attitude toward "visible things." For the fool:

> ... it [passion] will blind them with insatiable lust and burn their souls and become for them like a stake stuck in their heart which they can never dislodge.... And it has fettered them with its chains and bound all their limbs with the bitterness of the bondage of lust for those visible things that will decay and change and swerve by impulse.

But for the wise:

> "Everyone who seeks the truth from true wisdom will make himself wings so as to fly, fleeing the lust that scorches the spirits of men." And he will make himself wings to flee every visible spirit.[42]

For Gnostics, the rejection of conventional morality is a rejection of the world and the body and all that goes with it, a kind of practical self-nihilism as a way to escape the bonds of deception and deceit, to find the truth and become free. Thus the information of new texts, while correcting errors in Campbell's presentation, nonetheless is capable of supporting and elaborating the position he described.

Religious Experience and Metaphysics

But, as we have seen, despite Campbell's dislike for ethical laws, he wants to get away from a dualistic metaphysics that rejects the value of the body and life in the world. This set of factors leads to some confusion in his treatment of Gnosticism.

This confusion is amplified by his treatment of Gnosticism as a unified, coherent phenomenon. In fact, the modern label "Gnosticism" houses a wide variety of distinct mythologies. Although Campbell recognized this fact at least in part, he still treated the different perspectives as aspects of a single phenomenon. At least three positions on metaphysics can be distinguished in Campbell's discussion of Gnosticism in *Creative Mythology*.[43] There we see him noting some of the variety of metaphysics present in Gnostic traditions, but linking them together as parts of a single encompassing perspective.

For Campbell's purposes, each type serves only to illustrate a different aspect of his own outlook: he cites examples of radical dualism when he wants to emphasize the need to transcend physical and culturally conditioned restraints to spiritual experience, radical monism when he wants to show the ultimate transcendence of all illusory divisions, and mild dualism when he wants to stress the value of *amor* and life in the world. Each of these types can be illustrated and elaborated from the newly discovered texts: We have seen already a radical dualism expressing extreme repugnance for the world in the encratite *Book of Thomas the Contender*. Campbell's favorite passage from *The Gospel of Thomas*, "the kingdom of the Father is spread out upon the earth and men do not see it,"[44] illustrates the mild dualism of that text[45] (though it should be noted that the Gnostic character of this text itself is hotly debated[46]). The Valentinian *Gospel of Philip* expresses a radical monism, a view that the world with all its suffering is itself nothing, a lack or deficiency, which only deceptively appears to exist, and therefore cannot be truthfully described. The false dualism of opposites therefore produces illusory distinctions, while the truth itself is one.[47]

The final type of metaphysics, described by Campbell as "the 'hither shore' variety," can be illustrated from several texts that describe the "mythological end of days" in apocalyptic terms, for example *On the Origin of the World*[48] and *The Apocryphon of John*.[49] Both describe the end of the world and the final destruction or the eternal punishment of the wicked. "For," as *On the Origin of the World* says, "everyone must go to the place from which he has come. Indeed, by his acts and his *gnosis* ["knowledge"] each person will make his nature known."[50] My real problem with Campbell's treatment of Gnostic metaphysics here is that there is never any sustained analysis of particular Gnostic myths at all, even those easily available in the fifties and sixties. Instead, the bits and pieces of Gnostic myths he cites serve only as illustrations for his own preconceived views. Given this fact, one has the impression that the addition of further information made possible by the discovery of new texts would not alter Campbell's basic views at all. One can learn much about Joseph Campbell in reading his books, but very little about Gnosticism.

Conclusion

Campbell seldom considers the meaning and function of myths in their social and political contexts,[51] nor even the social and political implications of his own views. These deficiencies are consequences of his personal understanding and appropriation of the individualism and universalism associated with American Romanticism. They have led him on the one hand to an inaccurate portrayal of Gnostic myths, and on the other hand to reproducing naively views that in the past have been the sources of violence. As we saw in two cases (Torjesen's analysis of the pattern of social dominance and violence implied in Campbell's view of the self, and Campbell's denigration of Israelite ethical laws), ignoring social and political contexts has inherent dangers of seriously misunderstanding the beliefs and practices of others and leading to violence, either in domestic violence,[52] the psychic dissociation of the self, or in racism and religious discrimination. Consideration of myth apart from culture and history leaves us open to the onslaughts of unthinking violence. Social evils do not, however, seem to bother Campbell much.

CAMPBELL: People ask me, "Do you have optimism about the world?" And I say, "Yes, it's great just the way it is. And you are not going to fix it up. Nobody has ever made it any better. It is never going to be any better. This is it, so take it or leave it. You are not going to correct or improve it."

MOYERS: Doesn't that lead to a rather passive attitude in the face of evil?

CAMPBELL: You yourself are participating in evil, or you are not alive. Whatever you do is evil for somebody. This is one of the ironies of the whole creation.[53]

For those who do take a more active attitude toward evil and who experience a greater responsibility — and regret — for the ways in which we do in fact participate in evil, the study and analysis of religion cannot be limited to psychology and metaphysics, as important as those are, since even the most interior and world-rejecting traditions have clear social and political implications.[54]

In terms of possible socially-redeeming qualities, the most appealing part of Campbell's presentation is his attempt to fill the void of the "empty self and empty relationships"[55] with an identification with the traditions and community of the whole world.[56] This is essentially what he wishes to communicate when he insists that there is no special revelation or special truth.[57] Though his own approach is problematic and naive insofar as he ignores the particular social and cultural contexts of myths, this criticism does not diminish the value of comparative analysis as a way to further understanding and global peace. Of greatest contemporary value in Campbell's work — and in comparative study generally — is the implicit appreciation that every human culture has something of value to offer.

6

Joseph Campbell
the Perennial Philosopher:
An Analysis of His Universalism

Robert A. Segal

MOYERS: They [myths] just wear different costumes when they appear at different times?

CAMPBELL: Yes. It's as though the same play were taken from one place to another, and at each place the local players put on local costumes and enact the same old play.[1]

Universalists and Particularists

The ways in which human beings have been classified are endless. The classification that best fits Joseph Campbell and his critics is that into universalists and particularists. I contend that, despite contrary appearances, Campbell is a consummate universalist and is therefore subject to the common criticisms of universalists by particularists. At the same time I argue that those criticisms are question-begging — as question-begging as the conventional ones universalists make of particularists. To illustrate the circularity of the criticisms I cite a dispute analogous to that between the universalist Campbell and his particularistic antagonists in the study of myth: the dispute in the study of mysticism between universalist perennialists and particularistic non-perennialists. Finally, I claim that Campbell is himself a perennialist, not just a kindred universalist.

81

Universalists are those who emphasize the similarities among phenomena; particularists, those who emphasize the differences. Both groups usually stress the similarities and the differences *within* classes of phenomena, not across classes. Universalists maintain that all trees are at heart alike and that all humans are alike but not that trees and humans are really akin. Particularists maintain that the differences among trees and among humans outweigh the similarities.

The divide between universalists and particularists is only secondarily over the *fact* of similarities and differences. While universalists seek out similarities missed by particularists, and particularists differences overlooked by universalists, neither side necessarily denies the *findings* of the other. Rather, both sides deny the *importance* of each other's findings. Particularists can hardly deny that even after all the differences between one tree and another have been explicated, some similarities remain: exactly those characteristics that make any tree a tree. Particularists simply scorn those similarities as vague. Universalists cannot deny that even after all possible similarities have been extricated, differences remain: precisely those characteristics that make any two trees distinct. Universalists for their part merely dismiss those differences as trivial.

The opposition between universalists and particularists is especially prevalent in the humanities, where particularists, here often called "interpretivists," typically assert that humans and their artifacts are decipherable only in their distinctiveness. Universalists, or "explainers," reply that humans, like other subjects of inquiry, are best grasped as instances of ever broader categories.[2]

The difference between universalists and particularists, like that between Platonists and Aristotelians in philosophy, introverts and extroverts in psychology, and optimists and pessimists everywhere, is ultimately temperamental. As philosopher of religion Huston Smith, even in defending universalism, acknowledges:

> ...people differ according to whether they incline towards similarities or differences. Perennialists [i.e., universalists] are persons who are exceptionally sensitive to the commonalities that similarities disclose; they are drawn toward unity as moth to flame. Sensitized by its pull, they find tokens of unity profligate; they see similarities everywhere. It comes as something of a jolt, therefore, to find that others see their eye for resemblances as an optical defect — a far-sightedness that cannot read fine print.[3]

Arguments for and against Universalism and Particularism

Seemingly, there is no way to adjudicate the clash between universalists and particularists. To say, for example, that similarities are more important than differences is to beg the question. For on what basis save an *assumed* universalism can one say so? Likewise on what grounds beyond an assumed particularism can one declare differences more salient than similarities? Smith's own defense of universalism displays the circularity of the debate:

> Everything obviously both resembles and differs from every other thing: resembles it in that both exist; differs or there would not be two things but one. This being the case, when should we accent one pole, when the other? Claims for similarities or differences spin their wheels until they get down to *ways* and *degrees* in which things differ or are alike, and those variables shift with the problem we are working on. Does the fact that an Ethiopian's hunger is mediated by his African context cause it to differ from mine to the point where it throws international famine relief into question?[4]

Not even the most unbending particularist would deny that hunger is a crosscultural phenomenon. The issue is whether one is concerned with hunger anywhere or with hunger in Ethiopia. Even in feeding Ethiopians, not to mention in explaining the cause and effect of Ethiopian hunger, the nature of *Ethiopian* farming, diet, climate, politics, and history is not clearly secondary to the nature of farming, diet, and climate per se. What, moreover, is the "problem" that dictates universalism or particularism except one's concern in the first place with either all hunger or Ethiopian hunger — that is, with either universalism or particularism?

Violations of the generalizations of universalists would seemingly constitute an incontestable argument for particularism. For example, there are hero myths that clearly fail to conform to the differing patterns that universalists Otto Rank, Lord Raglan, and Campbell himself claim for all hero myths. But the challenge is therefore to the *fact* of similarities. It is not to the *significance* of them, which is where the central issue lies. Moreover, the failure of even all generalizations about hero myths would establish not that similarities are less important than differences but only that purported similarities are really differences. At most, the failure would suggest that few similarities exist. The real dispute is whether, if found, similarities would be more revealing than differences.

The demonstration of differences beneath manifest similarities would seemingly provide an alternative incontrovertible argument for particularism. For the differences would thereby go deeper than the similarities. Conversely, the demonstration of similarities beneath surface differences would seemingly argue indisputably for universalism, as Rank, Raglan, and Campbell mean to be doing. But to argue for either particularism or universalism both sides would have to agree on the starting point: on what constituted the *surface* similarities and differences. In all likelihood universalists would deem the differences superficial and the similarities deeper; particularists, the reverse. Each side would likely dismiss the other's *conclusions* as the mere *starting point*.

Still, there *might* be agreement on the starting point. Suppose particularists were to grant that beneath the manifest differences between the Greek hero Odysseus and the Roman hero Aeneas lay the pattern that Campbell presents in his *Hero with a Thousand Faces*.[5] Manifestly, it might be agreed, the two heroes, while both heroes, are very different. Odysseus is seeking to return home to Ithaca, which he left for the Trojan War. Aeneas, by contrast, is seeking a new home. His old home, Troy, has been razed by the Greeks. Odysseus is seeking to re-establish himself as husband, father, and ruler. Having lost his wife, his father, and his country, Aeneas is seeking to establish a new family and nation. Where Odysseus finally returns home, Aeneas finally finds a new one.

Odysseus wants to return home for his own sake. By contrast, Aeneas leaves Troy only because he has been commanded to go. Duty, not self-interest, impels him. Odysseus might have been acting selflessly in leaving for Troy in the first place, but Aeneas is selfless in leaving Troy now. He would have wished either to die there during the fighting or to rebuild it on its ruins.

Campbell, however, would argue that despite these undeniable differences the two heroes, like all other ones, are alike: both leave the security of home, where they are ensconced, for a dangerous trek to a strange, new world, with which they must come to terms. Odysseus leaves Ithaca for Troy; Aeneas, Troy for Italy.

A particularist, however, would point in turn to further differences. Aeneas, here *breaking* with Campbell's scheme, never returns home: where Odysseus' heroism is in part his resolve to return home, Aeneas' is his willingness to abandon his home forever. Odysseus, also breaking with Campbell's scheme, finds the strange new world not at Troy, which had been his destination, but only en route home from Troy. Furthermore, he returns to Ithaca not to inform others of the existence of the extraordinary places he has visited but merely to re-establish himself as King of Ithaca. Where Aeneas serves future Rome, Odysseus serves only himself. In sum, particularists would argue that beneath the similarities that lie beneath the surface differences lie still deeper differences. Universalists would reply that those deeper differences are in fact nothing other than surface ones, in which case whatever similarities do hold are deeper. Again, universalists and particularists would be contesting the starting point.

The Perennial Philosophy

Despite professions of particularism, Joseph Campbell, I will show, is an arch-universalist. The universalists to whom he is closest are exponents of a *philosophia perennis*, or "perennial philosophy," running through all religions and, for Campbell, myths. The phrase "perennial philosophy" goes back to Leibniz but was popularized in a 1944 book of that title by the novelist Aldous Huxley. The essential belief said to be found in all religions and myths is mystical: all things, including humans and god, are said to be one.

The exact claim varies from exponent to exponent. Less extreme perennialists like Huston Smith assert only that perennialism is to be found to some degree in all religions:

Exoterics [i.e., nonperennialists] will be quick to point out that the perennial philosophy is the minority position everywhere, even in mystical India, to say nothing of the form-loving West. Esoterics [i.e., perennialists] admit this statistical point, but insist that profundity is not determined by headcount.[6]

More extreme perennialists like Huxley assert that the core of all, or at least all world, religions is perennialist: "The core and spiritual heart of all the higher religions is the Perennial Philosophy...."[7] Similarly, Alan Watts, the popularizer of Eastern lore, declares that, with the lamentable exception of the insufficiently appreciative modern West, "there has otherwise been a single philosophical consensus of universal extent."[8]

Some perennialists — Huxley, for example — contend that *interpretations* of mystical experience are the same universally. Others — for example, the philosopher Walter Stace — acknowledge that interpretations differ but argue that the *experiences* themselves are the same. Still others — for example, the mystic Evelyn Underhill — allow for differing kinds of experiences as well as different interpretations but maintain that the experiences, if not also the interpretations, are the same within each kind, which itself is found universally.[9]

The Perennialist Argument for Universalism

The most striking characteristic of the debate between perennialists and their particularistic opponents is its circularity. Perennialists, as universalists, appeal to the *fact* of historical and worldwide similarities to establish the *importance* of those similarities and so the existence of a *perennial* philosophy. Stace begins by noting the fact of similarities in all places and periods:

> I shall, for the present, treat it as an hypothesis that although mystical experiences may in certain respects have different characteristics in different parts of the world, in different ages, and in different cultures, there are nevertheless a number of fundamental common characteristics.... The most important, the central characteristic in which all *fully developed* mystical experiences agree, and which in the last analysis is definitive of them and serves to mark them off from other kinds of experiences, is that they involve the apprehension of *an ultimate nonsensuous unity in all things*, a oneness or a One to which neither the senses nor the reason can penetrate.[10]

While Stace recognizes the need to establish the importance, not just the fact, of similarities, his evidence for the significance of the similarities is merely the recurrence of them:

> I shall also assume that the agreements are more basic and important, the differences more superficial and relatively less important. This hypothesis can only be fully justified by an elaborate empirical survey of the descriptions of their experiences given by mystics and collected from all over the world. But I believe that enough of the evidence for it will appear in the following pages to convince any reasonable person.[11]

So similar for Stace are mystical experiences among the world religions that the heart of mysticism simply *must* lie in those similarities.

Stace never denies differences. To begin with, he emphasizes the difference between "extrovertive" mystical experience, in which ultimate reality is found *through* the senses *in* the physical world, and "introvertive" experience, in which ultimate reality is found with the mind by blocking out the senses and thereby the physical world.[12] But Stace then declares that the similarities between extrovertive and introvertive experience override the differences:

> Meanwhile, the fact that there exist two such very different types of consciousness, to both of which the one adjective "mystical" is nevertheless applied, should not be considered inconsistent with the alleged existence of a universal common core of all mysticism. For ... the two types have important characteristics which are common to both. Indeed, this is evident even from the brief remarks which have already been made, since both, as we noted, culminate in the perception of, and union with, a Unity or One, though this end is reached through different means in the two cases. Nor is this the only thing they have in common, as we shall see.[13]

How Stace determines the greater significance of the similarities over the differences is the "perennial" question he fails to answer.

Stace never denies, further, the differences between the mysticism of one religion and that of another. Indeed, he acknowledges that Judaism, in its stress on the separation between humans and God, is *anti*-mystical: "Jewish tradition has always frowned on the kind of mysticism" — for Stace the only kind of true mysticism — "in which [outright] identity, or even [mere] union, with God is claimed."[14]

In analyzing Jewish mysticism Stace regularly defers to Gershom Scholem, not only the greatest scholar in the field but also an uncompromising *anti*-perennialist. Says Scholem:

> The point I should like to make is this — that there is no such thing as mysticism in the abstract, that is to say, a phenomenon or experience which has no particular relation to other religious phenomena. There is no mysticism as such, there is only the mysticism of a particular religious system, Christian, Islamic, Jewish mysticism and so on.[15]

Yet Stace nevertheless speculates that at least some cases of Hasidic mysticism, cases taken from Scholem himself, suggest union and even identity. While conceding that these experiences get *interpreted* non-mystically, Stace asserts that the interpretations are artifices imposed *ex post facto* on fully mystical experiences to preserve the Jewish belief in separation between humans and God:

> Thus Professor G. G. Scholem quotes one of the Hasidic mystics as saying: "There are those who serve God with their human intellects and others whose gaze is fixed on Nothing...." It is true that this does not mention the unity of the One. But the key word "Nothing" means the absence of all multiplicity and therefore of all empirical content. It is unquestionably the undifferentiated void which cannot be anything else but the introvertive experience more fully described [i.e., interpreted] in other traditions.[16]

Joseph Campbell as a Particularist

At first glance, Joseph Campbell is far from a universalist, in which case he cannot be a perennialist. He not only recognizes but even stresses differences — not among mystical experiences but among myths. "Myths," he says repeatedly, are "intimately bound to the culture, time, and place...."[17] He classifies mythologies worldwide as distinctively primitive, Occidental, Oriental, and "creative."

Even Campbell's hero pattern, by far his most rigid, allows for variations. The hero need only leave the everyday world for an unknown one, encounter female and male gods, and return victoriously with some power for his community. While at least in *The Hero with a Thousand Faces* the hero must be an adult male, he can be young or old, rich or poor, king or commoner, god or human. How and why he ventures forth, how he gains entry to the new world, what boon he secures, how he secures it, and how he returns home are all open-ended:

> The mythological hero, setting forth from his commonday hut or castle, is lured, carried away, or else voluntarily proceeds, to the threshold of adventure. There he encounters a shadow presence that guards the passage. The hero may defeat or conciliate this power and go alive into the kingdom of the dark (brother-battle, dragon-battle; offering, charm), or be slain by the opponent and descend in death (dismemberment, crucifixion). Beyond the threshold, then, the hero journeys through a world of unfamiliar yet strangely intimate forces, some of which severely threaten him (tests), some of which give magical aid (helpers).... The triumph may be represented as the

hero's sexual union with the goddess-mother of the world (sacred marriage), his recognition by the father-creator (father atonement), his own divinization (apotheosis), or again — if the powers have remained unfriendly to him — his theft of the boon he came to gain (bride-theft, fire-theft).... The final work is that of the return. If the powers have blessed the hero, he now sets forth under their protection (emissary); if not, he flees and is pursued (transformation flight, obstacle flight).[18]

Hero myths sometimes focus on only one or two elements of the pattern, sometimes fuse elements, and sometimes duplicate elements.[19] Campbell goes so far as to say that "the changes rung on the simple scale of the monomyth defy description."[20]

Furthermore, Campbell grants that a mythic pattern or archetype expresses itself only through a particular form: "...universals are never experienced in a pure state, abstracted from their locally conditioned ethnic applications."[21] Campbell even says that in the differences, the "infinitely various metamorphoses" of universals, lies the "fascination."[22]

Again and again, Campbell insists that a myth be interpreted locally as well as universally:

Such a recognition of two aspects, a universal and a local, in the constitution of religions everywhere clarifies at one stroke those controversies [between universalists and particularists].... The first task of any systematic comparison of the myths and religions of mankind should therefore be (it seemed to me) to identify these universals...and as far as possible to interpret them; and the second task then should be to recognize and interpret the various locally and historically conditioned transformations of the metaphorical images through which these universals have been rendered.[23]

Finally, Campbell does not merely note the differences among myths but also seeks to account for them. Where he explains similarities psychologically, he explains differences socially and above all geographically: "Myths take into their domain the conditions and even the geographical idiosyncrasies of the various landscapes. One will be in a desert land, another in a jungle, and so on."[24]

Joseph Campbell as a Universalist

As fully as Joseph Campbell emphasizes, not merely concedes, the differences among myths, he finally dismisses all differences as trivial. As he typically puts it, "...by casting off the [mere] shell of the local, historical inflection, one comes to the elementary idea which is the path to one's own innermost heart."[25] Again: "Dissolving, the ethnic [i.e., local] ideas become transparent to the archetypes, those elementary ideas of which they [i.e., the ethnic ideas] are no more than the local masks."[26] Campbell is ultimately a stalwart universalist.

While on the one, particularist hand Campbell says that the hero "evolves as the culture evolves,"[27] on the other, universalist hand he says that "essentially, it might even be said [that] there is but one archetypal mythic hero whose life has been replicated in many lands by many, many people."[28] Campbell argues that there is not just one hero myth but one myth per se:

> ...in the face of the ubiquitous myth itself, its long persistence and the basic consistency of its lesson, all variations of detail must appear to be of only secondary moment; all finally conspire to inflect the single lesson....[I]t is a story, therefore, which knows how to bend itself and reshape itself to the diverse needs of divers [sic] times and places; but there can be no doubt, it is one story.[29]

Near the end of his life Campbell remarked:

> I have been dealing with this stuff all my life, and I am still stunned by the accuracies of the repetitions. It is almost like a reflex in another medium of the same thing, the same story.... If you were not alert to the parallel themes [of myths], you perhaps would think they were quite different stories, but they're not.[30]

Just like Stace, Campbell concedes that Judaism constitutes an apparent exception to his universalist rule — for Campbell both because the Jewish god is the god of a single people rather than of all humanity and because that god is separate from his people rather than mystically one with it. Campbell's strategy for encompassing Judaism within his universalist scheme is bolder than even Stace's. He rejects the particularistic interpretations of Jewish myths by Jews themselves and argues that, unbeknown to its own adherents, Judaism in fact espouses both a global and a pantheistic God:

For the conditions, not only of life, but of thought also, have considerably changed since the centuries of the composition of that guide to truth and virtue [i.e., Bible], which with its deliberately restricted and restricting ethnocentric horizon and tribal "jealous God" (Exodus 20:5) is culture specific to such a degree that its "folk ideas" and "elementary ideas" are inseparably fused. The first step to mystical realization is the leaving of such a defined [i.e., local] god for an experience of transcendence, disengaging the ethnic from the elementary idea.... Also, the first step... is to recognize every such local image of a god as but one of many thousands, millions, even perhaps billions, of locally useful symbolizations of that same mystery beyond sight or thought which our teachers have taught us to seek in their god alone.... The Holy Land is no special place. It is every place that has ever been recognized and mythologized by any people as home.[31]

Like the perennialists, Campbell does not just announce his universalism but also argues for it. His argument mirrors theirs. He appeals to the *fact* of similarities as evidence of the *importance* of them:

Comparative cultural studies have now demonstrated beyond question that similar mythic tales are to be found in every quarter of this earth. When Cortes and his Catholic Spaniards arrived in Aztec Mexico, they immediately recognized in the local religion so many parallels to their own True Faith that they were hard put to explain the fact.... There was a High God above all, who was beyond all human thought and imaging. There was even an incarnate Saviour, associated with a serpent, born of a virgin, who had died and was resurrected, one of whose symbols was a cross.... Modern scholarship, systematically comparing the myths and rites of mankind, has found just about everywhere legends of virgins giving birth to heroes who die and are resurrected.[32]

So striking for Campbell, as for the perennialists, are the similarities that the meaning, not to add the origin and function, of all myths simply must lie in them.

Because Campbell analyzes myths rather than reports of experiences, he cannot, like some perennialists, distinguish between experiences themselves and interpretations of them. Hence he argues that the meaning, or interpretation, of all myths is itself the same.

The distinction he does draw is between the true, universalist meaning of myths and the false, particularistic meaning indoctrinated in believers in the West.

Particularists would say against Campbell what they say against the perennialists. They would deny either the existence or the importance of the similarities Campbell amasses. They would argue that the differences count far more. They would argue that the presence in even all myths of gods, virgins, heroes, saviors, death, and rebirth would beg, not answer, the key question: whether the similarities are as important as the differences and whether they mean the same in each case.[33]

Joseph Campbell as a Perennialist

Joseph Campbell is a perennialist because he is not merely a universalist — a necessary but insufficient prerequisite — but also a mystic. The "*philosophia perennis* of the human race"[34] is the mystical oneness of all things:

> The universally distinguishing characteristic of mythological thought and communication is an implicit connotation through all its metaphorical imagery of a sense of identity of some kind, transcendent of appearances, which unites behind the scenes the opposed actors on the world stage.[35]

Myths for Campbell pronounce all oppositions illusory:

MOYERS: Why do we think in terms of opposites?

CAMPBELL: Because we can't think otherwise.

MOYERS: That's the nature of reality in our time.

CAMPBELL: That's the nature of our *experience* of reality.

MOYERS: Man-woman, life-death, good-evil —

CAMPBELL: — I and you, this and that, true and false — every one of them has its opposite. But mythology suggests that behind that duality there is a singularity over which this plays like a shadow game.[36]

The unnamed brand of mysticism that Joseph Campbell finds in myths is equivalent to Stace's extrovertive mysticism, which finds ultimate reality within the everyday physical world known through the senses. Extrovertive mysticism embraces rather than rejects the everyday world.[37] Rather than, as in introvertive mysticism, rejecting earth for heaven, body for spirit, and humanity for god, Campbell's extrovertive mysticism finds heaven in earth, the spirit in the body, and god in humanity. Heaven and earth are identical, spirit and body are identical, and god and humanity are identical. Just as Campbell's hero returns to the everyday world only to find within it the strange new world he assumed he had left behind, so all who heed the message of myth eventually find ultimate reality within, not outside, the everyday world. As Campbell puts it, "...divinity informs the world."[38] The physical and nonphysical worlds are identical. Because Campbell interprets myths psychologically as well as metaphysically,[39] myth for him preaches the oneness of the unconscious with everyday consciousness as well as the oneness of ultimate reality with ordinary reality.

Campbell goes beyond other perennialists in claiming that all mythologies harbor not merely *some* mystical myths but *only* mystical myths. For him, not some but all myths espouse mysticism, and mysticism of the extrovertive variety. Campbell is scarcely unaware that mysticism is a minor strain in Christianity and Islam as well as in Judaism. His litany-like response is that the West misconstrues its own myths. Hence he continually berates Western religions for reducing their myths from pristine symbolic expressions of mystical truths to degenerate pronouncements of particularistic literal pseudo-facts:

> Mythology is very fluid. Most of the myths are self-contradictory [at the literal level]. You may even find four or five myths in a given culture, all giving different versions of the same mystery. Then theology comes along and says it has got to be just this way. Mythology is poetry, and the poetic language is very flexible. Religion turns poetry into prose. God is literally up there, and this is literally what he thinks, and this is the way you've got to behave to get into proper relationship with that god up there.[40]

Like other perennialists, Campbell maintains that the modern West needs to be reconnected to the tradition that has previously served all humanity. Indeed, Campbell employs depth psychology to recover what Smith calls "the forgotten truth." Where Smith and others blame science for severing moderns from "the primordial tradition,"[41] Campbell blames organized religion, which for him always misinterprets myths literally and therefore, for Campbell, both particularistically and nonmystically.

Where other, less daring perennialists seek to show that the mystical meaning of all *incontestably* mystical myths and religions is the same, Campbell seeks to show that all myths, which for him overlap with religions if not encompass them, are truly mystical.[42] The initial issue dividing Campbell and his critics is therefore over the facts themselves. Only subsequently would the division be over the importance of those facts. But Campbell would doubtless then assert that the recurrence of extrovertive mysticism throughout history and the world is so impressive that the meaning of all myths must lie in extrovertive mysticism per se rather than in the differing forms it takes.

PART THREE

Mythic Power:
Joseph Campbell's
Symbols and Stories
in Contemporary Culture

7

Masks of the Goddess:
A Feminist Response

Christine Downing

The mother is really a more immediate parent than the father because one is born from the mother, and the first experience of any infant is the mother. I have frequently thought that mythology is a sublimation of the mother image.[1]

While I was a graduate student Joseph Campbell was invited to participate in a colloquium that brought to our campus a series of brilliant and celebrated intellectuals. I remember many of those lectures, some more vividly than others, but Campbell's presentation stands out from all the others because he didn't lecture; he told stories. Actually he didn't so much *tell* stories as *dance* them; his whole body, his whole being, was engaged in his telling. (When a few months later I saw his wife, Jean Erdman, perform her dance based on *Finnegans Wake*, "The Coach With Six Insides," I understood how much each had given the other.) Campbell was a gifted storyteller. I remember him; I remember the stories; I still retell many of them. For me there is no higher praise: to tell the old stories in a way that honors them, renews their power, moves others — what a blessing!

But, of course, we never just retell the old stories; we use them to tell our own, and what I want to focus on here is the story Campbell uses the old stories to tell, the story he tells about the stories. For, though Campbell seems to respond more sympathetically to James Joyce's "creative mythologizing" than to Thomas Mann's, his own practice more closely corresponds to Mann's:

[Mann] explains, interprets, and evaluates discursively the symbols of his art, whereas Joyce simply presents, without author's comment. Furthermore, in his approach to symbols Mann comes to them from the secular world, through literature and art [as Campbell came to myth through Joyce's fiction], not by way of the ingraining from childhood of the iconography of a seriously accepted, ritually ordered religion.[2]

Campbell is addressing us, seeking to persuade us to a particular view of the history of mythology and of its function, and ultimately, like Mann, to a "lifeway."

Campbell's Natural History of the Goddess

It is to his great credit — from my feminist perspective — that in his history of mythology he accords an important place to the role played by goddesses, and that he did so already in the first volume of the Masks of God series (published in 1959) long before the revival of interest in the goddess among contemporary feminist scholars (which we might date as becoming visible in 1976 with the publication of Merlin Stone's *When God Was a Woman*). In the third volume he explains:

> I am taking pains in this work to place considerable stress upon the world age and symbolic order of the goddess; for the findings both of anthropology and archaeology now attest not only to a contrast between the mythic and social systems of the goddess and the later gods, but also to the fact that in our own European culture that of the gods overlies and occludes that of the goddess — which is nevertheless effective as a counterplayer, so to say, in the unconscious of the civilization as a whole.[3]

As Campbell understands the history of human religiosity the goddesses were there from the beginning. The goddess shows herself as *there* "at the very dawn of the first day of our own species." She "lures us beyond even our longest archaeological fathom-line." She can truly say, " 'No one has lifted my veil.' "[4]

He finds evidence of her presence in neanderthal burials. The supplies around the skeletons, the evidence of animal sacrifice, the attention to the solar axis in the placement of graves, the arrangement of the dead in sleeping or fetal position — all suggest that burial was understood as a return to mother earth for rebirth.[5] Campbell believes that the earth as both bearing and nurturing mother was prominent in the mythologies of both early hunting and planting societies.

The importance of the goddess among the earliest hunting, fishing, gathering peoples is confirmed by the many nude female figures (often with a highly stylized emphasis on loins, genitals, and breasts) found at early paleolithic sites. Their placement on shrines makes clear they were cult objects. Indeed, these female figurines were apparently the first objects of human worship. Thus among the paleolithic hunters as in the later planting societies "the female body was experienced in its own character as a focus of divine force, and a system of rites was dedicated to its mystery."[6] Campbell believes that in these small and relatively settled societies there was neither a strong patriarchal or matriarchal emphasis, but rather an essential equality, indeed, that even puberty rites did not distinguish significantly between male and female initiates. All worshipped the goddess, because from her womb came the game animals upon which their life depended.

> There can be no doubt that in the very earliest ages of human history the magical force and wonder of the female was no less a marvel than the universe itself; and this gave to woman a prodigious power, which it has been one of the chief concerns of the masculine part of the population to break, control, and employ to its own ends. It is, in fact, most remarkable how many primitive hunting races have the legend of a still more primitive age than their own, in which the women were the sole possessors of the magical art.[7]

Later the goddess's importance among hunting peoples declined. A second stage of primitive hunting societies came into existence with larger hunting groups ranging more widely for big game. The change to a warmer, drier climate during the late paleolithic and the appearance of great grazing herds of bison, antelope, and wild cattle, issued in a more continuously ranging nomadism; women's domestic work came to be disvalued and men developed a "fine sense of their own superiority."[8] In these societies men came to dominate in the religious and political sphere; women were excluded from the men's secret initiation rites, which included ordeals and mutilation. In the regions of the Great Hunt an essentially masculine psychology came to prevail, with an emphasis on achievement — and women became ancillaries to male achievement.[9] The paintings in the underground caves where the men performed their rituals focus on animals and male hunters; there are no female figures. The costumed shaman now exercises the magical role previously assigned the naked goddess. Outside these caves one sometimes finds female figurines so violently shattered as to lead to the suspicion that there had been a deliberate attempt to break their power.[10]

In planting societies, on the other hand, women who were responsible for the transition from gathering to cultivating enjoyed the magico-religious and social advantage. By their discovery they had made the earth valuable; thus they were seen as knowing its secrets. Woman did the planting and reaping "and, as the mother of life and nourisher of life, was thought to assist the earth symbolically in its productivity."[11] During the basal neolithic period between 5500 and 4500, characterized not only by the beginnings of agriculture but also by the domestication of animals, by pottery and weaving, and by settled village life, women probably predominated socially and religiously. Again, many female figurines have been found, attesting to the importance accorded the goddess in whose body are sown the seeds upon the growth of which human life depends.

Campbell comments on how reluctant male scholars have been to admit the significance of these sculptures:

> We have no writing from this pre-literate age and no knowledge, consequently, of its myths or rites. It is therefore not unusual for extremely well-trained archaeologists to pretend that they cannot imagine what services the numerous female figurines might have rendered.... However, we know perfectly well what the services of such images were in the periods immediately following — and what they have remained to the present day. They give magical psychological aid to women in childbirth and conception, stand in house shrines to receive daily prayers and to protect the occupants from physical as well as from spiritual danger, serve to support the mind in its meditations on the mystery of being.... They go forth with the farmer into his fields, protect the crops, protect the cattle.... They are the guardians of children. They watch over the sailor at sea and the merchant on the road.[12]

Campbell recites the many titles by which the goddess was known in the neolithic world; he lists the many symbols associated with her, and describes her characteristic postures: standing pregnant, giving birth, nursing a child, holding serpents, riding a bull. The goddesses are often accompanied by male gods who are both son and consort, who die (often as a ritual sacrifice) and are reborn. He explains how the rituals dedicated to these goddesses derive from a recognition of death as the presupposition of life, from the perception of harvesting as a killing — as a heroic act on the part of the reaper but as a sacrifice by the grain. He shows how this leads to rituals of sacrifice, including human sacrifice — sacrifices which are not so much gifts to the goddess or god but re-enactments of their gift of themselves. He interprets these often violent rituals as representing a "willed affirmation" of "the ruthless nature of being," a reconciliation to the "monstrosity of the just-so of the world."[13]

> In the neolithic village... the focal figure of all mythology and worship was the bountiful goddess Earth, as the mother and nourisher of life and receiver of the dead for rebirth. In the earliest period of her cult... [she] may have been thought of only as a local patroness of fertility, as many anthropologists suppose. However in the temples of Sumer (3500–2350)... [she] was certainly much more than that. She was already... a metaphysical symbol: the arch personification of the power of Space, Time, and Matter, within whose bound all beings arise and die... And everything having form or name — including God... was her child, within her womb.[14]

But then once again the goddess was obscured. In the neolithic village, men were close to being superfluous. "Small wonder," Campbell says, "if, in reaction, their revengeful imaginations ran amok."[15]

With the beginnings of plow agriculture, the preconditions for the establishment of the hieratic patriarchal city-state appeared. Planting became men's work; the greater productivity led to larger communities, to specialization and stratification. Writing, astrology, the calendar are introduced; there are male priests and male kings. For the first time social order was imposed from above by force. The "stars" — the five visible planets, the sun and the moon — and their hierarchical order were looked to as providing a model for a hierarchical social order. Myth was consciously used, not to foster the growth of the young to maturity, but to render the authority of the king unchallengeable.[16] The lunar bull is suppressed by the solar lion, the goddess by the god. "The progressive devaluation of the mother goddess in favor of the father... everywhere accompanied the maturation of the dynastic state and patriarchy."[17] In these monarchies the focus has shifted from the goddess to her son, with whom the king (by way of what Campbell terms an act of "mythic inflation") identifies himself. The new mythology implies a new psychology, the rational, divisive functions of the mind under the aegis of the male hero overcome the dark mystery of the deeper levels of the soul represented by the goddess.

The move away from the goddess correlated with the appearance of the city-state was then aggravated by invasions of nomadic hunters with *their* masculine ideology, both into areas where it simply amplified a transition already underway and into areas still dominated by the neolithic village perspective. Toward the end of the Bronze Age (c. 1250 B.C.E.) the mythology of the mother goddess was radically transformed, reinterpreted, and, in large measure, even suppressed by suddenly intrusive, patriarchal nomadic herder-warriors like the Hebrews who entered Canaan and the Aryans who came to Greece, Persia, and India.

Campbell traces the impact of this patriarchal god-worshipping invasion on both oriental and occidental mythology. But everywhere, he finds, the sense of the power of the mother remains as an ever-present threat. He uncovers the ubiquity of the goddess, even in myths where she is not supposed to be playing any part.

He shows how in India, the old neolithic Bronze Age goddess reappears when the Upanishadic view triumphs over the Aryan gods. "The enduring power in that land has always been the same old dark goddess of the long red tongue who turns everything into her own everlasting, awesome, yet finally somewhat tedious, self."[18] In her first appearance in Hindu literature the goddess presents herself as guru of the gods; she teaches them to know brahman. And in Mahayana Buddhism with its viewing of the world as a Buddha Realm, woman returns as prime symbol of the positive way — "a living image of the wonder of the world in which we live."[19]

In the West, on the other hand, the freely willing hero wins — and yet, as Campbell shows, in the myths of Israel and Greece the ultimate life and spiritual depth continue to rest with the dark presences of the earth, which "though defeated and subdued, are with their powers never totally absorbed."[20]

In a detailed reading of the Genesis stories as carriers of symbols borrowed from the deep past, Campbell explores how biblical mythology inverts the meaning of images drawn from the neolithic organic nonheroic vegetal-lunar goddess complex. "There is consequently an ambivalence inherent in many of the basic symbols of the Bible that no amount of rhetorical stress on the patriarchal interpretation can suppress. They address a pictorial message to the heart that exactly reverses the verbal message addressed to the brain."[21] He also reminds us how the Bible itself testifies to how important goddess worship remained in Israel until the Babylonian Exile.

When he turns to Greece Campbell applauds Jane Ellen Harrison's discovery of how vestiges of the pre-Homeric goddess survive in later epic and tragedy. In the myths of the gods subduing the titans, of heroes slaying monsters, he discerns an anxious protest against the worship of the Earth.[22] He also acknowledges that in Greece, unlike Israel, the patriarchal gods married the goddesses of the land and so the goddess survived in agricultural cults, in women's ritual life, and in the Orphic and Eleusinian mysteries. And where he criticizes the Hebrew emphasis on obedient submission to transcendent male deity, he communicates how he values the Greeks' emphasis on human reason, on their having learned to live as neither servants of a god nor "of the ever-wheeling, cosmic order."[23] He also appreciates how the Greeks (like the Orientals) recognized that their gods were "masks," human images, how they never confused the Olympians with "the ultimate Being of being," but understood that, "like men, they had been born of the Great Mother."[24]

Campbell does not minimize the role of goddess worship in early history nor settle for a simple linear evolutionary view which would relegate the goddess only to those archaic beginnings. He accords value to both the perspectives of the early hunters and the early planters, of the hero-worshippers and the goddess-worshippers, though he clearly regards the former's focus on life as opposed to death as "childlike" and "superficial" compared to the integration of life and death characteristic of the latter. He recognizes the violence and loss involved in the suppression of the goddess, though he sometimes writes as though it were just a matter of an oscillating alternation of female- and male-oriented mythologies.[25]

Campbell discerns how many male myths and rituals are really reaction formations, attempts to deny the mother's power or to take it from her. He describes male puberty rituals that assert that though women gave birth to the boy's temporal body the men will give him spiritual birth as attempts to arrogate women's birthgiving function to men. Many of these rituals involve forced separation from the mothers; many include the infliction of a sub-incision wound which is identified as a vagina. The boy undergoes a painful metamorphosis into a self-sufficient androgynous being.

Campbell is also sensitive to the distortions imposed by our reliance on male sources:

It is one of the curiosities and difficulties of our subject that its materials come to us for the most part through the agency of the male. The masters of the rites, the sages and prophets, and lastly our contemporary scholars of the subject, have usually been men; whereas, obviously, there has always been a feminine side to the picture also.[26]

But perhaps he has not always been fully aware of the male bias which informs his own view of the goddess — and of mythology in general.

Campbell's Male Perspective

He writes that woman is a "permanent presence" in mythology

both in her way of experiencing life and in her character as an imprint — a message from the world — for the male to assimilate.... the mystery of the woman is no less a mystery than death. Childbirth is no less a mystery, nor the flow of the mother's milk; nor the menstrual cycle — in its accord with the moon.... Woman, as the magical door from the other world, through which lives enter into this, stands naturally in counterpoise to the door of death, through which they leave.[27]

However, he says this without ever quite acknowledging how much his own account — quite naturally — falls on woman as a mystery to *men* rather than on woman as *she* experiences life. His accent falls on the goddess as mother, on the mother as sons experience her, not as daughters relate to her nor as mothers know themselves.

Despite his attempt to acknowledge that the goddesses of the neolithic world were more than fertility goddesses and cannot be understood only in relation to the fertility of the crops, the herds, and human mothers, his accent always falls on their motherly aspect. Little is said of the warrior goddess, the artisan goddess, the celestial goddess, or the vulnerable goddess.

The accent also falls on the *mysteriousness* of the goddess, rather than on the sense of familiarity and kinship she may have inspired in her female devotees. In his *Primitive Mythology* Campbell observes that prehistory corresponds to a layer of our own experience, so that in archaic mythology we find clues to "our own most inward expectations, spontaneous responses, and obsessive fears."[28] He reflects on how the earliest experience of the relation to the mother is an imprint that functions to shape the imagination of all humans, our remotest ancestors and ourselves. He notes there how this is particularly true for sons. The mythology of our entire species, he says, gives "innumerable instances of the unrelenting efforts of the male to relate himself effectively" to the mystery of motherhood and the fearfulness of woman.[29] Mother images serve as almost inevitable symbols of the mystery of life and the image of the child in the womb provides us with our most powerful image of bliss — a bliss that myth and ritual seek to help us regain.[30]

For Campbell the mother goddess typically suggests fantasies of bliss and fusion:

> The image of the mother and the female affects the psyche differently from that of the father and the male. Sentiments of identity are associated most immediately with the mother; those of dissociation, with the father. Hence, where the mother image preponderates, even the dualism of life and death dissolves in the rapture of her solace.[31]

Daughters are more likely to recognize that one can be close to the mother without dissolving in her; sons more typically see only the radical alternatives: autonomy and separation or dissolution and fusion.[32]

Rapture and bliss: Campbell often tells us that the most important function of mythology is to lead us to experience the rapture of being alive, the wonder of existence, to elicit and support a sense of awe before the mystery of being. He says it beautifully and yet again I see this as in part a man's perspective. Bliss and rapture are for him so intertwined with images of reunion with the mother. All myth is seen as an expression of the longing for that return (or as an attempt to deny or overcome it). As he acknowledges to Bill Moyers in the comment that serves as the epigraph to this essay, "I have frequently thought that mythology is a sublimation of the mother image." But what if there is a mythmaking that does not proceed from fusion-longing or from fusion-fear, but from a celebration of intimacy and diversity?

Campbell has a deep appreciation for the role of the goddess in ancient mythology and modern psychology, though, not surprisingly, his understanding of her is shaped by his male perspective. It is my sense that this perspective informs not only his view of goddesses but of all mythology. I think, for example, of his emphasis on its homogeneity, on the universality of its central themes. He recognizes diversity, recognizes how landscape and history shape the details of particular mythologies, acknowledges how diffusion always includes "creative absorption," but what matters in mythology is "the one, shapeshifting yet marvellously constant story."[33] Thus to him all the goddesses — the Virgin Mother, Aphrodite, Cybele, Hathor, Ishtar, and the rest — are really one;[34] Zeus's many mistresses and wives are each "a local manifestation of the goddess-mother of the world."[35] He applauds the Greek identification of Isis and Demeter, Shiva and Dionysus.[36] Many feminists would protest that this is to ignore the affirmation of the particular, the concrete, the earthbound in contrast to the universal, the transcendent, the heavenly that is so central to goddess worship. But our celebration of the many rather than the one, of the local deities rather than the universal, is denigrated by Campbell as a religion of the extroverted and the superficial. He distinguishes two types of mythology — one where the stress is placed on the historicity of the episode — the other where the episodes are *meant* to be read symbolically.[37] The deeper thinkers, the "tender-minded," see the local as merely a vehicle, recognize myth as myth, the gods and goddesses as masks; they see the psychology beneath the history.

For in our time, Campbell believes, mythology is left with only one function: the psychological, initiating the individual into the realities of his own psyche, guiding him toward his own spiritual enrichment and realization. Thus in *his* myth about myth all the history of human mythmaking he reviews in such detail is in a sense but an allegory; the different stages of mythology are equated with different levels of the psyche. To know the history is to know ourselves. Campbell speaks of the "vanishment" of all the earlier masks of god, which are now recognized as simply images of developing man himself. I have retained the sexist language here because I believe it may be more appropriate than Campbell intended. The hero of his myth, the autonomous creative individual, is in some sense inevitably a male figure.

And the *celebration* of the outmoding of mythology's cosmological and social functions may also represent a male vision. For surely we need myths to remind us of our emotional and erotic bonds with the natural world and of our interdependence with all that lives. Science has not superseded this function; it may have made it more pressing. Much of the energy for feminism's rediscovery of the goddess has come precisely because she may help us recover a more whole relation to the natural world — before we autonomous humans destroy it.

Campbell also devalues mythology's sociological function in his claim that disengagement is a deeper truth than social engagement. Thus in his reflections on the costs of the disappearance of the goddess from modern consciousness, he emphasizes the psychological costs, in a tone reminiscent of Jung's regrets over the loss of an integrated relation to the anima on the part of most modern men. But he rarely reflects on how a patriarchal mythology has served to support the social oppression of modern women. He does recognize how mythologies have been used oppressively, but proposes as an alternative not more generous, more inclusive mythologies but a turning inward, away from the social realm.

In India women rarely chose the Forest Path, perhaps because they were often prohibited, but perhaps in part because they glimpsed a different truth. Perhaps the masks of *god* are but masks of the creative *individual* — perhaps masks of the *goddess* are masks of women *with* women (and, I would want to say, with men). And perhaps "masks" is not quite the right word either — since it implies that we would see more truly if we removed them.

For one of the strange things about this wonderful storyteller, Joseph Campbell, is that he sees myths as penultimate, gods as but convenient means.[38] The ultimate function of mythology, he tells us, is SILENCE.[39] Unfortunately, "not all of us are philosophers;" many of us need the stories.[40] Yet, for Campbell, there is always the regret that, too often, taken literally, the symbol, the myth, occludes truth.

He is persuaded that "the known myths cannot endure. The known God cannot endure." The only honest possibility is that each of us become our own "creative center of authority," each of us become our own mythmaker, beginning with our own experience and finding images for it. Having listened to the stories of the past, we are encouraged to "an intelligent 'making use'" of all the mythologies of the past "to activate...the centers of [our] own creative imagination."[41]

I, too, following Monique Wittig, would recommend that we "remember *and* invent." But not alone. I so much value that my own mythmaking about the goddess has been done in the context of a community of women engaged in the same task.

8

The Flight of the Wild Gander:
The Postmodern Meaning
of "Meaning"

David L. Miller

CAMPBELL: People say that what we're all seeking is meaning for life. I don't think that's what we're really seeking. I think that what we're seeking is an experience of being alive....

MOYERS: You changed the definition of a myth from the *search* for meaning to the *experience* of meaning.

CAMPBELL: Experience of *life*.[1]

Myth Is Powerless

There is an irony in the power that has been exhibited in the television series, *The Power of Myth*. The irony is that the very person who embodies the power of myth again and again speaks of the powerlessness of myth in our postmodern time! If Joseph Campbell speaks of the power of myth powerfully, it is so that he can speak of its powerlessness. Joseph Campbell tells Bill Moyers succinctly: "What we have today is a demythologized world."[2]

This theme of the powerlessness of traditional mythologies is, to be sure, familiar. Nietzsche (a favorite of Campbell's) spoke of the "death of God." Wallace Stevens wrote that "here / In Connecticut, we never lived in a time / When mythology was possible."[3] And these are just the beginning of the testimonies that are by now well known. What is surprising is to hear the man who stands for the power of myth speaking of its powerlessness. But speak of it he did, and not only in the popular television series.

In an essay entitled "The Symbol without Meaning" — an essay originally delivered as a lecture at the Eranos Conference in Ascona, Switzerland, in 1957 — Campbell made the powerlessness point most powerfully, if absurdly. He first recited the most recent data from physics and astronomy about the distances across the galaxies proximate to ours. Then he juxtaposed with those modern accounts the dogma of the Assumption of the Blessed Virgin. "Is one to imagine," Campbell asked rhetorically,

> a human body rising from this earth, to pass beyond the bounds of our solar system, beyond the bounds, then, of the Milky Way, beyond the bounds, next, of our supergalaxy, and beyond the bounds even of what may lie beyond that? If so, then — please! — at what velocity is this body moving? For it must still be in flight! Having been launched less than two millenniums ago, even if traveling at the speed of light (which for a physical body is impossible), both the body of our Lord Jesus Christ (which began its own ascent some fifteen years earlier) and that of His Most Glorious Virgin Mother Mary, would now be only some two thousand light-years away — not yet beyond the horizon of the Milky Way.

Campbell acknowledged what everyone must: "The image is ridiculous."[4] Traditional mythologies, including the Christian one, simply cannot bear literal belief. They are powerless.

In his last book, the second volume of the Historical Atlas of World Mythology, at the very end, the same impossibility of belief is affirmed, and even more forthrightly than in Campbell's Eranos essay. Mythology is a lie, for

> ... there was no Garden of Eden antecedent to the Lower Paleolithic finds of c. 3 to 4 million years ago, no time when the Serpent could talk, no Fall, no Exile from such a Paradise with sword-bearing cherubim at its gate: the unequivocally documented history of the evolution of life and mankind on this planet has wiped that fairytale off the map. And if there was no Fall, what then of the need for Redemption? What god was offended and by whom? (Some especially touchy cave bear whose skull had been improperly enshrined?) What devil then took

mankind in pawn, so that we all had to be redeemed? And there was no Universal Flood, no Noah's Ark, no Tower of Babel, no scattering of the peoples, after Babel, over the planet, no Seven Plagues of Egypt, no drowning of any pharaoh and his army in the Red Sea, and no stopping of the sun and moon so that Joshua, God's special friend, might finish off in a battle the residents of a neighborhood he was invading. It is not the sun that moves in the sky, but the earth that revolves on its axis, and if this spinning had been suddenly stopped, every man, woman, and child, and every dog, elephant, and giraffe, would have been sent flying in trajectories east at a speed of some 1,500 feet a second, like Aunt Sarah through the windshield when her Cadillac hit the tree. So let's be serious![5]

Could anything be clearer? Campbell is serious about the powerlessness of traditional mythologies when they are interpreted in traditional ways, which is to say, in the way of belief. Yet Campbell's entire life is dedicated to these mythologies! How can we understand this irony?

The Powerlessness Is the Power

It is not precisely that *myth* is powerless. It is rather that the *misreading* of myth by modern men and women has rendered myth powerless. To paraphrase Nietzsche, it is not that *myth* has died; it is rather that *we* have murdered myth by turning it into belief and meaning.

In an essay on fairy tales, Campbell wrote that "mythology is psychology misread as cosmology, history and biography."[6] This is to observe that some people believe that myths refer to the cosmos, the world, and so understand them as early versions of science. But so to understand mythology is to render it irrelevant in a later time when there is a new science. Other people read mythology as history or biography, believing the images and tales to refer to past events and to chronicle human lives. But so to read myths is to make them irrelevant in the face of contemporary histories that supplant the myths and show their characters to be fictitious. Our modes of interpretation murder mythology in the name of the meaning we seek.

All the while, according to Campbell, mythology itself shows a psychological truth, a truth that shows forth in metaphor and image, imagination and fiction, story and poetry. This is why Campbell tells

Bill Moyers that one way to overcome our misreading of myths is to "read other people's myths, not those of your own religion, because you tend to interpret your own religion in terms of facts — but if you read the other ones, you begin to get the point."[7] The point being (as Campbell told Sam Keen in an earlier interview) that "all the gods are within us."[8]

The myths are our stories, images of our thoughts and feelings, figures of our behaviors and fantasies. "The latest incarnation of Oedipus, the continued romance of Beauty and the Beast," said Campbell in an often-quoted sentence from *The Hero with a Thousand Faces*, "stands this afternoon on the corner of Forty-second Street and Fifth Avenue waiting for the traffic light to change."[9] And at the end of *Hero* Campbell noted, as he did also at the end of the *Atlas*, that the postmodern individual should live *as-if*: not in belief, but in the make-believe of myths, "as though the day were now,"[10] because today, as he thought, the group (whether family, society, nation, state) receives its significance through its creative individuals rather than, as formerly, the individual getting his or her meaning through the medium of the collective unit.

In the interview with Sam Keen, Keen noted that a reduction to a private psychological focus might accompany such a point of view.[11] Indeed, it is the accent on the creative individual, the hero, the freedom of the courageous spirit that has prompted many to associate Campbell with the depth psychologist C. G. Jung, who also emphasized the archetypal psychological function of mythology in a time when the gods seem to be dead and dying, powerless to influence everyday life. Like Campbell, Jung saw that when a person gives up literal metaphysical belief (which places the meaning of myths in past history or in future eschatology), then the myths can take on symbolic significance as metaphors of psychological states (which places the meaning of mythology in the here and now). Both Campbell and Jung are asserting a sort of paradox: when myth is powerless, it can become powerful, and only then. This paradox can begin to account for the irony of why Campbell, so powerful in his exposition of mythology, speaks of that very mythology's powerlessness. Yet, if Campbell and Jung agree in being ruthless against dogmatic and literalistic religious belief, they nonetheless make something of an odd couple.[12]

The Irish Catholic and the Swiss Protestant

What is at stake in the religious and mythological iconoclasm of both Campbell and Jung is the question of "meaning." Even more, it is the question of "the meaning of 'meaning,'" which is the title of an important book by C. K. Ogden and I. A. Richards written in the twenties. Meaning — to put it bluntly — is a myth. This is the implication of Campbell's correction of Moyers in the epigraph to this chapter. Campbell explained this most clearly in his seminal essay at Eranos, "The Symbol without Meaning." Campbell argued that recent discoveries in archaeology and in the history of religions lead to a radical insight concerning the meaning of "meaning." In a stunning display of the history of religions from the time of the Riss-Würm interglacial age (*circa* 200,000 B.C.E.) through both paleolithic and neolithic periods to the time of the hieratic city states, Campbell noted a shift in the function of the religious symbol from one of disengagement to that of engagement.

Drawing explicitly upon Jung's distinction between "sign" and "symbol,"[13] Campbell placed religious and mythological discourse in the realm of the symbol (i.e., in the domain of expressions of what a person does not and cannot in principle know). But Campbell further differentiated the symbolic nature of religious and mythological discourse into two types. He called these two types "engagement" (or "reference") and "disengagement" (or "transport").[14] "When...the symbol is functioning for engagement, the cognitive faculties," Campbell explained, "are held fascinated by and bound to the symbol itself, and are thus simultaneously informed by and protected from the unknown. But when the symbol is functioning for disengagement, transport, and metamorphosis, it becomes a catapult, to be left behind."[15]

In his review of the history of religions, Campbell noted that characteristic of the mythology of paleolithic persons are shamanism, with its motifs of magic, vision, trickster, and fire-bringer, on the one hand, and animal mastery, with its motifs of returned blood, buffalo dance, lady of mammoths, and master bear, on the other hand.[16] But with the coming of the neolithic period, these "same ideas have been given a fresh turn and organization, which amounts, indeed," as Campbell puts it in another work, "to a new and certainly magnificent, though somewhat horrifying, crisis of spiritual growth."[17] Characteristic of the neolithic mythology are motifs of immolated kings, ritual love-death, virgin descent and ascent, and serpent creation. This transformation in the themes of religious consciousness is parallel to the sociological change from hunting to planting modes of existence.

In the earlier hunting societies, religious meaning is centered in the individual. There is an emphasis on "the individual fast for the gaining of visions" or on "hierophantic realizations." However, spiritual significance does not imply among such peoples "a rupture with society and world." Rather, it is a separating of oneself from the "comparatively trivial attitude toward the human spirit and the world that appears to satisfy the great majority." There is a conversion, in this symbology, from family to universe, from tribe to deep psychic structure. Meaning is in *dis*-engaging from the collective unit. So, a common theme is "death and personal rebirth" or "a passing back and forth of an immortal through a veil."[18]

This all changes, according to Campbell's argument, as the social mode of being moves from the hunter to the planter. Whereas in earlier religion the central motif is death and rebirth, in planter-religion the interdependence of death and sex (fertility) is emphasized, with the result that killing and consuming are fulfilled in propagating and dying, while sex and murder become the fundamental rituals.

Prior to the situation of life lived as "sex and murder" there seems to have been an Edenesque "dreamlike state of essentially timeless being." But now in time and history, the sociology of nonmystical reality dictates that religious meaning be discovered in ritual, that is, in the rituals of the collective unit (family, religion, tribe, state, nation). Conversion is not from family to universe or deep psychic structure; it is from family to tribe.[19] There is little room for individual deviation and variation in the religious realm of this later concept of religion and its sense of so-called "meaning." Spiritual significance is to be found, if at all, in relation to neighbor, village life, and calendar.[20] *Extra ecclesium, nulla salus:* "outside the group there is no individual salvation." In history- and agriculture-based consciousness, so-called religious meaning has its locus in the social unit. Individualism is suppressed. Religious mythology functions to *engage.*

But people today no longer live in an agriculture-based society or consciousness. Ours is a life and world of science and computer technology. The meaning of our "meaning" is different. "Dig below the geometrically composed floor of the neolithic walled town and search the mystery of the paleolithic cave,"[21] says Campbell, and you will find the meaning of "meaning" most appropriate to the postmodern moment. As Campbell tropes it, the meaning of "meaning" that implies engagement (attachment) is now "like the carapace of a crayfish or cocoon of a butterfly that has been cracked, sloughed off, and left behind. They [mythologies of engagement]... have been cracked... and should be left behind."[22] Such types of mythology and such readings of mythology are powerless today.

But the powerlessness of mythologies of engagement can become an opportunity for a rediscovery of an at once older and newer power: that of disengagement, disidentification, dislocation, or (as Jacques Derrida says) *différance*.[23] Campbell finds this postmodern mode illustrated in paleolithic mythology and in yogic philosophy.

The shaman, the yogic saint, the artist and the contemporary free soul (all of whom Campbell calls "wild gander") are flying. Their flight corresponds to the sign of the bow and arrow. As Campbell explained at Eranos, "the bow, in order to function as a bow and not as a snare, must have no meaning whatsoever in itself — or in any part of itself — beyond that of being an agent for disengagement — from itself."[24] So it is also with a symbol, with mythic or religious discourse. If someone assigns a so-called "meaning" to a myth or symbol, this "meaning" serves for engagement of energy and consciousness to itself. For the symbol to work properly (if indeed the symbol, the myth, and the religious text do indeed refer to something unknown and unknowable), "meaning" must be withdrawn so that the symbol, like the bow, may function to disengage the arrow.[25]

So Campbell said boldly in 1957: "The world, the entire universe, its god and all, has become a symbol — signifying nothing: a symbol without meaning. For to attribute meaning to any part of it would be to relax its force as a bow, and the arrow of the soul would then lodge only in the sphere of meaning."[26] "Our meaning," said Campbell, "is now the meaning that is no meaning; for no fixed term of reference can be drawn."[27]

On this matter of the "myth of meaning," Jung is very much in agreement with Campbell.[28] Jung referred to so-called meaning as a "conjecture."[29] One day late in his life, Jung was talking in his home to a group of psychiatrists from America and England and, after telling them they needed to create a myth of meaning for themselves, Jung added, "then you have to learn to become decently unconscious."[30]

For Jung, the problem with the meaning of "meaning" as it has been construed in the modern world is that "the myth of meaning is the myth of consciousness."[31] So-called meaning is imagined to be something that will be conscious, and it thereby neglects repressively such dimensions of the self as are not conscious.

Jung observed that the "archetype of meaning" tends to present itself in the dream-life of an individual in the figures of Old Wise Woman and Wise Old Man. But such figures always have two sides (light and shadowed, kind and terrible, helpful and threatening). Hence, the "meaning" of such figures must be deferred. They have different "meanings." They do not have a monolithic identity with which the dreamer can identify simply. The psychologist, therefore, in the face of such figures, must be, like the alchemist, agnostic, ironic, and humble.[32] Jung noted that if a one-sided and single "meaning" is insisted upon, then there will be what he called a "bold enantiodromia," a turning of the "meaning" into its opposite — "meaninglessness."[33] So it is that meaninglessness is built into the archetype of meaning as one of its constituent elements. When someone seeks meaning or asserts a meaning consciously, the fear or the experience of meaninglessness is already present as meaning's unconscious shadow.

So, when Jung was fifty-four, he wrote words very much like Campbell's: "Life is crazy and meaningful at once. And when we do not laugh over the one aspect and speculate about the other, life is exceedingly drab, and everything is reduced to the littlest scale. There is then little sense and little nonsense either. When you come to think about it, nothing has any meaning, for when there was nobody to think, there was nobody to interpret what happened. Interpretations are only for those who don't understand."[34] Jung may as well have said: so-called meanings are meaningless.

Thus it is that both Campbell and Jung speak in good postmodern fashion about difference rather than identity, about dislocation rather than attachment, about infinite deferral of signification rather than referral of signifiers to fixed signifieds. Myths are like poems. They do not mean, but simply are. Myths and poems are like flowers. "They toil not, neither do they spin." They are disengaged. "What," asks Campbell, "is the meaning of a flower, and having no meaning should the flower then not be?"[35] "There's no meaning. What's the meaning of the universe? What's the meaning of a flea? It's just there. That's it."[36]

The Myth of Power

Even though Campbell and Jung concur on this matter of meaning, there is still an oddness about linking the Irish Catholic and the Swiss Protestant, neither of whom practiced their religion in a traditional manner. The difference between them is not incidental nor trivial, and it can be seen by looking once more at Campbell's Eranos lecture.

Three times Campbell invoked the name of Prometheus.[37] In his final paragraph, he wrote: "Within the time of our lives, it is highly improbable that any solid rock will be found to which Prometheus can again be durably shackled."[38] Again, Campbell was speaking about meaning. "Meaning" proceeds now, as it did prior to neolithic times, under the aegis, not of identity, but of disengagement or difference. Prometheus is unbound. We are free of the rock.

It is just at this point that Jung might not have been so sanguine. Jung once wrote:

> The stronger and more independent our consciousness becomes, and with it the conscious will, the more the unconscious is thrust into the background, and the easier it is for the evolving consciousness to emancipate itself from the unconscious, archetypal pattern. Gaining in freedom, it bursts the bonds of mere instinctuality and finally reaches a condition of instinctual atrophy. This uprooted consciousness can no longer appeal to the authority of the primordial images; it has Promethean freedom, but it also suffers from godless hybris. It soars above the earth and above mankind, but the danger of its sudden collapse is there, not of course in the case of every individual, but for the weaker members of the community, who then, again like Prometheus, are chained to the Caucasus of the unconscious."[39]

We began with an irony about the work of Joseph Campbell, and we end with an irony. Could it be that the very flight of the wild gander tempts a failure of flight and freedom? Campbell himself was not unaware of this irony, writing, as he did, that we may still be "in a trap; for we are attached... [now] to the idea of enlightenment, release from the bow, disengagement."[40] Jung seems to be warning that a notion of disengagement or of difference (whether of Campbell, or Derrida, or some other postmodern theorist) can itself come to be understood — ironically and unconsciously — from the point of view of identity. One becomes identified with difference, attached to detachment, engaged by disengagement. If this were to be the case, then, when Prometheus is loosed from the rock (consciously), he may all the more be chained to it (unconsciously).

To be sure, Campbell never forgets suffering, even in all of his talk about bliss and freedom. In the conversations with Moyers, Campbell said: "I know no story in which death is rejected."[41] "Life is pain;

life is suffering; and life is horror...."[42] "I can't think of any [myths] that say that if you're going to live, you won't suffer."[43] Campbell was surely not naive about his Promethean, heroic ideal of Nietzschean freedom and individual bliss. But Jung did not hold that ideal. He wrote that "the goal is important only as an idea,"[44] because the end-product of therapy, like that of alchemy, "always betrays its essential duality. The united personality will never quite lose the painful sense of innate discord. Complete redemption from the sufferings of this world is and must remain an illusion."[45] So, in his autobiography Jung confesses that he "had to abandon the idea of the superordinate position of the ego."[46] Jung gave up the myth of the heroic ego lest the power of myth lure men and women into the myth of human power.

Campbell wanted to take the risk. He wanted to risk "the rapture that is associated with being alive,"[47] a rapture beyond meaning and meaninglessness. This is what the myths taught him. They taught him that it is all myth. As he himself put it, quoting the *Vajracchedika:* "Stars, darkness, a lamp, a phantom, dew, a bubble; a dream, a flash of lightning, and a cloud: thus should we look upon the world."[48] We should look upon it mythically, without meaning.

9

Harney Peak Is Everywhere:
The Place of Myth
in a Planetary Future

Daniel C. Noel

In the vision, Black Elk saw that the hoop of his nation was one of many hoops, which is something that we haven't learned at all well yet.... He says, "I saw myself on the central mountain of the world, the highest place, and I had a vision because I was seeing in the sacred manner of the world." And the sacred central mountain was Harney Peak in South Dakota. And then he says, "But the central mountain is everywhere."

That is a real mythological realization. It distinguishes between the local cult image, Harney Peak, and its connotation as the center of the world.[1]

To wonder about the place of myth in a *planetary* future is to call forth the exploits and imagery of what has become known as the Space Age, the late-modern period of history that has taken us to the surface of the moon and confronted us with the icon of the earth floating among the stars. Joseph Campbell was one of the very few commentators to realize the great psychological and religious importance of these Space-Age developments and to begin a much-needed interpretive exploration.[2]

The moon voyage, Campbell said as early as 1970, "has transformed, deepened, and extended human consciousness to a degree and in a manner that amount to the opening of a new spiritual era."[3]

118

Likewise, in the same lecture he exclaimed that "that fabulous color photograph of our good earth rising as a glorious planet above a silent lunar landscape is something not to forget."[4]

He never did forget, and for the next seventeen years, whenever he spoke about the possibilities of an emerging new mythology he referred to this Space-Age perspective. He readily acknowledged that "to predict what the imagery of the poetry of man's future is to be, is today, of course, impossible"[5] — we cannot make such a confident prediction, Professor Campbell frequently reminded us, for the same reason that we cannot predict what we will dream tonight, nor can we sheerly *invent* any myth worthy of the name.

However, he felt that the most promising possibility lay in a remark of the Apollo astronauts that the earth to which they returned was " 'like an oasis in the desert of infinite space.' Now *there* is a telling image," wrote Campbell: "this earth, the one oasis in all space, an extraordinary kind of sacred grove, as it were, set apart for the rituals of life; and not simply one part or section of this earth, but the entire globe now a sanctuary, a set-apart Blessed Place."[6] This is a telling image of earth indeed, one worth returning to. But what is important to note at the outset is simply that despite barriers to predicting what the emergent mythos may be, all the most evocative clues point in the direction of a *planetary* mythic focus, a guiding set of psychocultural images resulting from our new, technologically-assisted line of sight on the earth in space. In fact, when the theologically-trained interviewer Sam Keen asked him what heroes and events he judged to be "symboliz[ing] modern man's self-understanding," Campbell replied without hesitation: "The astronauts are the heroes and the moon walk the event that I find most significant."[7]

That was in 1971. In 1986, conversing with Bill Moyers for the PBS *Power of Myth* television series, he forcefully drew one implication from his championing of the lunar voyage:

> ...the only myth that is going to be worth thinking about in the immediate future is one that is talking about the planet, not the city, not these people, but the planet, and everybody on it....
>
> When you see the earth from the moon, you don't see any divisions there of nations or states. This might be the symbol, really, for the new mythology to come.[8]

If this is the likely symbol for the new mythology to come, what may be its meanings?

No More Horizons

Campbell's mention of the lack of national boundaries visible on the earth as seen from space echoes a prominent theme of returning astronauts: the *boundary-less* view of the planet, unified across old borders by a newly-shared sense of home. Here is the popular image of "the whole earth" — or holistic earth — promising a balanced and harmonious world beyond the territorial strife of Beirut or Belfast. In a time of *glasnost* the sociopolitical interconnectedness sponsored by a whole-earth mythos seems not only positive but possible.

Joseph Campbell's whole-earth vision, however, pointing toward the place of myth in a planetary future, went farther than a sociopolitical agenda, even a huge and hopeful one. His own *mythographic* agenda proposed something more drastic: the end of *all* horizons and the privileged spatial centers from which they are seen. "No More Horizons," proclaims the title of the postscript essay in his 1972 collection *Myths to Live By*,[9] and to announce that the lunar horizon is or should be our very last one is a significantly more cosmic statement than the call for international cooperation. It rearranges our perspective in a manner that is equal to the vastness Campbell took to be the proper scope of the mythic. As he voiced it in this same essay:

> The concept of the state... is yielding rapidly at this hour to the concept of the ecumene, i.e., the whole inhabited earth.... There is therefore neither any need anymore, nor any possibility, for those locally binding, sociopolitically bounded, differing forms of religion.... [10]

In other words, the ramifications of our Space-Age efforts at "planetization" extend to the virtual *abolition* of what we have known as *both* state and church and suggest a very different set of social and spiritual options for the future that is coming to birth.

But the rearrangements that Campbell foresaw are not even limited to the superseding of social and spiritual *institutions*. For him the Space Age had transformed the very semantics of our symbolism — the engine, so to speak, driving the reference-system, the ability to *mean*, of the mythic images surfacing in private dreams and the arts of culture. The hero-journey of the astronauts, by lifting us above the horizons that have shaped all our prior semantics, offers us (perhaps forces upon us) a cognitive frame once available only to those few persons called to follow some metaphysical path. Instead of local-historical denotations, the space perspective, the planetary perspective, gives us cosmological connotations that finally pertain as much to inner psychology as to outer space, "privileging" what Campbell took to be *spiritual* references.

Moreover, this shift is a boon for mythic images, or for Professor Campbell's theory about them, because he saw their prime and proper sense as always spiritual, a reading he felt the moon voyage had now fully endorsed and made evident. The title of a late work, *The Inner Reaches of Outer Space*, signals his conviction that the Space-Age perspective had publicly vindicated a psycho-cosmic spirituality earlier relegated to ancient or Asian esoteric traditions, while its subtitle tells of the semantic issues now at stake: *Metaphor as Myth and as Religion*. The difference between these latter combinations expresses in capsule form Campbell's understanding of the conflicting ways in which any myth, or any image with mythic resonance, may be construed today. To link metaphor with myth is to interpret either "anagogically" (mystically), that is, symbolically, spiritually, and truly. On the other hand, linking it with official religion — certainly the biblical religions dominant in Western culture — gives rise to the local-historical reading of a metaphor's meanings, or a myth's, which he constantly criticized as an inappropriately narrowing literalism, the enemy of the spiritual knowledge myth offers.

And it is the new technology and cosmology of space and planetization that serve to point up such semantic constriction in the local-historical preoccupations of some religions, urging us with all the power of myth to launch ourselves beyond our horizons toward a metaphoric vision of the spiritual "space" within.

In his Space-Age stress on "metaphor as myth" rather than "metaphor as religion" Joseph Campbell seemed to be in accord with the only other prominent writer to comment at any length on the mythic significance of outer-space exploration. The novelist Norman Mailer, in his characteristically quirky and provocative volume of 1970, *Of a Fire on the Moon*, remarked that

> ... we might have to go out into space until the mystery of new discovery would force us to regard the world once again as poets, behold it as savages who knew that if the universe was a lock, its key was metaphor rather than measure.[11]

While the term "savages" can be an offensive one, it is clear that Mailer is here *affirming* the wisdom of indigenous or primal peoples, equating it with the sophisticated expressions of the poet or artist as a crucial resource for informed vision in a planetary future. And, again, Professor Campbell would appear to agree, given his high estimation not only of the semantic workings of metaphor but also (as any number of passages from his works would suggest) of the "primitive" shaman — and of the artist as his or her modern counterpart in a purported cultural re-cycling of hunter/food-gatherer spirituality.[12]

Unfortunately for the tidy harmonizing of the views of these two imaginative Space-Age commentators, however, there turns out to be a subtle yet very significant disagreement between them. More to the good, if probed with some care it can deepen our sense of the future place of myth as well as our assessment of Campbell's contribution.

This disagreement can begin to reveal its complexities through an investigation of what is implied by Mailer's positive use of that troublesome term "savages," and by our consulting another author who has commented — albeit more briefly — on the relation of "primitive" perspectives to Space-Age semantics. Other issues, crucial issues concerning the artist or poet and the role of metaphor in myth-making, will thereby open up.

Savages, Poets, and Metaphoric Perception in the Space Age

The equating of the savage with the poetic in Mailer's statement — and each as equally representative of a needed metaphoric vision — is already an intriguing one. It can best be explained, and then carefully set over against Campbell's standpoint, if we look at the philosopher William Barrett's book *Time of Need*, a study of "forms of imagination in the twentieth century." There Barrett discusses among many other matters the impact of spaceflight on the evolution of consciousness, especially as concerns the cultural function of the arts. He wonders about the connection — which art, he argues, has always maintained — between our current culture and those of archaic peoples: "Earlier civilizations," he notes, "still hugged, whether they knew it or not, that primitive forebear to their bosom and preserved his ways. Their knowledge did not depart too far from the world of the senses that he first set in order. Their myths repeated the patterns of his."[13] Continuing this line of thought, Barrett raises, and tentatively answers, a very large question:

> We seem to be headed toward a civilization that would be the
> first to break its ties with that primitive being. To accomplish
> this would be more audacious than the mere physical leap into
> space.... Will it succeed? Art seems to say no.[14]

Here is a question that directly pertains to an understanding of the place of myth in a planetary future, and William Barrett's surmised answer in the negative already implies the lurking contrast I am claiming in the approaches put forward by Norman Mailer and Joseph Campbell: We can readily imagine Mailer agreeing with Barrett's negative answer, opposing art to the spacefaring agenda, and Campbell, with his mythographic endorsement of the latter, emphatically *dis*agreeing. Upon closer inspection, in other words, it seems that two different views of art are involved here.

A second question — and its likely answer — can further clarify this hidden clash of perspectives: How can both Mailer and Campbell *endorse* the value of poetic metaphor, and yet the former equate its use with a "savage seeing" enclosed by the limiting horizons of traditional cultures, while the latter links it to a mystical spirituality that he deems to be in harmony with the horizonless technology of computers and spaceflight? A key text in Joseph Campbell's impressive corpus of writings suggests the answer.

Lowly Vehicles for Lofty Tenors

In his 1960 essay "Primitive Man as Metaphysician" Campbell follows the lead of Paul Radin's *Primitive Man as Philosopher* (1927) while addressing the crucial theme of the "savage" or the "primitive being" as a metaphor-using participant in the operations of myth. Here certain anthropologists are criticized for having advanced as primal humankind's *metaphysical* ideas what Campbell sees as only "images, symbols, or vehicles" — for instance, belief in a land of the souls of the dead with its attendant imagery, or the idea of a multiplicity of worlds, each concretely described. "Such images," responds Professor Campbell, "are not the final terms of our subject, if it is metaphysics we are treating. They have often served...as vehicles of metaphysical expression...but we miss our proper point if we rest with them as they stand."[15]

There are several emphases central to Campbell's idea of the semantics of mythic symbolism in this essay, hinted in his response to the anthropologists, and they all bear upon his view of the nature of the metaphoric process. First is a well-known distinction by the philosopher I. A. Richards between "vehicle" and "tenor," a way of differentiating the major elements of a metaphor or symbolic image. Similarly to Marshall McLuhan's later description of the "medium" and the "message," the concrete, sensuous, specific, "local" *content* used as the vehicle or medium — the image itself or the "stuff" of the symbol — carries a tenor, a message, that is often less material and more abstract or universal than the vehicle that has conveyed it. Thus, in the simplest example, the cloth, shape, design, and colors of a flag combine to be a vehicle for the principles and emotions of patriotism that comprise the tenor.

For Joseph Campbell, ever wary of a literalistic identification of lofty tenors with their more lowly vehicles and intent upon the communication of universal metaphysical or mystical principles, the metaphors and metaphoric understandings that make up a myth are always merely masks for the "God beyond God," the disembodied idea in the depths of space or the depths of the psyche that can never be literally named. And this core emphasis is very much in line with his vision of myth's role in a planetary future about which he began to lecture and write in the early seventies. Indeed, partly under the influence of Leo Frobenius's notion of a "World Culture" superseding a "Monumental Culture," he had already been espousing a vision of global spirituality well before the moon walk and earthrise of 1969. A full *twenty* years earlier, for example, he had decided that "the community today is the planet, not the bounded nation...."[16]

Meanwhile, back in the 1960 essay, "Primitive Man as Metaphysician," he seems to *incorporate* the archaic thinker into his horizonless semantics of mythic symbolism, interpreting the particular local imagery of a Pima Indian origin myth as identical in *tenor* to one of the Upanisads and one of the Puranas of Hinduism, to the Norse Eddas, to the Babylonian "Epic of Creation," to the Latin poetry of Ovid, to the Memphite theogony of ancient Egypt and the Vedantic philosophy of India, and to the writings of Kant and Goethe! In other words, Campbell, it is clear from this essay, endorses the archaic metaphor-wielding and myth-making human being — but only as a *proto-philosopher*, an early and perhaps unconscious example of the abstract thinker, who supplies particular vehicles that he or she may or may not understand as carrying a transcendental tenor, a mystical, spiritual reference. Although his avowed linkage of the modern artist with the archaic shaman has been acknowledged, this description of "primitive man as metaphysician" seems a far cry from the sensibility of most poets or painters. Surely few poets would be attracted to his closing pronouncement in the essay that "the bedrock of the science of folklore and myth is not in the wisps and strays of metaphor, but in the ideas to which the metaphors refer."[17]

What, then, *is* the status of the arts in Campbell's theory?

Poetry Overdone and Underdone

In his 1964 volume *Occidental Mythology* in the Masks of God series Professor Campbell distinguishes between "the true poetry of the poet, the poetry overdone of the prophet, and the poetry done to death of the priest" — a strong vote of approval, implicitly, for the Western poet's properly mythic spirituality as contrasted with the proponents of organized religion. Moreover, this apparently supportive assessment of the poet is immediately succeeded by straightforward praise for "the sensitized, creative, living minds that once were known as seers [among which he includes the shamans of indigenous cultures] but now as poets and creative artists."[18]

However, there is a significant proviso in all this mythographic adulation: Campbell also *criticizes* the poetic enterprise (and by extension the other arts) for what he designates "poetry underdone," an inclination to "rest in the whimsies of personal surprise, joy, or anguish before the realities of life in a universe poets never made."[19] That is, for Joseph Campbell, poets concerned with the local vehicles supplied by personal imagery are simply not practicing true poetry. In fact, it is necessary at this point to infer that Campbell's version of the poet's or artist's authentic role makes this figure a metaphysician, just like the savage shaman: a servant of the intellect and the spiritual idea.

And yet, Norman Mailer and William Barrett would almost certainly retort that the modern poet or artist (along with the native practitioner of any primal religion) is on the contrary a servant of the *imagination*, which is to say a worker in the local field of the image-vehicle, following its hook-and-eye connections with other images on a largely horizontal quest for insight, always grounded in the earthy immediacies of the here and now, the near and dear. Admittedly, they might say, the poet no less than the mystic would resist the literalistic, but usually there is all the difference in the world between the aims of the poet as such and those of the mystic as such: if the former would refuse to take revealing imagery *literally* he or she would nonetheless take it very, very *seriously*. The imaginary gardens of poetry, Marianne Moore once remarked, contain real frogs, and the surrealist painter René Magritte spoke for the vast majority of his fellow artists in extolling "the mystery of the *visible*."[20]

There are far-reaching reverberations from this subtle (but once seen, sharp) clash of views between Mailer and Barrett on the one hand, who express their *resistance* to equating the poet or artist with the mystic or metaphysician, and Joseph Campbell on the other, whose vision of the place of myth in a planetary culture *depends* in part upon affirming this very equation. It has already become evident that the situation of the "savage" or "primitive being" is implicated: In the first of these two viewpoints he or she shares with most modern practitioners of the arts an allegiance to the "local field," the particularities of concrete imaginal vehicles and the horizon-bound contexts they come from. Contrariwise, Campbell finds the figure of the archaic shaman to be a "seer" who offers up visionary vehicles that succeed semantically only when used as propellants into "the higher mysteries" of metaphysics.

It is as though, in pursuing the important task of protecting the cross-cultural significations of myth, its universally *shared* messages, from what he saw as the reductive and literalistic interpretations of orthodox social scientists and orthodox religionists alike, it proved difficult for Professor Campbell to honor the need of both artistic and archaic vision to "stick to the image," to stay with the vehicle, to relish the paint, the clay, the particular words, the prayer-sticks or ritual feathers — and to let any supernatural revelations arise, as he himself put it in a less metaphysical moment, like the "bouquet" of the natural. Seen from the heights of mysticism or perhaps the perspective of outer space, this need of poetic and savage seeing can no doubt seem dangerously materialistic and literal-minded. Moreover, the wish — which Joseph Campbell voices so very eloquently — to avoid the excesses of parochialism in politics and religion, to transcend the often-bloody strife of ingrown groups, each defending its own "local field," is a worthy one. Who can deny the attractiveness of this pacific ideal of the global vision broadcast by the Space Age?

Nevertheless, it should be obvious from the foregoing that there is an alternative vantage point from which to view the place of myth in a planetary future, a line of sight taking its lead from an alternative assessment of the activity of archaic and artistic vision in myth-making — and, in effect, a late-modern or postmodern vision alternative to that implied by Professor Campbell. In order to explore this alternative further, to confront the additional questions it provokes, and to draw some tentative conclusions, let us engage in a brief case study: tracking Campbell's reading of the testimony of the famed Oglala Sioux medicine man Black Elk.

The Case of Black Elk's Center

Even a less-than-exhaustive survey of Professor Campbell's extensive writings reveals several discussions of this Native American vision (as recorded in one instance by the Nebraska poet John Neihardt and in another by the Religious Studies scholar Joseph Epes Brown[21]). It is not Black Elk's entire testimony that is pertinent here, however, but only Campbell's interpretation of a single major consideration within it: the nature of sacred place as the center of the circle of the world.

The earliest reference significant in this regard is a discussion within an essay from 1959 entitled "Mythogenesis." Here Campbell reacts to Black Elk's description, recounted in Brown's *The Sacred Pipe*, of the building of a ceremonial lodge as having "established...the center of the earth...and this center, which in reality is everywhere, is the dwelling place of Wakan Tanka [the Great Spirit]." The reaction is to compare this perception to that of the fifteenth-century metaphysician Nicholaus Cusanus: Campbell reasons that Black Elk's description is "a counterpart, exactly," of Cusanus's reflection on God as a sphere whose circumference is nowhere and whose center is everywhere. This leads him to exclaim that "it is amazing indeed to catch the echo of such a metaphysical statement from the lips of an absolutely illiterate old Sioux....What are we to think," he wonders, referring to similar parallels he has cited, "of all these coincidences? Whence come these timeless, placeless themes?"[22]

Recalling the alternative perspective represented by Mailer and Barrett, we could react otherwise than to marvel at Black Elk as a Renaissance metaphysician, asking instead whether the claim of such a coincidence does not actually obscure the very real *differences* between Cusanus's center and Black Elk's, the integrity or distinctiveness of each. Certainly few artists would fail to note that the *vehicles* in use here are hardly timeless and placeless. For Professor Campbell, nonetheless, the parallels are persuasive, and he proposes another by referring to Neihardt's record of Black Elk's childhood vision: "...the culmination was the arrival of the boy, still riding his bay horse, on the highest mountain of the world, Harney Peak in the Black Hills. 'But anywhere,' said Black Elk, 'is the center of the world.'"[23]

It is not difficult to see that such a statement appears to support Campbell's Space-Age idea of no more horizons, as the following comment from 1964, five years after the "Mythogenesis" essay, makes plain with its familiar allusion to Cusanus: "...there is no more any fixed horizon, there is no more any fixed center, any Mecca, Rome, or Jerusalem. Our circle today is that announced, c. 1450, by Nicholaus Cusanus...."[24] Still, much may hinge on a subtle difference in verbal vehicles. Black Elk's description to Joseph

Brown of the ceremonial lodge, built by human hands, led to the profession that "the center is *every*where." The testimony to John Neihardt about the natural sacred mountain, Harney Peak, had prompted Black Elk to add an alternative declaration: "But *any*where is the center of the world."

What comparison might be made here between the ceremonial building constructed by human culture and the place existing in the local landscape apart from our designs, or between *every*where and *any*where? Could we say that "anywhere" can be a *place* while "everywhere" cannot?

Blessed Place or Spiritual Space?

In *Creative Mythology*, the final volume in the Masks of God series, published a year before the Apollo 11 moon landing, Campbell especially emphasizes the psychological function of myth. Thus we learn that "the mythogenetic zone is the individual heart...each the creative center of authority for himself, in Cusanus's circle without circumference, whose center is everywhere, and where each is the focus of God's gaze."[25] The inner psychospiritual reaches of outer space are here indicated as the non-place of Cusanus's intelligible sphere of God, and by extension are seen as the non-place of Black Elk's expressions of centeredness. And yet again a question must be put to Professor Campbell's mythography from our alternative angle: Does his approach do full justice to the Native American sense of sacred place, their perceptions of what Europeans have called the *genius loci?* Or perhaps this very line of questioning, Campbell might have replied, does too *much* justice to the "poetry underdone" of the local vehicle, the unique integrity of a particular mountain or the specific word "any" as contrasted with the specific word "every."

By 1970, Campbell's timely article on the moon walk had seemed to settle the matter, announcing that "all the old bindings are broken. Cosmological centers now are any- and everywhere."[26] But that was the same article where, at the outset, we found him praising the astronauts' vision of the whole earth as an oasis in the desert of infinite space: "Now *there* is a telling image," he had written, "this earth, the one oasis in all space, an extraordinary kind of sacred grove set apart for the rituals of life...the entire globe now a sanctuary, a set-apart Blessed Place."[27]

Surely Joseph Campbell's regard for this telling image amply demonstrates his *capacity* to respect the vehicle of a metaphor as much as any artist or poet — as much, even, as Mailer and Barrett in their aesthetic perceptions of the Space Age. Unhappily, his enthusiastic acceptance of the whole earth as a "Blessed Place," *set apart* like any little horizon-bound local field or particularized mountain peak against the desert of space, is scarcely in accord with his Space-Age vision of the future myth of the planet. Nor, apparently, does it add much to our attempt to resolve all this when we read the remark in the moon walk essay that "spiritually...the center is where sight is."[28] On the other hand, a clue may lie in the word "spiritually" and in the entire approach to myth — Campbell's approach to myth, as we have seen — which places myth and its semantics of metaphor totally in the service of "spirit," the disembodied Ideal of metaphysics or most mysticism.

Joseph Campbell is, of course, not alone in speaking of "global spirituality" — others have done so at least since Teilhard de Chardin's notion of the "noosphere." And recently the Roman Catholic theologian (or "geologian," as he calls himself) Thomas Berry has produced work that is in many ways extremely similar to Professor Campbell's on these matters.[29] But neither Teilhard nor Thomas Berry includes *myth*, so named and discussed, as a central ingredient in his *spiritual* vision of a planetary future. This implies that a spiritual focus stressing transcendence suits the elevated vistas of the Space Age but may constitute a destructive force for the mythic.[30]

That is — to frame this suspicion as a series of questions — how can myth survive *as* myth without being tethered to the "local fields" of earth, its sources of non-literal imagery taken seriously? What *place* will there be for myth if we all become spiritual astronauts? What future? Will the placeless, timeless spiritual *tenor* of myth be able to jettison its earthy *vehicles* and remain myth? Would myth — like art in William Barrett's statement — seem to say no to the success of our efforts to break archaic connections to the earth?

For such a radical disconnection, after all, is just what Professor Campbell envisioned: a relinquishment of the particular and the concrete that is both symbolized and, in a real sense, culminated by the planetary perspective achieved in the Age of Space. The very first image in the *Power of Myth* television series is probably the most "telling" one: the fire of the rocket engine at blast-off, the image of the "launch vehicle," a vehicle that is indeed jettisoned after lifting us above the earth. Reflecting upon this video imagery in the light of Joseph Campbell's mythography overall, it becomes obvious that for him "the power of myth" is the power of the ascending rocket — its "spiritual thrust" — to elevate us out of the horizon-bound fields of the planet and into an outer space without places and a future without the familiar times of sunrise and sunset at home. Here once again the TV imagery tells us much: A view of a gaseous nebula in deep space beyond superimposed primitive masks accompanies the opening title and closing credits of each episode of the Campbell-Moyers conversations.

Viewed, then, from the alternative perspective on poets, "savages," and metaphoric perception in the Space Age suggested by Norman Mailer and William Barrett, it looks very much as if, unless myth can *do without* its thousand faces and many masks, it will be *dis*-placed by a future that only sees the earth from above and beyond — as an empty circle or receding zero with no inner differentiation of locales, tantamount to nothing.

Another encounter between Joseph Campbell and Black Elk's vision — one previewed in our opening epigraph — can point up this troubling possibility.

Harney Peak Is Everywhere — Myth Dis-placed

The justly-praised series with Bill Moyers contains Professor Campbell's last references to Black Elk. This time, no doubt because of the extemporaneous oral mode involved, John Neihardt's text is slightly misquoted. Instead of Black Elk's actual words about Harney Peak — "But *any*where is the center of the world" — we hear or read Campbell's informal recollection of the account, together with his accustomed interpretation:

> And then he says, "But the central mountain is *every*where."
> That is a real mythological realization. It distinguishes between the local cult image, Harney Peak, and its connotation as the center of the world.[31]

In the ensuing discussion comes another allusion to Nicholas of Cusa: "God is an intelligible sphere — a sphere known to the mind, not to the senses — whose center is everywhere and whose circumference is nowhere. And the center, Bill, is right where you're sitting," Campbell continues. "And the other one is right where I'm sitting. And each of us is a manifestation of that mystery.... You are the central mountain, and the central mountain is everywhere."[32]

No one can fault Professor Campbell for a minor misquote in the midst of a dazzling display of memory and erudition, and surely the ethical sensitivity here to the central role of the *other* is to be applauded as a wise application on the personal level of his opposition to in-group exclusivisms. It is nevertheless fair to wonder whether a view of myth as more spiritual than sensual (or, finally, as *totally* spiritual) — a view rooted in mystical-metaphysical philosophies like Cusanus's, read into indigenous shamanism as well as modern art, and fueled by the earth-abandoning impulses of a planetary technology — is not responsible for this innocent error.

There is by now little need to wonder, as Campbell did in the mid-seventies, whether the planetary culture *will* come about: The technology of the communications media alone is seeing to that, and more so by the day. A recent TV commercial shows a young Australian aborigine on his "walkabout" striding up to a remote outback shack with a satellite dish and an American-brand soft-drink machine. He enters to watch the pop singer Madonna — a name with its own mythic overtones — strut her stuff for the worldwide market of the same soft drink. At about the same time, a critic of television, writing in the *Whole Earth Review*, tells of the introduction of satellite receivers into the native villages of Canada's Northwest Territories. The Dene Indians and the Inuit along the Mackenzie River now find their children watching *Edge of Night* and *Dallas*, no longer interested in the stories told by the elders for generations.[33]

As with these examples, there are indeed what the perceptive Los Angeles writer Michael Ventura calls "pitfalls" to fear from such a technologically-globalized future. "The worst," he says, "is the possibility of a homogenous planet, Americanized as the Western cities are now, under a world government that enforces its will through satellite laser weapons."[34]

In other words, what has so often been called "Spaceship Earth" — more a technological than an ecological image, in any event — could turn out to be *"Battleship* Earth," or "the world in a man-of-war," as Herman Melville foretold it in the subtitle of his navy novel of 1849, *White Jacket*. And what would become of myth in such a future, homogenized either by military or more subtle means? With these prospects, is not a "free fall into the future" (as Campbell once approvingly termed it) *worth* fearing, not least because of its possible *abolition* of all that human cultures have known as the mythic?

Where, for example, would Black Elk, any more than the young aborigine or the Dene and Inuit children, be left by such planetization? Without *their* stories, what place is left for myth? Where is Harney Peak if it is no longer *any*where but instead *every*where? Can myth dispense so happily with its "local cult images"? Despite the dangers of semantic literalism and bloody sociopolitical divisions, does not myth need the *local* to be *located*, to have a *place* at all? Will a rocket-launching culture jettison the local vehicles of metaphoric imagery in the arts of its own creative myth-makers like a collective discarded catapult or a bow after its last arrow has been shot?

Meditating at our private (and infinitely portable) "bliss stations," will the desert of outer space begin to seem *preferable* in the New technological Age, heavenbent on its spirit fantasies? That is, will it become preferable, as mystics and ascetics have often decided, to the endangered oasis of earth, supposedly set apart as a Blessed Place but in a universe that has no more horizons, and therefore no longer *recognizes* anywhere as set apart — least of all an oasis, a "sacred grove" with its messy profusion of flora and fauna rewarding the senses and distracting the mind from disembodied contemplation of the intelligible sphere of God? Finally, if such unintended but ironically myth-destroying side effects of Professor Campbell's spiritual vision of a planetary future are real possibilities, are there any remedies?

Telling Tales and Terrestrial Reconnections — A Place for Myth

If there are, they hardly lie in assuming technology will *not* make us a planetary culture, so only a globalizing technology put more in the service of the mythic and less exclusively in the service of the spiritual — a difficult balancing act in a supposedly materialistic culture where the spiritual seems the needed antidote — would be of any help. Here a thoroughgoing critique of technology that lays out its subtle and highly problematic support of spirit's essentially earth-denying aspirations is certainly called for.[35] Here as well Joseph Campbell's episodes with Bill Moyers are themselves cause for a modest but real hope.

These conversations, after all, put the technology of television in the service of mythic storytelling. This is also to say that Campbell's *practice* of storytelling, as contrasted with his *theory* of the future mythos, is the hopeful factor. It is this activity, interlaced with mythographic theorizing during a long career, that can be an example of the kind of attention to particularity and place we need in order to make the postmodern future safe for the mythic. He relished every detail, every telling image, in his beloved anecdotes, and relished the telling and re-telling, returning to *this* particular tale, *here*, again and again, with *these* particular turns of phrase, voiced just so. His writing, in its practice if not its preaching, showed this same regard for the local vehicles of language as his oral interviews and lectures. Incontestably, he wrote more delightedly and more delightfully, more faithfully to the specific ethnic voices of English — with many an Irish inflection — than any critic he ever encountered.

Whatever our differences may be with Joseph Campbell the mythographer (and his accomplishment here was enormous by any account), Joseph Campbell the teller, the bard or verbal shaman, almost the artist, makes a place for myth by preserving in his tales the semantic value of down-to-earth settings.[36] Such telling reconnects our imagination to the particular places of the planet, and if this, too, is an unintended side effect from Professor Campbell's perspective, it is a hugely fortunate one for our planetary future. By focusing on it we not only contribute to the survival of myth but also see to it that Harney Peak — or any central mountain — is *some*where to be envisioned among the likely dislocations of that future.

10

Let Talking Snakes Lie:
Sacrificing Stories

Lynda Sexson

We're kept out of the Garden by our own fear and desire in relation to what we think to be the goods of our life.[1]

If Jesus had plucked a curling leaf, would he have been, also, a gardener?

One of the most compelling stories of the Christian tradition is in the Gospel of John, after the crucifixion when Mary Magdalene comes to the tomb, while it is still dark, and where she discovers that the stone has been rolled back and the body is missing. She turns around and Jesus is standing in the garden; and so she mistakes him for the gardener. "Sir, if you have carried him away, tell me where you have laid him, and I will take him away." "Mary," he says. Then she recognizes him and reaches toward him, "Rabboni," Teacher. Lord. *Noli me tangere.* "Do not hold me," he says.[2]

In that moment between Mary's seeing the man and her recognition of the beloved, *supposing him to be the gardener*, if he had reached out and trimmed a branch — not restored it like Lazarus, nor withered it like the fig tree, nor made an analogy to his viny, winy self — but *tended* it, would Mary have been able to rescue us before we needed rescue; with her error in mistaking him for the gardener, could she have saved the story from Christian dualism and the need for salvation? The Christian paradigm is founded on the ontological split between earth (gardens) and spirit (Garden), healed by the

134

sacrificial drama (on the cross/Tree). But Jesus, in the story from John 20, did not tend the garden, nor did Mary touch Jesus — *Do not hold me* — and flesh and spirit were severed, and male and female, sex and death, and the serpent was silenced again, and we lost, once more, the Garden.

Although Campbell speaks of myth, I speak of story, lest we forget that "dreams are the myths of individuals"[3] and that any lies I might tell about the old stories are as true as tradition. (So, why not, Mary, go forth from the garden proclaiming a gardener?)

Joseph Campbell's steady appeal has burst suddenly into the mass imagination as a result of Bill Moyers' television series; and now clergy draw upon him homiletically, workshops discuss him to death, lecturers close their appeals for reason and for funding with Campbell's summons to our need for myth.

All this talk, all this enthusiasm, raises questions: Why would the "demythologizing" West become so fascinated by the relentless story-teller and gentle scholar who mingles the polytheistic and nonthe-istic, nondualistic stories of the Orient with the sacrificial split of Western tales? Why would the church open its doors to this master of disguises when the academy has more often resisted his entry? Why does story itself seem safe now, all of a sudden, these stories that put West in its place and put East in focus, and even place so-called pri-mal traditions along an equivalent horizon? Have these homilies and discussions let the snake, the genius of the Garden, back in the pic-ture? Is it simply that we hunger from the deprivation of stories? And that they seem so good for food, a delight to the eyes, to be desired to make one wise? Or is it New Age nonsense, that no matter how much Campbell assured us this telling of stories is not a therapy, he tutored us on everything necessary to get better, including the "bliss station," so we might be made as charming and thriving as himself? Do the stories give us a fantasy of immortality, or the immortal soul, or at least of an orchestrated humanity uttering the one song, and therefore a meaningful song? Is it symptomatic or emblematic of the post-Christian era, so that only now can the many stories be revealed? Is it a hidden affirmation of conservative political values? Or is it a hidden affirmation of radical transformation in society?

The controversy is genuine, and the genuine responses are mul-tifold. It seems unlikely that a careful examination of Campbell's work will provoke a simple conclusion about its value; his signifi-cance and brilliance is wound up right along with his exasperating refusal to do what he has called us to do: to read, to hear, to enact the possibilities inherent in story. Though consistently indicted as a popularizer, Campbell, with his gift for story, takes up subtle phenomena that many of his denigrators choose to ignore. Though he may oversimplify or even trivialize method and metaphor, Campbell nevertheless brings us back to the heart of religion.

In the following pages, we will take up several aspects of myth or story that Campbell seems both to illuminate and to betray; indeed they are points Campbell seems to refute, but also to demonstrate: (1) that aesthetic consciousness is the ground of reality; (2) that all cultural manifestations come from that aesthetic ground; (3) but that myth or story is not only the primal heritage, but also the freedom to make the contemporary world on any model we like; (4) also that stories are not archetypal systems, but are stories by their very particularities; (5) those seemingly infinite particularities subvert the very systems that carry them and provide the creative energies for other versions of myth; (6) stories, if we must attach a term for metaphorical exchange, might better be named desire or laughter rather than sacrifice; and (7) whatever stories we tell, they do not tell us how to proceed; they surprise us. Finally, (8) Campbell's concentration on the heroic paradigm may blind us to stories, characters and events, and to thoughts about stories, especially to the strategies of the gardener.

1. *Aesthetic consciousness is the telling, the reading, the making of the universe.*

Along with Campbell, and without appealing to occultism or pop psychology, story does not give meaning to life but makes life "readable." The ambiguity and multivalence of story make it possible for many readers to be carried along and gathered to a narrative, despite time or space. Parcels of meaning, seeds of desire, envelopes of feeling open at every turn, every syllable, every gesture. Story and image are the basis of culture, of language, the basis of human expression; we are a bundle of metaphors, *skandhas*, skeins of threads — texts, sutras, suras, lines, twine, strands, yarns. Myth is located in the telling of it, the making and making up of it. Story makes possible ways of seeing/thinking that do not translate into other formal linguistic or rational systems. Campbell's task is to persuade us that myth is at the heart of human experience, that human experience is primarily imagistic, and, moreover, that the images are embodied in narrative. Our being is in our stories.

However, Campbell's reading does not tend to enhance or amplify or refine a story — leaping as he does so quickly between comparativism and exclamation — so Campbell's reader learns little about the art of reading. He decidedly narrows the possibilities for reading; we tend to approach stories from the same doorway, over and over, follow the maps we already had in our back pockets before we came to the terrain of the new story, which is by definition a land with a missing map, no cartographers, and unfamiliar constellations. With Campbell's structure and interpretive maneuvers, I may be freed to leap geographical and chronological barriers, but it is still difficult to slip out from the restraints of a phallocentric, heroic paradigm.

2. *Everything from theology to technology is located in story, is aesthetic formation.*

The return from theology to mythology, of relocating reality in the blood and bone of narrative rather than in excuses and abstractions, is the compelling power of Campbell's best work, the major reason, perhaps, he appeals so broadly — and perhaps so deeply — to his audience. The most frequently cited reason for his popularity is that the stories themselves draw us to them, theories about them be damned. Western monotheisms suppress their own divine images, treat their own god stories iconoclastically. Thus it is possible to see the popular interest in comparative sacred stories as something akin to the Protestant Reformation but in the opposite direction. However, the move from theological premises (which mask their sources, which are, of course, stories) to mythological premises is not merely the move to give up idea or reason for the sake of the carnival or display. Mythic or story language has its logic, its structure, and Campbell consistently alludes to story language, or the thought of fiction. Feeling is not the opposite of thinking. Although the language of metaphor is neither mere analogy nor mere moral lesson, it can, alas, even by the most sympathetic of tale bearers, be pressed into the service of all sorts of systems.

While Campbell seems to offer refuge particularly to the Christian caught at the end of theological assumptions, sometimes he just trades them for another set of artificial assumptions about reality. Stories insist — even those dogmatic or hagiographical stories — that there's more to tell. Christianity, after its iconoclastic purges, especially the Reformation, and after its historical quests, and after its long affairs with linear rationality, and after its prolonged ideological contortions, perhaps, will spring back to its flurry of stories: for "Inasmuch as many have undertaken to compile a narrative of the things which have been accomplished among us," Luke testified, the record has been one of closing the gaps, silencing the dissension, keeping the secrets. Western iconoclasm's dominating story is the one of cannibalizing its own stories, of purifying itself of narrative, of sacrificing myth (rather than myths of sacrifice). This may help us to see why Campbell, in returning us to polyvalent memory nevertheless keeps us within the confines of the paradigm of sacrifice. We cannot tell stories, participate in any dramas, unless we have the capacity for lying and laughter — both of which were locked up with the snake in Paradise. A monotheistic theology cannot bear the deluge of stories as Campbell presents them, perhaps even those stories from within that tradition itself. Each one opens a chink in the wall. Part of the history of Christianity is the urge to cleanse itself iconoclastically of stories. Campbell, for all of his appeals to the ancient, great traditions, is opening the canon, and is to be celebrated for releasing fecund, dangerous stories onto the culture.

Yet, Campbell's critics might well complain of a Christian bias, or a Gnostic Christian bias, which informs the stories he recalls, as well as the style of understanding attached to them. Campbell's considerable work on the Grail illuminates his telling of the underside of the Christian tradition; he enhances the Christian stories, moving from the tradition's theologies to its metaphysical realms. This minor or esoteric tradition breaks through for us, un-doing the ideo-story of the dominant tradition. "The idea of the supernatural as being something over and above the natural is a killing idea."[4] But it is the idea that has prevailed in Western culture. This increasing interest in myth, in seemingly esoteric stories that offer alternatives to the killing idea, may indicate the culture's story is shifting toward stories in which ecological as well as Christian values can be presented in rich, pluralistic existences.

3. *Rather than the yield of the archaic or arcane mind, or the ancient truth, story is today's little mistakes and last night's illusions.*

Novices sometimes have the impression that there's a primordial story or an authentic source, even though Campbell disdains scholarly complexities or contexts, for the authenticity he seeks is the psychic one. But where is it located, how is it discovered? One of the flaws in Campbell's work, found more in his followers than in himself, is the presumption that there is a system to which the story refers, and the references are psychic realities. And although Campbell distinguishes between the shamanic and the priestly function, he may have become a priestly figure in today's popular culture: the shaman risks the dream; the priest trusts the system.[5]

Story is metaphor and metaphor is made by giving the name of one thing to something else, as Aristotle said. It's all a fruitful mistake. Stories emerge, as they do in dreams, in slips and collisions. To return to the errors in our garden, there is a French Saint, "Saint Rabony," who could "improve bad husbands," as the term *rabbonir* is "to improve wine." "Saint Rabony apparently originated from a phylactery which pictures the Magdalen's recognition of the resurrected Christ and emphasizes it with the word *Rabboni* coming from her mouth."[6] One error gives way to another; story continues. Myth can be made of anything, lies as fertile as any strait-laced truth.

Are we, though, too distracted and fragmented to be able to form myth in our time? There is, perhaps, some irony in that surely as noble as PBS and Moyers are, it is nevertheless the fragmenting, distracting, dulling effects of television through which its antithesis, mythic narrative, has the task to reveal itself. Television is the fire around which the tribe hunkers now, but without a cohesive hearth — or with one that consistently shatters with demands for outside consumer activities. TV reality, time in tiny segments, repetitions, characters formed around products, news formed around polls, is the medium through which this mythic magnitude became known. Cinderella's sisters cut off their toes, their heels, to try to fit in the slipper; in some sense, television reduces its viewers and its stories always to the role of the ugly sisters, mutilating the body of the text to try to arrange the psyche into the time segment.

What is it that is filtered through a medium used to introduce easily to such diverse and vast audiences something they would have wanted before if only they had been knowledgeable of it, if only it had been distributed before? Is it an obvious question to ask, how is it that the sudden blossoming interest in Campbell came via television? Or, maybe it's obvious in the way that Grail riddles are obvious. Or is it possible that Campbell represents one of the TV gurus, not only charismatic on the tube, but also a teacher of electronic enlightenment: that I can have it easily and in segments, that my television consciousness is truth?

As well as television, Campbell has influenced the popular film. The Skywalker quest of *Star Wars* is embedded in a Gnostic universe informed by Campbell; thus as Joseph Campbell cites George Lucas's work as evidence for or example of his own hero archetype, it is a self-validating theory. "May the force be with you," and "follow your bliss" then, may seem to amount to the same sort of heroic cry in a self-imposed dualistically Gnostic scheme.

4. *Story is its own particularity, its own bundle of details not subordinate to a system in which narrative must forfeit its detail, its body and blood.*

The serpent thrust us into story, the mortality of story, not the immortality of it, the particularity of it, not the typology of it. A story is as delicate and particular as the tear Jesus shed for Lazarus, brought by an angel to Mary Magdalene to preserve in a vial. No other tear, condensation, or rainfall will do. Jungianism has long been suspect for its claims to universalism — most glaringly, cultural assumptions about social differences in gender have been codified into claims about universal, deep psychic realities. Yet myth bestows on us a tolerance for ambiguity, indeed, the grace of mystery, the ability to live within story without certitude. Between the story and the system, lies the dilemma. Somehow, we still depend upon systems to justify the narrative consciousness. Or is it that Campbell and others use the richness and depth of narrative to mask their adherence to abstract systems that may be as artificial, ultimately, as the newspaper horoscope? But this renewed appetite for stories belongs, perhaps, to a culture that is ready to give up the constricting embrace of literalism or hierarchical systems, to give up the literalism of social codes read into story and computed into the psyche.

On one end of the spectrum, following Campbell's way with stories includes a set of presuppositions about human nature (and to whose worldview are these notions comforting, reassuring?); at the other end his story-telling may be used by his enthusiasts as self-help in disguise. Story is not theology or therapy. Though Campbell protests that it is not meaning, but experience[7] that is his objective — and ours — he undermines that assertion with the system he arrives at given the human "nature" from which he begins. Jung, one of Campbell's primary influences, reduces story — that which moves itself, ourselves, and cultures — from the dynamic to the static; and Campbell sometimes falls into that Jungian stillness, the fantasy of a spiritualized eternity, where characters and events are signposts or puzzles. The nature of story is that it seems to tell us space/time stuff; but the treachery of story is that the snake lies: space/time is annihilated into narrative consciousness, which is not an archetypal rigidity, but a dynamic of story, of aesthetic perspective.

Despite Campbell's presuppositions about human nature, it seems to me that we must remember that our nature is our culture, and whether Freud or Augustine is behind the scenes, we cannot accept readily someone who "knows" the dark passions, the "irrational savage" within us, a peculiar mythic system that may not serve us well now.[8] The system does not necessarily go with the story; stories metamorphose through their readers; even the great system makers, such as Freud and Augustine, are reimagined, their systems become their stories, and their stories are re-formed by their readers. Augustine has become, in part, a Freudian story; and curiously, one of the exhilarating *re*-mythologizing projects is Freud's story of envy and desire as it is being reimagined, reread, by feminist thinkers. All essayists and all readers, including you and me, have worldviews, mythic premises about reality. It's not that Campbell should be "objective" (a term from another mythic system) but that we should recognize the implications of his worldview, particularly those aspects of which he seems oblivious — the place where cultural views are given biological or metaphysical labels. Both the biological and the metaphysical are worldviews, made up of narratives, serpent tales. Campbell does not show us varieties of systems, but tends to lead us astray into supposing that the systems themselves generate or sustain the stories, that the analog is the narrative.

5. *Stories, no matter what systems they promulgate, carry the seeds of other stories, other tellers, other views on the Garden.*

Campbell's work can inadvertently promote damaging, conservative values: hierarchialism, dualism, heroic and patriarchal social views, sexism; and yet it validates the entry into story that is the exit from those constrictions. The power of myth is the power to alter politically, to imagine, to name and describe the gods, the humans, their relationships, their contexts, their order, chaos, and chance. Campbell seems to retain many of the values of the old order, but confoundingly gives away the secrets to undermining it.

Is there a cultural chauvinism, a romanticism, behind the clinging to the old ways of expression? Campbell has tried over and over to place our myth on the streetcorner, under our own pillows, nevertheless convincing us the real stuff, or the good stuff, is Way Back There. But Campbell's Way Back There is often a nineteenth-century American romanticism — along with Emerson, Campbell codifies and sentimentalizes animals and Indians. He tells, in fact, of his entry into myth by means of the commercial Indians of Buffalo Bill's Wild West Show. "Ours is one of the worst histories in relation to the native peoples of any civilized nation,"[9] he says, but fails to comment that Indian "lore" — the stories — is one of the ways to invent reservations, as important as being "put into wagons and shipped under military guard out to what was then called Indian Territory,"[10] which the colonialists imagined as they eradicated the native peoples of this continent. That, too, is a legitimate mythic

entity, but the white man's Indian is not to be confused with the people who lived here before the sweep of European myth across the
continent; indigenous people are not to be confused with Edward S.
Curtis's haunting, romantic Apache by the pool.[11] Campbell seldom
examines the ideo-story of any of the narratives that he tells so well.
His mythic mind is informed by nostalgia rather than irony when he
speaks of the cathedral decentered by government, then superseded
by commerce.[12]

An exquisitely argued and controversial book by Sam Gill examines the American myth of Mother Earth, a given for those who grew
up on the feminine figures who were stations along the hero's journey. Gill finds that "Mother Earth has come into existence in America
largely during the last one hundred years and that her existence
stems primarily from two creative groups: scholars and Indians."[13]
What might be the implications for our studies of myth and history
and human consciousness, for our own playful means of creating
the world we inhabit, of interacting analytically with the heritage?
Although ecological descendants of this continent or others rhetorically and prayerfully call upon Mother Earth, the words may well fall
upon ears accustomed to thinking of the womanly body as an inferior
element of heroic matters — or as a sacrifice. If we are mythically
conscious, there is no Back Then — it's a right now — and commerce
and politics are the mythic terrain; we should not fantasize that the
old stories are without their political baggage. The virgin mother
serves as a doorway for the heroic venture, but to apply that image
to environment, to sexuality, to many women's or men's narratives,
prevents the varieties of virginal tales from being told, distorts or
stops them. To view the image exclusively from patriarchy is another
spiritual rape, another surprised maiden assaulted by the word from
on high. But our virginal selves will tell other stories; and in their
resistances are not likely to give birth to heroic culture. The serpent
in the Garden told an enormous lie: not that the fruit was good, a
delight to the eye, desirable to make one wise, but that there was
a boundary around the Garden — or that other sly old devil, Yahweh, did that. Now Campbell's going along with it — when he's not
refuting it, of course.

6. *What we call story may look more like desire rather than like sacrifice;
the exchange medium of story is not necessarily heroic contest; matters of
gender may change the game.*

These qualities of story — the aesthetic base of mind and its animated particularity — are demonstrated and simultaneously under-

mined by Campbell's work. His suppositions about the heroic sacrifice may serve as illustration.

Perhaps his most appealing contemplations regarding story consciousness have to do with marriage and love. Love may be the transformative experience that makes us so vulnerably just ourselves, the miracle that turns us into what we already are; but Campbell once again seeks to exalt the spiritualization of it rather than the manifestation of it, the system rather than the narrative. His remarks about marriage, particularly the "second half" of marriage, although revealing a cultural conservatism also reveal a graceful sense of multiple perspectives.

The Western pious tradition teaches the giving up of passion, but Campbell's views are more complex, as in that famous Zen story of an old woman who had given a monk a little hut and food, supporting his twenty-year meditation. Finally she wondered just what he had learned in all this time; she became curious about the story in her backyard. To find out (and unwittingly to make the story) she told a desirable girl to embrace him, then ask him suddenly: "What now?" The girl did as the old woman told her; but when she asked the monk her question, he replied, "An old tree grows on a cold rock in winter. Nowhere is there any warmth." *Noli me tangere*. Do not hold me.

The rejected girl returned and told the woman, who exclaimed, "To think I fed that fellow for twenty years! He showed no consideration for your need, no disposition to explain your condition. He need not have responded to passion, but at least he should have evidenced some compassion." She went at once to his hut and burned it down.[14] The compassion shown was the old woman's, forcing that warm monk onto winter's cold rock and into another realm of the story, into the Garden.

Campbell's theories of spiritualized romantic love do not question outdated scholarly speculations regarding the invention of what Campbell calls *amor* in the twelfth century, nor do they question the value of spiritualizing the metaphors of romance; nevertheless, his quaint views on love and the image of embrace almost release him from the image of sacrifice and the hero.

His comparative study of the hero is an enduring classic. However, he never seems to have called into question the notion of the hero story as the model for storytelling, that the hero is the model of life's adventure, nor raised the question whether patriarchy can be redesigned. ("Society is always patriarchal. Nature is always matrilineal."[15]) Rather than letting the varieties of stories suggest varieties of models, he often stuffs and trims a story to fit the model.

Nowhere is it more evident than his assertion, "Giving birth is definitely a heroic deed, in that it is the giving over of oneself to the life of another."[16] However that falsifies and diminishes the experiences of birthing or of parenting, it also falsifies, or causes us to ignore, the complexities of heroic stories as well. Nevertheless, Campbell himself informs us that story doesn't have a monolithic model:

> Mythology is very fluid. Most of the myths are self-contradictory. You may even find four or five myths in a given culture, all giving different versions of the same mystery. Then theology comes along and says it has got to be just this way. Mythology is poetry, and the poetic language is very flexible.[17]

7. *Stories are not recipes: not therapy, not ego-management, not blueprints for civilization, not veiled mysticism.*

He thinks that myth might straighten out the delinquent, bring about a kinder, gentler culture, but avoids examining his own basis for investigation: the deep stories that underlie the patriarchal assumptions. Campbell began his work when historians, though distrusting his typological study, essentially agreed with the worldview that history is made by heroes, individuals, especially in wars and struggles. History is no longer told from a heroic paradigm — great men in great clothes with great toys — but Campbell's myths are. That is, the hero may not be the fundamental paradigm within the stories Campbell reads; rather, he may be only demonstrating this particular inherited way of reading, not what he puts forward as the inherent *contents* of reading. It comes as no surprise, then, that from his perspective, myth represents heroic struggles within or for the soul. Perhaps the act of reading, of receiving and telling stories, is the work we have to do; that is the task, not the work of the hero, but the work Campbell set for himself, the way of the stories. But, Campbell's reading instructions may encumber, ultimately, our abilities to read — to discover varieties and particularities. Campbell's notion of the hero is bound up in a notion of soul that may be a masquerade of ego. The soul that has individual identity and a historical job to do in the land — despite the claims of the West — is the ego. Individual consciousness is ego consciousness, not eternal truth. Though the "soul" may run up the tree to escape the mad elephant, nevertheless Shankara's famous parable reveals: ego (King and Shankara), tree, and mad elephant, as well, and we might add, "soul" of Western individualism, are ephemeral — maya.[18] The soul has no work to do. No place to go. Shankara prayed forgiveness for his, and our, story consciousness: forgiveness for using words, for the Divine is silent; forgiveness for worshiping in images, for the Divine is formless; forgiveness for going on pilgrimages, for the Divine is everywhere. As the Zimmer/Campbell text points out, referring to Shankara's bhakti (devotional) verses to the Goddess Shakti-Maya-Devi:

> They reveal a surprising aspect of his spirituality; for though he dismisses maya in his philosophical writings and goes relentlessly beyond to the ineffable transcendency of Brahman, the "One-without-a-second," here he gives devout praise to the "second" — Maya, Mother of the World — and with all sincerity; expressing the mode of divine dualistic experience on the plane of bhakti, where the devotee regards and understands himself as the creature and servant of the deity-in-human-form.[19]

The homely paradox of story, perhaps, resembles the mystical paradox of Shankara. Campbell himself, as he too deftly reduces stories to story, claims the ego is extinguished.

> In the Christian tradition, Jesus on the cross is on a tree, the tree of immortal life, and he is the fruit of the tree. Jesus on the cross, the Buddha under the tree — these are the same figures. And the cherubim at the gate — who are they? At the Buddhist shrines you'll see one has his mouth open, the other has his mouth closed — fear and desire, a pair of opposites. If you're approaching a garden like that, and those two figures there are real to you and threaten you, if you have fear for your life, you are still outside the garden. But if you are no longer attached to your ego existence, but see the ego existence as a function of a larger, eternal totality, and you favor the larger against the smaller, then you won't be afraid of those two figures, and you will go through.[20]

Is there any *you* left to go through? Will story existence, too, evaporate? Campbell is sometimes dismissed because he celebrates the mystical qualities he discovers in the great stories; it is perhaps one of the most crucial elements of his work. Mysticism can abandon story like a heap of old clothes; conversely, stories are so busy changing their clothes, their shapes, and our minds, that they seem the antithesis of the mystical. What is it, then, that Campbell is about? Is he using story merely as a premise to lead us to mystical awareness? Or, on the contrary, is he using mystical analysis as a beatification of story? Whichever is ultimately in service of the other in Campbell's work, it is a peculiar combination for mainstream Western culture to accept; both story and mysticism are devalued and often suppressed forms in Christianity as well as the secular culture. Campbell, though, alludes to ways that stories can subvert linear, exclusivist thinking and offer a synthesis of time and text, space and soul. It is, after all, the dualist's assumption that mysticism is spirit, that it is a soul bereft of body, or that story is confined within analytical boundaries.

8. *The hero's sacrifice is a great story, but if it is the dominant story, we cannot imagine other ways out of violence, other ways of reading.*

And, it seems to me, if he had examined both mysticism and myth more carefully in relationship to one another, he would not have staked his story claim on heroic sacrifice. Yet his eloquence on the interconnectedness, or the participation of subject and object in ritual activity, for all of its dauntless speculation about ancient thought and culture, is appealing:

> ... the hunter and the hunted beast — in ritual terms, the priest and his sacrifice — would have to have been experienced in some psychological dimension as one and the same — even as the mixed form of the presiding presence of the Sanctuary, the semi-human, semi-animal, dancing Animal Master, already suggests. The beast to be slaughtered is interpreted as a willing victim, or rather, as a knowing participant in a covenanted sacred act wherein the mystery of life, which lives on life, is comprehended in its celebration.[21]

But does life need consecrating, do actions need imitations? Stories, perhaps, are not counterfeits of raw experiences, but are themselves primal. Campbell's theory seems to ride on Platonic-Christian structures. If anything, though, it is Oscar Wilde's playful parody of Platonism, that life imitates art, which stands up in the best of Campbell's work. Yet, whether stories are consecrating life or life is consecrating stories seems somehow to miss a finer point: we are not simply acting out, but making up. Stories permit us to critique our givens as well as repeat them; they permit us to transmute our categories as we receive them. Stories make claims, file false statements, lie all the time, that they are nothing grand. The premise of story-telling is playfulness, not contest; giving, not giving up. Sacrifice may not be the fundamental exchange system, but may be one form that follows the fundamental model in myth — not giving it up but making it up; within the fluid exchanges of the Tao, how could one be sacrificed to another? The story of sacrifice may have little room for the laughter of Chuang Tzu, the iconoclasm that engenders image. On the other hand, the iconoclasm of phallic significance (the Doubting Thomas) that purges variety is reduced to only one victim/offering/story.... a purifying encoding of body. Sacrifice must answer to the corpse. Do not hold me. The corpse blossoms, and until it does the story is comic: how do we hide the body? (Do not hold me.) There are, in this universe of metaphors, of tales, no symbols that point to the real stuff: there is nothing to guide us, no disguises:

> After many years as an agnostic and monistic materialist, I learned from the Ndembu that ritual and its symbolism are not merely epiphenomena or disguises of deeper social and psychological processes, but have ontological value, in some way related to man's condition as an evolving species, whose evolution takes place principally through its cultural innovations. I became convinced that religion is not merely a toy of the race's childhood, to be discarded at a nodal point of scientific and technological development, but is really at the heart of the matter.[22]

If we find meaning in myth, as Campbell, too, warns us about, we will sacrifice our freedom in stories, their mindfulness.

The prophet Amos is our first recorded voice in the West who undermines part of the sacrificial model of religion: his Yahweh despises the people's offerings, saying instead, "But let justice roll down like waters, and righteousness like an everflowing stream." Nevertheless, those chosen people are to suffer, even "of hearing the words of the Lord." And, though the sacrifices of cultic worship are scorned, the metaphor, in the form of the maiden, continues: "Fallen, no more to rise, is the virgin Israel; forsaken on her land, with none to raise her up" (5:2). The image of the people is destroyed by their god, with only the hope of a sacrificial remnant surviving, "a piece of an ear." Israelite prophetic religion, in its developing monotheism, gave up sacrificial worship and created the great sacrificial victim, the chosen, suffering servant. Campbell flows with that current, without questioning either the image that troubled the prophets, nor the image they made. The great story of Abraham and Isaac is that laughter survives beyond the sacrificial impulse; the disturbing story of Jephthah's (unnamed) daughter is that she bewails her virginity and dies for the sake of her father's rash promise. (The son is rescued, the daughter is bargained away.).

Cutting away, giving up, promising, purifying: foreskin, maiden, blood of animal or body of old king, handful of grain, first born, one hundred horses, folded paper into fire, poem into river, the skins of flayed prisoners. Will just anything do to change the status of the voyeurs, the witnesses? Sacrifice is the model of the patriarchal, voyeuristic culture. Stories, on the other hand, do not send in substitutes, but drag us in, are not distant enough to be seen, observed.

In India, too, sages withdrew from sacrificial practices recorded in the Vedas and sought the Self beyond the one in the mirror, the one in dream, the one in deep sleep, and discovered Self in which there is "no cessation of the knowing of a knower," which is not a second thing.[23] But alongside the *Upanishads*, other views arose; in the *Bhagavad Gita*, *yajna*, or sacrifice, is the key to release from *samsara*. "The good of all and the origin of all are grounded on the sacrifice."[24] Buddhism told story after story of sacrifice. In the *Jataka Tales*, when the Buddha was on earth as a rabbit, after shaking vigorously so as not to sacrifice, inadvertently, any insects that might be living in his fur, "throwing his whole body into the jaws of his generosity,"[25] he sacrificed himself to the fire to enable the prayers to go forward, so impressing the disguised Sakka, who squeezed the ink from a mountain and drew the image of the rabbit on the moon, where we can still see him. But the extinction of this ego may not be parallel to ego-sacrifice in the Western tradition. The Vedanta tradition, however, keeps to the Upanishadic and *jnana* path, giving up the model of sacrifice and its binding images. The Indian traditions have told many stories in which we will not be ensnared by the image of sacrifice.

Much has been made lately of adoring the American flag; those who idolize its presence call up the sacrifices soaked in its red stripes, and occasionally refer to the victorious image of sticking the flag in the moon. Stories are in their telling, pictures in their perspectives; a nationalistic emblem jammed into the cool goddess, or on the divine drawing of the Bodhisattva rabbit, is a conflict of story worldview. Sacrifices are, sometimes, the literalizing of one set of stories to the exclusion (or sacrifice) of others, the giving up of story images to an ego-centered tradition.

If the world is information, if our perceptions are constructions, if we are with Shankara up the illusory tree along with the snake in the Garden, what are all these lies? Then let us go back and ask: Can Sedna, the goddess of sea mammals, save us from the oil spill? If we all knew her story would it alter our use of the earth? In her story, her father betrayed her, first by marrying her off (sacrificing her) to a mysterious bird husband, and then again by chopping off her fingers, to throw her from the boat, sacrificing her to the storm. Her friends comb her hair, fingerless as she is, at the bottom of the sea, and her severed fingers, the seals, otters, walruses, whales, try to endure the ravages of our leaks and avarice. Can the story of Sedna help? Will her dismemberment evoked again, the sacrifice performed again, over and over, heal us? Or will the repetition of the story ensure the repetition of the acts of the father? Is the difference that within the story the sacrifice of the daughter is generative act, whereas within the contemporary sacrifices the numbers of her offspring are diminished? Shall we celebrate all of those sacrificial stories? Or must we ask the question whether or not the seeds of our contemporary slaughters are bound up with those old stories of sacrifice? If Campbell is right — which is certainly problematic — that the sacrifice is central, we still are compelled to ask if we want to imagine another story anyway, despite great claims of mythic heritages.

Stories that are not told and events that don't happen have their consequences, too: "The Martians have perhaps done us more harm by their non-existence than by their imagined invasion of the world," Frederick Turner suggests, who celebrates the sacrificial and the heroic, but spins them into an open, poetic future in which we are not cast in the old bloody molds, but imagine, for example, the "gardening of Mars":

> I don't want to resuscitate the myth of life on Mars. But let us imagine another myth instead. In one of Ray Bradbury's stories an Earthly colonist of Mars takes his daughter down to a canal to show her a Martian. She is told to look into the water, and there she sees her own reflection. Suppose we *ourselves* were the Martians. Suppose we could go to Mars and make the place our own. By we, I do not mean just us human beings. If the ecology movement has taught us anything, it is that we cannot exist without a biosphere of other species about us; they *are* us.[26]

One story is not as good as another — we have had too much of the individualistic hero who brings it all back to the masses. If Campbell insists on a sacrificial victim, perhaps we can at least concentrate on one where we keep the body. (Hold me. Eat me.) We must ask what worldview demands are implicit within each story — even the ones we are writing and which are therefore mysterious or opaque. What is the difference between the seemingly reassuring, comforting talk about sacrifice from Campbell and the disturbingly more pointed work of René Girard, who calibrates sacrifice in his key term, violence?[27] Both scholars may present a view of human culture that demands victimization of their readers' choices. A myth may be a mask of eternity, of god, of reality, but it is not necessarily on a higher plane. Otherwise, once again, dualism creeps in, and stories become the rubble of civilization.

To the adventurers of the "age of discovery" the notion was that the speaker/viewer created the center of the world and that their god — ever adaptable, portable — went with them. Columbus took his first name seriously, as Christ-bearer to those misnamed strangers who charmed him, who, he said, would be easy to convert for they had no religion, and whom he took readily into slavery. The move to heliocentrism, which happened along with the Columbian geographical revolution, did not remove "man" from the center; the geocentric worldview was god's eye on the sparrow, the heliocentric was the human eye on itself. It was a god's eye, not humanity's eye, which made for pre-Renaissance perspective. Renaissance perspective is the illusion that the viewer is the center. The age of discovery is the illusion, too, that the center is where I am. The hero story has been colored by those shifts in vision. But there are other shifts in perspective now; and when Columbus rolls around for another hero's send-off, the story will change: we cannot pretend that the land was "undiscovered" before European invaders came, or that people can be misnamed and eradicated; the land cannot again be named for Europe and the people for Asia,[28] given the sacrificial impulse that went with those acts. Sacrifice is a technique of naming: to name what is profoundly valuable in order to preserve what is real; or, to transform what is unworthy in order to use up what is unreal or forsaken.

When considering sacrifice, we must ask some riddles. (If we do not answer a riddle properly, we sacrifice our necks. The following riddles are filled with holes, are without answers; we will read them at our peril if we seek conclusions.)

The first is God's: Can you give me something that does not already belong to me?

The second is the woman's: "Is there any known human culture in which still-fertile women are allowed to practice blood-sacrifice?"[29]

The third is the hero's: Who, me?

The fourth is the child's: Shall you take my laughter?

The fifth is the animal's: Can you be in the mouth (myth)?[30]

The sixth is the mother's: I am still here, you still suck at my breasts, how can you claim I am sacrificed or that the milk does not flow bountifully?[31]

The seventh is another Divine Player's riddle: Does not sacrifice place humanity over against the gods, preempting a god's rights as well as its own blood thirst?

The eighth is the story's: Does the sacrifice construct a crisis that keeps us from facing another risk?

The ninth is the maiden's: What am I surrogate for: for giving up the greatest pleasure — for sacrificing the possibility of the great marriage/love Campbell extols — or of other stories that do not fit his scheme?

The tenth is the garrulous carrot's: Is not the Christ sacrifice, more parallel to my own vegetable cycle, a mockery of human frailty; or is it a mockery of the sacrality of everyday life, which is in no need of redemption?

The eleventh is the scapegoat's: If the difference between me and him (the third riddler) is consciousness, whose mind has been sacrificed to the paradigm? Can violence banish violence?

The twelfth is Brahman's, the silent: "I am food." Is this the way from death to sex?

The thirteenth (the numeral often sacrificed in mythic systems) is the dream's: Did I not, back at the beginning of our brains, offer a theater of possibilities, including this theater of cursing and spilling? Is sacrifice and the hero the only play I gave you?

If the paradigmatic myth is the mouth, the liar in the Garden, the sacrificial hero has but one small role to play, and gives up exclusivism.

The serpent insists upon its riddle, too: To whose version did I sacrifice our Good Times; and knowing the cycle by which I shed my skin, what, do you think, is the cycle by which I shed my legs, my wings, my breasts?

Finally, stories are not only reflective but also formative. We create the universe as we go along, evolving, by flesh and by story. Campbell takes up the ways in which we construct our lives by our story participation, but he does stop short of saying that it is all story — he seems to lose his nerve and peek behind the curtains for the charlatan, the one who will explain it all. In Lu Chi's *Wen Fu*, the Chinese classic, the mystery of writing is revealed to be the curtains themselves: a yard of silk, the paper and pens, the lies:

> The pleasure a writer knows is the pleasure all sages enjoy.
>
> Out of non-being, being is born; out of silence, the writer produces a song.
>
> **In a single yard of silk, infinite space is found;**
>
> Language is a deluge from one small corner of the heart.
>
> The net of images is cast wider and wider; thought searches more and more deeply.
>
> The writer spreads the fragrance of new flowers, an abundance of sprouting buds.
>
> Laughing winds lift up the metaphor; clouds rise from a forest of writing brushes.[32]

Campbell's often-cited four functions of myth leave out a fifth for us to discover in the body of his work: the aesthetic. The four functions — the cosmological, the natural, the social, the psychological — show his fascination with the East but betray his Western taxonomy. The fifth category, the unnamed, but always present, releases us from that separating self, which imagines itself apart from nature or society or the universe (or that they need our blood to abide).

In Kyoto, walking with my friends from an impressive temple through the cicada-orchestrated gardens, I suddenly saw in the trees a monk and a gardener, bending together, consulting over the green. And, I felt not like a tourist seeing Oriental gardens, a delicate, landscaped forest, and I felt not like a Buddhist, nor like a Christian, but I felt like another transformation of the one who makes an error. I saw both the teacher and the gardener. I saw the sensibility of Japanese Buddhism through the Christian tradition. I looked up, and saw: both the monk and the gardener. No confusion. A parable of simplicity. No supernaturalism. I heard the chorus of cicadas, present here as they had been present in Socrates' outing beyond the city walls. He had reluctantly gone out to the "garden" or countryside only for the sake of conversation, for entertainment, and heard the cicadas, who had once been men, he reminded Phaedrus, transformed to insects and singers, by beauty — by the Muses.[33]

I, then, as a cranky tourist, wanted my parable photographed; and my friend hopped after them asking permission for me to take their pictures. They, of course, didn't cooperate for the kind of photo-graph I had wanted, the rabbi and the gardener in the Garden; instead they graciously, formally and formidably, posed standing still and straight beside each other on the path, each in the costume of his occupation, each with the dignified composed face, looking toward the woman who wanted their picture. I wanted to explain to them, don't you see, it's an embroidery on John 20, it's a parable on the resurrection, it's a naturalizing, a normalizing of the miracle. As Campbell says, "Eden is."[34] But neither did my English-speaking friends understand me.

I tried to explain, unless the Garden is experienced, body is certainly in vain, and the resurrection is grotesque and the sacrifice is redundant. But in that frivolous East/West fantasy, the teacher and the gardener were both real, no mistake, and both leaned tenderly over a plant with complete attention to the plant. If Mary had seen Jesus pruning leaves, think how the gospel might have changed; though she did in Kyoto, and let me see, too. It's a little reminiscent of the Zen story of the man, chased by a tiger, who leaps over a cliff and clings by a single vine, which, he sees, is gnawed by mice; and below him, he sees, mad elephants await his fall. Then he notices one more thing: a ripe strawberry growing in a cleft of the rock. With one hand holding the vine, he reaches with the other, plucks the berry, pops it in his mouth and says, "How delicious." When the Jainists told it, the story showed how foolishly distracted the man was; the Zen turn on the story makes the moment poetry, makes us all edible. What if Jesus, with that body in abeyance, had plucked something in the garden and eaten? Offered to Mary a fruit? If the offering was not a sacrifice, body without violence, but a gift of abundance, can there be a sacrifice in Paradise? ("Eden is," says Campbell.) Another riddle, Campbell's riddle as well as the serpent's: Does Jesus have a Buddha nature? Campbell does a disservice when he conflates systems, but he sets us dreaming when he demonstrates how one story critiques, as well as engenders, another. Do not hold me; eat me. Jesus is not the only story in the only Garden. Mary is not a gardener, nor does she work in the kitchen; she has chosen the better part: mistaken identities. Story telling.

What is the forked-tongued, story-telling serpent asking of us? To turn away from what we already know — that if we already know the structure, meaning, harmony, point of the story, it is no longer a story — he's telling us another. And the serpentine curse is that the tale is all 'sinuation.

APPENDIX

Joseph Campbell and the History of Religions— Two Reviews

11

The Dreams of Professor Campbell: Joseph Campbell's *The Mythic Image*

Charles H. Long

> Every one of us is like a man who sees things in a dream and thinks that he knows them perfectly and then wakes up to find that he knows nothing.
>
> —Plato, *Statesman*

1. Introduction

Not since the publication of Erwin R. Goodenough's *Jewish Symbols in the Greco-Roman Period*, between the years 1953 and 1968, or perhaps Heinrich Zimmer's *The Art of Indian Asia* in 1955 (²1960), has the Bollingen Foundation presented us with such a prodigious text. It must for Professor Campbell surely represent a labor of love. One feels when going through the volume that Bollingen acceded to Campbell's every wish in the production of this volume, for literally everything — choice of paper, typestyle, format, photographs, and so forth — has been carefully chosen; each page is marked by the precise sense of the author. No compromises seem to have been made, and thus the volume represents in every detail the intent of the author. It is an unstinting, handsome, lavishly illustrated text. Such meticulousness is obviously a sign of the regard which the publisher holds for the author, but in this case the attentiveness and

Reprinted from *Religious Studies Review* 6 (October 1980) 261–71, by permission of the Council of Societies for the Study of Religion.

pains for detail are directly related to the basic orientation of the work; the objective of the book could not have been accomplished in any lesser edition.

Campbell suggests two approaches to his work. We might, first of all, deal with the volume as a pictorial essay since "Pictures invite the eye not to rush along, but to rest a while and dwell with them in enjoyment of their revelation. In the fashioning of this book, therefore, my thought has been to let the spirit of the pictures rule, and to arrange it so that the reader might enter into the pages at any turn he liked" (xi).

If we take this approach and browse through the book, we begin with a beautiful reproduction of Michelangelo's *The Creation of Eve*, find ourselves enticed into the dreamlike moods of William Blake and Gauguin, are confronted suddenly with the monumental architecture of the Ancient Near East and Meso-America, are forced to ponder mathematically arranged astronomical and chronological charts, experience the wild and erotic images of Tantric Buddhism, and then are lulled again into the archaic and ephemeral beauty of paleolithic South African rock paintings. Thereafter we are taken up by voluptuous Venuses, Yakas, sleeping Buddhas, crucified deities, gruesome sacrifices, winged genii, and so forth. From this first approach we are indeed made to experience the text as a dream, for in this sense there seems to be no necessary connection among the images that appear to us, at least no necessary connection in the historical sense, neither in the methodological nor ideological senses of the disciplines of the human sciences. In this sense the images are discrete — residues, survivals, leftovers from other times and places; and they float before us in a panoramic vision which flows from and back into another time and place.

Now, while we are invited to enjoy the book in this manner, Campbell has not left the issue of order simply to our devices, for he offers us a second approach, contradictory and complementary to the first one.

The principle of this second approach is stated in the first section of the text and can be discerned from meditation upon the Table of Contents. It is his argument "that through dreams a door is opened to mythology, since myths are of the nature of dream, and that, as dreams arise from an inward world unknown to waking consciousness, so do myths: so indeed, does life" (xi). The Table of Contents may be seen as a method for the elucidation of this thesis. It begins with a first chapter entitled "The World as Dream," followed by chapters on "The Idea of Cosmic Order" (II), "The Lotus and the Rose" (III), "Transformations of the Inner Light" (IV), "The Sacrifice" (V), and, finally, "The Waking" (VI). If we continue our meditation with a perusal of the quotations at the beginning of the text, we move to another stage of our initiation into the method of this book. These quotations are as follows:

> We are such stuff
> as dreams are made of, and our little life
> Is rounded with a sleep.
> —Shakespeare, *The Tempest*

> There is a dream dreaming us.
> —A Kalahari Bushman

> The Chinese sage Chuang-tzu dreamt he was a butterfly and on waking wondered whether he then had been a man dreaming, or might not now be a butterfly dreaming it was a man.

> That we come to this earth to live is untrue: We come but to sleep, to dream.
> —Aztec poem, Anonymous

> La Vida es Sueño: "Life is a Dream"
> —Title of a play by Calderón

And so it is dream and myth that we confront in this text. It is no surprise that we should meet this problem in this latest work of Professor Campbell. From his early work, *A Skeleton Key to Finnegans Wake*, through his four volumes on the Masks of God, to this text, the relationship of the dream to myth has been his central concern. In many circles he has been called a Jungian, but it is my feeling that his Jungianism is secondary to the central problem of dream and myth, and that he has used Jung as a guide, a helper, in the endeavor to unravel this problem that haunts him. Both this problem and Campbell's interpretive orientation have a venerable tradition.

Dreams and oneiric modalities are part and parcel of almost all religious traditions. In the Western tradition of interpretation we may note the use of the dream in Plato, Augustine, and Vico, to mention only a significant few from the past.

If we look at *The Mythic Image* within the context of the Campbell *oeuvre*, it appears as if it should have been the first of his published works, and that his works beginning with *The Hero with a Thousand Faces* and the Masks of God should find their places as extensive commentaries and footnotes to *The Mythic Image*.

The key to this interpretive relationship is found in *Creative Mythology*, the fourth volume of the Masks of God, where he states that,

> In the context of a traditional mythology, the symbols are presented in socially maintained rites, through which the individual is required to experience, or will pretend to have experienced, certain insights, sentiments, and commitments. In what I am calling "creative" mythology, on the other hand, this order is reversed: the individual has had an experience of his own — of order, horror, beauty, or even exhilaration — which he seeks to communicate through signs; and if his realization has been of a certain depth and import, his communication will have the value and force of living myth — for those, that is to say, who receive and respond to it of themselves, with recognition, uncoerced.... The first function of a mythology is to reconcile waking consciousness to the *mysterium tremendum et fascinans* of this universe *as it is:* the second being to render an interpretive total image of the same, as known to contemporary consciousness.... It is the revelation of waking consciousness to the power of its own sustaining source (4).

Again, on pages 671–72 of this same work, we read:

> In art, in myth, in rites, we enter the sphere of dream awake. And as the imagery of dream will be on one level local, personal, and historic, but at bottom rooted in the instincts, so also myth is delivered to the sphere of bliss of the deep conscious, where it touches, wakes, and summons energies; so that symbols operating on that level are energy-releasing and -channeling stimuli. That is their function — their "meaning" — on the level of Deep Sleep: while on the level of Waking Consciousness the same symbols are inspirational, informative, initiatory, rendering a sense of illumination with respect to the instincts touched, i.e., the order subliminal of nature — inward and outward nature of which the instincts touched are the life.

Campbell's previous works have attempted to show how myths arise at specific times and places during the history of humankind. In their localized appearances, myths become the archetypes for order, meaning, and behavior, for idiosyncratic local, ethnic, or nationalistic groups. In this sense the mythologies and myths are "charters for conduct," to use Malinowski's phrase; and in Campbell's words, they are "the public dreams that move and shape societies; and conversely, one's own dreams are the little myths of the private gods, antigods and guardian powers that are moving and shaping oneself..." (Campbell, 1974, 362). But even in their localized settings, myths express an intentionality that goes beyond their limited context and a meaning that pushes toward universality. Myths, however, arise from the dream so that the primordial order of all myths is that of sleep and the activity of sleep, the dream.

It is Campbell's attempt to write a book within the structure of sleep and dream that renders the text essentially esoteric and exotic. But such esotericism and exoticism come about, not because sleep and dream are distant and foreign, but because of the common and surdic nature of dream itself! The dream, like language and sexuality, is commonplace and complex, simple and totalizing; but unlike sexuality or language, it occurs as a passive modality, seemingly unrelated to or defying in its passivity, the volitional consciousness. In spite of its occurrence during the passive mode of sleep, the dream, like all languages of the body, is "incomparably more ambiguous and more overdetermined than the most overdetermined uses of ordinary language." Pierre Bourdieu, to whom we owe the above insight, continues this discussion of the problematic character of "languages of the body" by saying: "This is why ritual roots are always broader and vaguer than linguistic roots, and why the gymnastics of rituals, *like dreams*, always seem richer than the verbal translations, at once unilateral and arbitrary, that may be given of it" (Bourdieu, 1977, 120; italics added). With this introduction let us continue to the substance of the text.

2. The World Dream

The first chapter of the text is entitled "The World as Dream." If the world is a dream, then who is the sleeper, and who the dreamer? In one sense, Campbell suggests that each culture, each people, each person is a dreamer; but if the world is a dream, our problem is a bit more complex. It is of the very nature of the dream phenomenon that only the awakened one is able to relate the dream; and thus the dreamer, the sleeper, and the interpreter often constitute a continuity, if not an identity.

The first section of this first chapter is entitled "Sleep," and it is sleep as the context for the dream that undergirds the entire text; for the myths and mythological motifs are presented in every other chapter and section as dream phenomena. Sleep thus envelops the text.

The images of sleep presented are those of the ultimate dreamer, Vishnu, floating on the Cosmic Milky Ocean, couched upon the coils of the abyssal serpent, Ananta, the meaning of whose name is "Unending" (7). But it seems that even within the dream a reflexive and reflective structure is present — a nonwaking, nonrational order of reflection and reflexivity. The dream is not therefore a chaos; it manifests its own logic.

> For in dreams things are not as single, simple, and separate as they seem, the logic of Aristotle fails, and what is *not*-A may indeed be A (8).

> We opened this work with a motto from the lips of a Kalahari Bushman: *There is a dream dreaming us;* and we are closing under the spell of a suggestion from the pen of Schopenhauer, of this whole universe of milky ways and ourselves within it as *a vast dream, dreamed by a single being, in such a way that all dream characters dream too* (497).

If there is an oneiric logic, it is of the most complex kind, and it is only in the light of such a logic that we may hope to understand the character of this text. Instead of attempting simply to reduce such a logic (if there be such) to written languages, we are also invited to allow images to appear before us. There is yet another pattern present — a pattern that possesses a beginning, a middle, and an end. The beginning is the first flow of symbols of life and birth. But within the death-like nature of sleep, life as expression appears with the symbolic orders of death. In a sense, the first life is already a resurrection from the dead; this initial form of life is presented as the duality of life-death — the totality of the image of life and/or of death. The mythology and iconography of Isis and Osiris form the first structure of the images of the beginnings, and this leads us on to the symbols and myths of the Wonder Child. But if there is the symbol of the child as new life and Savior, there is simultaneously the symbol of the Mother. In the forms of Mother and Mighty Goddess a cosmogonic principle of veiling, projecting, and revealing power is manifested. Following the etymological roots of Māyā, from the Sanskrit root *mā* — to measure, to create, construct, exhibit or display — the feminine is shown as the creator-revealer and limitation of life. The pictures accompanying this description are Christ in the

Virgin's womb, the *Vierge Ouvrante*, a boxlike sculpture which, when closed, shows the Virgin with child and, when opened, reveals Christ upon the cross against the background of a Father God holding up the cross.

The first emergence or episode of the world-dream in the images of death and resurrection, the wonder child, and the mighty goddess are still closely related to the modality of the passivity of sleep-death. The images of the world-dream, while creative and totalizing, are still closely bound to the instinctual rhythms of life.

The next section or episode of the world-dream is that of the "Idea of a Cosmic Order." Campbell introduces this section with a discussion of methodological issues. Beginning with a discourse on the similarity of the emblematic numbers designating eons of years in India, the Icelandic *Poetic Edda*, and in Berossos, he observes that such similarities are not due to the sheer independence and contingency of mind or culture. He proposes at this point a theory of cultural diffusion which is a variation of his theory of the mythogenic zones put forth in *Primitive Mythology*, the first volume of the Masks of God. This theory states that at certain times, in particular areas of the world, radical transformations of life have occurred, the effects of which have been diffused to the quarters of the earth.

The second methodological issue has to do with the distinction between literate and nonliterate cultures. Campbell makes clear that as a first principle of method one must make a distinction

> between literate and nonliterate orders; and further — in relation to the latter — to recognize a distinction between truly primitive traditions, such as those of the bushmen of the Kalahari desert, and those, like the Polynesian, that are, at least in part, regressed, i.e., provincial forms, survivals and local transformations of traditions originally stemming wholly or in part from one or another of the major matrices of literate civilization (74).

He continues,

> The present work is devoted chiefly to *literate traditions: firstly, because for these we possess dependable written interpretations from the hands of those who developed and employed them*; secondly, because it is necessary to become acquainted with the main figures, themes, and motifs of the literate traditions before attempting to distinguish between primitive and regressed fea-

tures in the nonliterate. But finally and principally, because it has actually been from the one great, variously inflected and developed literate world-heritage that *all* of the philosophies, theologies, mysticisms, and sciences now in conflict in our lives derive (74–75; italics in first sentence added).

These methodological principles may be sound and will not be under criticism at this point, though we shall take them up at a later point. What is striking is the appearance of this discussion at this juncture in *The Mythic Image*. First of all, the title of this chapter is not "The Cosmic Order," but "The *Idea* of a Cosmic Order." How does an idea appear within the structure of the world-dream? A clue may be found in the distinction made between the literate and the nonliterate. Campbell makes the argument from continuity the basic reason for his distinction. Our culture and our dilemmas are derivative from the diffused mythological and cosmological traditions of the citied traditions of the world. He does not, however, tell us anything about the relationship between literacy and religious symbols and images. What effect does writing, which is usually part of the complexity of urban centers, with division of labor, hierarchial social structures, imperialistic possibilities, and so forth, have on dreams? Not only has this issue not been discussed by Campbell, but he is equally silent regarding that very fundamental change in human culture from hunting-gatherers to citied traditions which is the context for literacy. In any treatise on the world-order as the world-dream, such an issue is of paramount importance. What theory of dream or of the order of psychic structure explains this radical shift?

After having made so much of the distinction between literate and nonliterate, in several instances Campbell nonetheless bases his case on examples from nonliterate traditions. On page 184 there is a photograph of Northern Aranda Australian Aborigines sitting before a sacred ground-painting, which is the center and mythological representation of the beginnings. Again on pages 424–25 we are given pictures of a rain sacrifice and a ritual murder scene from rock paintings from South Rhodesia and Basutoland in South Africa. It is worthy of remark that in announcing the exclusion of primitives and nonliterates from his text, he excluded the one group who spoke of the world-process as a dreaming. I am, of course, referring to the Australian aborigines whose primordial time is called *Alcheringa*, the dreaming.

The next two chapters, "The Lotus and the Rose" and "The Transformation of the Inner Light," are designed to deal with the cumulative episodes of the world-dream, the contradictions of the beginnings, the objective centering in the cosmologies of the literate traditions, and the tensions among these episodes. In "The Lotus and the Rose" the resolution and/or the raising of the contradictions to a higher level are discussed under the aegis of feminine symbolism. Hence we meet with the feminine not only in the form of creatrix and mother but as transformer and integrator. She is *shakti*, the Sanskrit term whose meaning covers power, capacity, energy, faculty, or capability. In Campbell's usage, the term denotes the energy or active power of a male divinity as embodied in his spouse.

> Carried further still: the word connotes female spiritual power in general, as manifest, for instance, in the radiance of beauty, or on the elemental level in the sheer power of the female sex to work effects on the male. It is operative in the power of the womb to transform seed into fruit, to enclose, protect and give birth. Analogously, on the psychological plane, it is the power of a woman to bring a man to his senses, to let him see himself as in a mirror, to lure him to his realization — or destruction: for it is the power also to bewilder and destroy (217).

This image may be seen in the Madonna, Queen Dedes of Java, Shri-Lakshimi, Tara, and in Dante's Beatrice. Power of this kind is supported symbolically by vegetative symbolism and more precisely by the rose and the lotus. It is equally manifested in water symbols and in the alchemical germ that is able to transmute the common into the most valuable.

If the lotus and the rose are symbols of the ultimacy of feminine principles, then the succeeding chapter, "Transformations of the Inner Light," describes the forms of transformation as masculine modes. In this movement the symbols of the former chapter are internalized, abstracted, and overcome through ascetic disciplines. A great deal is made of yogic techniques and the Tantric lore of the doctrine of the seven circles or lotuses which must be passed through or overcome if one is to achieve freedom. Whereas in the previous chapter the lotus is externalized and made the support or basis for the exfoliation of a cosmos, in this chapter the lotus is internalized and constitutes the support for the ladder of chakras through which the images of cosmic creativity are surpassed.

In the next to the last chapter, Campbell raises the issue of annihilation within the context of a discussion devoted to sacrifice. While accepting Frazer's theory of sacrifice as magic — religious and moral — he adds to these intentions a third, the mystical or the mystic, who, "thinking neither of God nor of man as an ultimate term but simply in awe of the marvel of being and absorbed in the difficult task of self-transformation, striv[es] to extend the range of his own realization of the Body of Truth" (431). From this point of view one is able to observe similar nuances in the death of Christ and in the Bodhisattva doctrine of Buddhism, but of special interest in this chapter is his discussion of the pig and the boar as symbols of deity and the numerous responses of awe and fascination which surround these animals in various cultures and religious contexts.

3. The Waking: The Boar, the Blacksmith, and the Buddha

The last chapter of the text is given over to a description of the symbolisms of the Last Supper of Jesus Christ and the Parinirvana of the Buddha; the symbolism of the Parinirvana is dominant. A parallel is made between Chunda and Judas, Ananda and Peter, and Jesus and the Buddha, who are the willing victims of the sacrifice. A text from the *Mahapari-nibbanasutta* of the early Pali scriptures is quoted *in extenso*.

The Buddha in the company of his faithful disciple Ananda proceeded from Bhogama to Pava where he was invited to share the hospitality of one Chunda, a worker in metals. After listening to the Buddha's discourse, Chunda prepares a meal of rice, cakes, and boar's meat. The Buddha instructs Chunda to serve the rice and cakes to the other listeners and reserves the boar's meat for himself. After eating his fill, the Buddha tells Chunda to bury the remainder of the meat in a hole; for he knows of no one in Mara's or Brahma's heaven, nor of gods nor men, who is capable of eating and assimilating the boar's flesh. After eating the flesh, the Buddha is taken ill and dies. While in his death throes, the Tathagata says,

> The offering of food after which, when a Tathagata has eaten, he attains to supreme and perfect insight; and the offering of food after which, when a Tathagata has eaten, he passes away by that utter passing away in which nothing whatever remains behind: these two offerings of food are of equal fruit and of equal profit, and of much greater fruit and much greater profit than any other (488).

We learn from the *Parinibbana-sutta* that the Buddha comes to his death in a very ordinary manner; he dies from eating swine served to him by a blacksmith (Chunda). The blacksmith is a religious symbol of transmutation through his technique of making hard metal from the soil of the earth; the blacksmith symbolizes the transcendence of the human condition. Swine, the flesh eaten by the Buddha, is a symbol of the divine itself. In the previous chapter, Campbell has this to say regarding pig sacrifice in Malekula:

> Whereas, on the other hand, the sacrifice of such a pig by a master eligible to assimilate its spiritual charge confers a degree of authority beyond the touch of any threat whatsoever, either of life or of death. He becomes one who has incorporated in his person not only the powers of all pairs of opposites — male and female, life and death, being and non-being, and the rest — but also whatever powers beyond such polarizations a man who had become verily a superman might be imagined to subsume (460).

The Buddha is the Awakened and Enlightened One, for he transcends all the opposites of the dream and goes beyond them. He shook ten thousand gods in ten thousand worlds by eating the flesh of divine ignorance. He destroys the dream and takes one to the other shore by showing that the other shore never existed. *The Mythic Image* began with the ultimate symbol of sleep, Vishnu, reclining, and in his sleep dreaming the universal in all of its forms, contrasts, and integrations. It ends with the reclining figure of the Buddha in his *parinirvana*, who has exhausted the dream in his waking moment of Enlightenment. Within this mythological structure, the boar is a symbol of the desires of the flesh that created the limited, illusory, and false consciousness expressed in the specific myth-dreams of the historical cultural mythologies. The eating of the flesh of the boar at once identifies the Buddha with the valences of the particular myth, while, at the same time, it transmutes the Buddha beyond the limitations and barriers of the specificities and false consciousness of particular myths.

The Buddha is thus the paradigm of the Savior Figure. Other archetypal paradigms of the symbol are Jesus as the Christ, who is obedient, even to the death of the cross, or Vishnu as the Cosmic Boar. The Savior or the Enlightened One (The Buddha) is that symbol in the world-dream that is able to partake of all the limited modes of human consciousness, but in partaking of these modes (a meal that leads to existential death and annihilation) the Savior Figure transcends the existentiality and the particularity of both the personal and cultural ego.

The Savior Figure manifests, for Campbell, the true and absolute consciousness, beyond the contradictions of male/female, nature/culture, existential/ontological. This consciousness, following the rhetorical style of the text, is the true consciousness that has dreamt the dream of life and has awakened from the dream: "That is to say, not only is the mighty Savior one with the cosmic dreamer of the dream into which he has entered as an incarnation, but *all* beings, all *things*, are also of the substance of that dream, at one with it in essential peace" (497).

Campbell ends with a paraphrase of Schopenhauer: Everything, the entire universe and ourselves within it is *"a vast dream, dreamed by a single being, in such a way that all the dream characters dream too"* (497). Thus we are enveloped within a dreaming dream. We are, in our personal and cultural beings, a dreaming, but not only this; our own personal and cultural dreams are at the same time dreams being dreamt by the world-dreamer. There is a dream dreaming us!

4. Oneiric Structures: Myths, Dreams, and Narratives

What now are we to make of this world-dream and its awakening in the revelation of the symbolism of the Buddha? Many will take exception to Campbell's choice of iconography, photographs, and paintings and to his general interpretation of these materials as part of his theory. Feminists and certain minorities could have a veritable heyday at this level of criticism. I will not engage in this kind of critique, for I have been at pains to render in skeletal form the basic intent of the work. My criticism will be addressed to the general theoretical and methodological issues generated by the problem of the authorship of the text, attending to detail as necessary to support this criticism.

Earlier in this essay I noted that there is an "oneiric logic" that holds together the major theory of this text, but that this logic is complex. It is through such a logic that we may hope to understand the character of this text. Nevertheless, how does one "take hold" of the text? It is a text whose context is dream and whose loci are myths. From the point of view of dream interpretation we are warned that the oneiric does not follow the normal expectations of logic; the myths, which give expression to the modality of the dream, have been interpreted in a precise manner, and Campbell has made rather explicit decisions, not only about the specific genre of myths, but more precisely about where these myths appear within the unfolding of the world-dream. We are presented with a narrative in the form and modality of the oneiricism of a world-dream. To "get at" or to "get hold" of this text we must treat it *as a narrative* that possesses, if not a logic, at least a pattern that expresses a beginning, a middle, and an end.

Since the Enlightenment in the West, several theories of myth have been put forward. There are evolutionary theories based on the correlation of the development of human consciousness with historical-cultural changes in the world. These theories may range from the *Urdummenheit* theory of Theodor Preuss, who viewed the earliest stages of human cultures as manifestations of a primordial stupidity, to Wilhelm Schmidt, who saw this early primordiality as the birth of the transcendental human consciousness that finds its symbolism in the "high god." Subsequent states of human consciousness in history reveal a degeneration of this transcendent meaning.

Other, mediating theories and positions have dealt with the appropriateness of myth as expressions of various historical stages and strata of culture. These theories extend from E. B Tylor's notion of "animism" and Lévy-Bruhl's notion of "pre-logical mentality," through Max Müller's "disease of language," to Malinowski's marriage of myth and social structure in his formulation of myth as "charters of conduct," and finally to the "concrete logic" of Lévi-Strauss.

Strangely enough, none of these positions is taken up or even alluded to by Campbell, not even the theories and interpretations of Mircea Eliade, who deciphers the meaning of myth as revelatory of an ontology — a position that at first glance might seem close to Campbell's. Why this coolness and distance from the interpreters of myth *en vogue?* In the first instance, the probable reason is that most of these interpreters locate and understand myth as a primary expression of primitive cultures — cultures which Campbell has consciously eliminated from his consideration in this study. In the case of Eliade, who incidentally emphasizes the a-historic and oneiric nature of myth, Campbell is, in the *The Mythic Image*, setting forth a different and alternate meaning of the history of the religious symbol than that put forward by Eliade in his *Patterns in Comparative Religion* and *From Primitives to Zen* or in his *History of Religious Ideas*.

Campbell in the work before us has more of a purely literary concern; he is, it seems to me, attempting to write an epic, but not an epic that is limited to local or provincial histories or cultures, but rather a world epic based upon the traditions, myths, and memories of all literate cultures. Two structures are employed to hold together this world epic, one empirical, the other speculative and rather vague. On the one hand, he makes use of the empiricity of cultures with written languages, and this is allied, on the other hand, with the oneiric order of the dream. So we have, if you will, an oneiric epic.

Epics, generally, consist of a series of myths and legends connected through the webs and rhetoric of kinship and are composed in a metric style appropriate for the oral recitation of the culture. Though the epic may be spoken through the mouth of a story-teller, the true epic is of anonymous authorship, and its origins are coincidental with an exemplary expression of the cultural language itself. Epic as a genre arises in literate societies.

It is obvious that one person, Joseph Campbell, is the author of this text, but the literary style evoked by its language, photographs, colors of pages, and so forth — the entire kaleidoscopic and panoramic presentation — seems contrived to convey the sense of the anonymity of authorship and the passivity and sheer "givenness" of the images and meanings. We are invited to experience the world, "worlding" or doing whatever the world does in its aseity. The dream and the mythological languages of the cultures discussed are analogies and substitutes for the family antagonisms and kinship structures that undergird the true cultural epic.

The mythical events of the text, even when they are expressions of the active, volitional, and passionate, are in point of fact really expressions of an anonymous, autonomous, passive expression of the world showing itself under the aspect of the dream. The paradigm for this special vision can be seen in the great epic, the Mahabharata, or in any of the various reconstructions of the Indo-European epics produced by Georges Dumézil.

Closer to home, however, the use of the dream as the basis for the epic structure can be noted in the medieval writer Macrobius, who classified and analyzed the literary typology of dreams as literary devices (see Macrobius, *Commentarii in Somnium Scipionis*).

Macrobius classifies dreams into five types: (1) *insomnium* (the nightmare); (2) *visum* (the apparition); (3) *visio* (the prophetic vision); (4) *oraculum* (oracular dream); and (5) *somnium* (the enigmatic dream). The first two types, according to Macrobius, are of little worth since they have little prophetic significance. The third type, *visio*, is a dream in which future events are so clearly seen that little or no interpretation is necessary. The *oraculum* is a dream in which a parent, revered person, divine/demonic being, or the voice of any one of these personages reveals something to the dreamer and suggests what action is to be taken or to be avoided.

The enigmatic dream of *somnium* provides the greatest possibilities for literary use, for it is a symbolic dream in which what is revealed to the dreamer is ambiguous and requires an interpretation. The *somnium* can be further divided into five subcategories: (1) the personal, in which all actions and experiences are those of the dreamer; (2) the alien, a dream in which someone else is the locus of action; (3) the social, which involves the dreamer and others; (4) the public dream, which reveals public misfortune or benefit; and (5) the universal, in which some change takes place in the heavenly bodies or regions of the earth.

A case could be made that Campbell was consciously aware of Macrobius or that Macrobius' theories are a part of Campbell's heritage as far as the literary use of dreams is concerned. Steven Fischer (1978) has clearly shown the literary use of the dream in the *Song of Roland* and *Tristan and Isolde*. In the case of these legendary epics, the story falls upon the ears of those who have been prepared to respond to the epic by the folkloric sediments of the story. While there were exemplary story-tellers and bards, even in their presentations they remained anonymous since the archetypal motifs of the story formed not only the structure of personal consciousness, but were actually archetypal for the common cultural consciousness. As I have said earlier, Professor Campbell seems methodologically anonymous throughout this text. Could it be that one of the difficulties in "getting hold" of this text stems from the fact that as a dream-epic told as such, the posture of anonymity does not fall within a common public or cultural language? Our cultural language is fragmented in such a way that there are no common folkloric sediments to Campbell's story. For, while the dream has always been a private matter, its discussion, language, and rhetorical valence was, during the medieval period, a matter of the public cultural arena.

To turn to another issue that is essential in the use of dream as a literary device in the modern period — the introduction of the dream as a phenomenon of depth psychology — raises several imponderables. For of all, the introduction of the dream as a serious motif must immediately deal with the demythologizing and remythologizing of this phenomenon within depth psychology. Second, the work of depth psychology must also be seen within the context of the Enlightenment and post-Enlightenment subjective epistemologies; the dream was "rediscovered" in our time as the symptom of a private pathology; the prophetic and public nature of the dream receded and could only be recovered as a primordial structure dependent on the science of biology or the general laws of nature.

In other words, though the literary devices of dream interpretation might seem apt, the phenomenon of the dream itself has changed, and different problems are presented by this change. The loss of correlation between a public language and a language of dream interpretation common to the public situates the dream and its interpretation within an arena of privacy. This private locus cannot easily be transferred to a public, much less a global, arena. Campbell plays fast and loose with us when he interprets particular and specific cultural myths as if they were "universally-private," that is to say, as if the archetypes revealed in these myths are at once local and provincial *and* expressions of universal archetypes. In point of fact the myths, or myth-dreams, that he makes use of are myths and dreams revealed and narrated as a public language within their original cultures. It is precisely for this reason that in traditional cultures dreams could become the basis for epic narratives and why the interpretation of dreams in traditional societies is so conservative. Roger Callois (1966, 25) remarks that "the human mind seems strangely conservative on these topics. I suppose it is so of necessity, for human nature in its essential difficulties allows for very little modification.... The interpreter must therefore reduce their [the dreams'] infinite multitude to the small number of events that are certain to occur to everyone in the course of his brief life."

The myth-dreams do not seem to be subjected to any systematic method and thus are reported by Campbell as if they were original dream experiences. None of the critical or hermeneutical strategies of the Enlightenment or post-Enlightenment are employed, but neither the a-causal logic of the dream nor its "literal narration" can substitute for a post-Enlightenment theory and method of dream and/or myth interpretation.

5. The Enlightened One and the Post-Enlightenment World: The Buddha and the Professor

This is the fundamental issue of *The Mythic Image*. What is the relationship between the Enlightenment and the "Enlightened One"? Does the Enlightenment have reference to the hermeneutical stance of Professor Campbell — a stance that would place him within the *Methodenstreit* of interpretation theory? Since issues related to interpretation theory do not constitute a part of this work, are we not justified in seeing some analogies between the Buddha as the "Enlightened One" and Professor Campbell as interpreter? The Buddha, in his moment of Nirvana, saw the ten thousand limited and illusory worlds of gods and humans pass before him in succession. The style of Campbell's text tends to approximate the Enlightened One's experience. However, beyond the stylistics of the text, the fundamental question of method recurs: "Who is the dreamer, and what is the dream?" Let us be absolutely clear about dreams. A statement of Samuel Weber's is quite appropriate when thinking about the nature of dreams:

> In recalling a dream, we seem to be reproducing something that has already taken place, at a particular time, usually the night before, while we are asleep. This something, however disjointed or absurd it may appear in our memory, will generally be supposed to have possessed a certain formal coherence. That is, it will be considered to have *begun* at a certain point in time, to have *unfolded*, and then to have reached an *end*, or — as is often the case — to have been interrupted; in any case, to have stopped. We thereby tend to cast ourselves, the morning after, in the role of a spectator seeking to conjure up something that was, that we then seem to watch as we would view a film, a sequence of images vis-à-vis, even if we are more or less dimly aware that we cannot simply be the spectator in such a process, but must at least double as the narrator (or, to stay within the film metaphor, as the projectionist). In any case, this vague awareness does not usually alter our sense of being somewhere quite apart and detached from the dream we seem merely to see before our mind's eye, as we remember it.... The simple model of a subject facing an object, of a mind repeating something that once was, progressively falls apart. We come to realize that we are not simply the spectator or projectionist of a dream, but the projector, the screen, the camera and film, the actors, extras, stagehands, and stage-props, in short: the entire production crew and the conditions of production (including the various forms of censorship, disseminated, *un peu partout*). What is remarkable in all this, however, is that although the dream is thus "our creation" or "product," we, as creators or as producers, are not situated outside, above, or beyond our *work*. On the contrary: we are, quite literally, part and parcel of a process that "we" — our conscious selves — can never entirely *comprehend;* and yet which at the same time we cannot but *apprehend*. Were we not to apprehend it, in one way or an-

other — and it is perhaps apt here to recall that one of the meanings of the word, not dormant, was to "feel the force of, be sensible of," in short: to be *grabbed* by... it could hardly be *said* to exist, or in any case to be discussed *as such* (Weber, 1978, 22–23).

This raises the problem of the meaning of language in dream interpretation. This is a problem separable from the meaning of myth, for whatever else myth may be, its arena is public. Campbell has enveloped the myth within the language of dream and thus used the oneiric to camouflage any access we might have to a critical interpretation of myth. So be it. Let us deal with the a-causal nature of the dream. Now, while the dream is private, it becomes a dream — a specific kind of discourse — only when it is told to another.

Emile Benveniste (1971, 66) has described this kind of discourse as follows:

> For if he [the analyst] needs the patient to tell him everything and even to express himself at random and aimlessly, it is not in order to recover an empirical fact, which will not have been registered at all except in the patient's memory; it is because empirical facts have no reality for the analyst, except in and through the "discourse" which gives them the authenticity of an actual experience, without regard to their historical reality and even (perhaps, especially) if the discourse evades, transposes, or invents the biography which the patient gives himself.

Benveniste concludes that the "syntax" in which these unconscious symbols are strung together does not obey any logical necessity; it recognizes only one dimension, that of succession, which, as Freud saw, also signifies causality. This "language" of overdetermination should not be confused with an organized or empirical language. "As infrastructure, it has its source in a region deeper down than that in which education instills the linguistic mechanism" (Benveniste, 74). It is finally with style rather than syntax that we are concerned. It is in the realm of the metaphor, the metonymy, and the synedoche that this discourse resides, and this is where Campbell is most problematical.

Because of the confusion of dreamer and interpreter in these tropes, the problem of double narration runs through the text. This is an old problem in dream interpretation but becomes even more crucial for Campbell. E. B. Tylor (1958, 25) alludes to this issue in Augustine:

> St. Augustine tells one of the double narratives which so well illustrate theories of this kind. The man who tells Augustine the story relates that, at home one night before going to sleep, he saw coming to him a certain philosopher, most well known to him, who then expounded to him certain Platonic passages, which when asked previously he had refused to explain. And when he (afterwards) enquired of this philosopher why he did at his house what he had refused to do when asked at his own: "I did not do it," said the philosopher, "but I dreamt I did." *And thus, says Augustine, that was exhibited to one by phantastic image while waking, which the other saw in a dream.*

The problem of double narration is present in two ways. First, what is expressed by fantastic image (the myths), while awake, is known to the other as a dream. Who is this *other* who knows in the waking state what is expressed by fantastic image in the dream? Is this *other* Professor Campbell or the world, and are the two identical? Second, the place, situation, and language of the dream must define a public arena of discourse. This is in fact the meaning of dream as an *interpretation* of the dream.

The meaning of dreams is problematical only in the waking state, but the waking state is obviously different from that of the dream. Campbell as an interpreter of the "world-dream" fails to establish a locus for his interpretation; he fails to let the reader know his methodological stance in relation to the authorship of his text. Is he a dreamer or is he an "Awakened One"? He fluctuates between the two. He wishes to give us the sense that he is an "Awakened One" who is within the dream and who is thus able to render an interpretation of dream from within the dream itself such that those of us outside of this dream will be able to understand the "dream as dream"; but then again, he is the Enlightened One who stands on the other side of the dreams and the dreamers, and is thus able to establish the *true* meaning of the dream and the dreamers. One is therefore confused about the nature of the discourse as well as the posture of the author. It does not evoke the rhetoric of cause, neither does it posses the precision of the language of decipherment, and it is not the kind of "motivational language" that issues from the patient and the therapist in psychoanalysis (cf. Benveniste, 1971, for a fuller statement on motivational language). It is the language, not of the critical professor, but of the ultimate knower, of the Enlightened Buddha.

I mentioned above Campbell's treatment of primitive or nonliterate cultures in *The Mythic Image*. In every case his treatment emphasizes the primitive/civilized distinction. The most telling mark of this distinction is that of writing. From this distinction that other distinction, nonhistorical/historical, follows. While these distinctions may be descriptively valid, the value placed upon them as a definitive taxonomy of humankind has given rise to a history of misinterpretation, exploitation, and terror.

For this distinction to appear in *The Mythic Image* is most unfortunate. Here is a work devoted to a new understanding of religion in the entire history of the world, and, furthermore, a work that makes use of the *dream* as the basis for continuity of religious meaning. Now, the dream is precisely that human phenomenon that is in fact present in all cultures at all times, and thus one would think that in this work the old primitive/civilized or literate/nonliterate dichotomy would be seriously attenuated if not destroyed. Such is not the case — the distinction is continued on the same old basis of writing and history.

Campbell renders his oneiric interpretation invalid when he makes crucial distinctions in terms of history, as he does when he sees our dilemmas as expressive of the literate heritage of the human community. Neither Freud nor Jung delimited the meaning of dream in this manner. In point of fact, all dreams in all cultures are "pre-historic" in a certain sense, and this is what accounts for their enigmatic character. Some of the fundamental theories about myths and dream have emerged from attention to and study of the so-called primitive societies.

There may be valid problems related to writing and dreaming, but they are of another kind. What, for example, is the effect of writing on society, how does this phenomenon affect not only the public nature of culture, but the deeper strata of the psyche? What is the relationship between repression and writing, power and expressiveness, sexuality and knowledge, and so forth? These are the kinds of questions that might have been explored through the oneiric analysis, but none of them is raised.

Professor Campbell has given us a large and beautiful text, but what are we to make of this "literate dream" when we awake? Are we left with a pictorial essay designed simply for our enjoyment, or has the oneiric pattern elucidated a deeper meaning? The answer to these questions should be sought in the symbol of the Buddha, who at the end of the essay is the Awakened and Enlightened One.

There are, however, two interpretations that are evoked by the Buddha, and perhaps, a third if the two interpretations are combined. Upon being confronted by his disciples asking his responses to the four metaphysical positions set forth in the *avyakṛta* — (1) whether the world is eternal or not, or both, or neither; (2) whether the world is finite (in space), or infinite, or both, or neither; (3) whether the Tathagata exists after death, or does not, or both, or neither; (4) whether the soul is identical with the body or different from it — the Buddha's answer was silence — a silence which is symbolic of the Enlightenment and Nirvana. But though Nirvana is inexpressible, its meaning involves a grasp of the true nature of the multiple forms of existence.

Knowledge of these multiple forms of existence, analogous to the myth-dreams of Campbell's text, as ways to Nirvana or as Nirvana itself is gained through a knowledge of what the Buddhist refers to as skillful means (see Pye, 1978). It accounts for the meaning of the practical and the pragmatic, the common itself, in gesture and discourse, as equivalent to or identical with salvation. Thus Buddhist hermeneutic requires a subtlety of interpretation and a precision in the hermeneutical act. It is the lack of this aspect of the Buddha symbol that accounts for the loss of a common structure of interpretation in *The Mythic Image*. The notion of skillful means frees the Buddha from even the *desire* to save others. The soteriological structure of *The Mythic Image* has not extricated itself from this desire, noble as it may be. But if one is not freed of this desire, one is thrown into the arena of common discourse or into silence. Without skillful means, one must simply remain "the professor" or the "wise man"; or if one remains silent, it must be a silence enveloped in common language and discourse.

6.522 There are, indeed, things that cannot be put into words. They *make themselves manifest*. They are what is mystical. . . . 6.54 My propositions serve as elucidations in the following way: anyone who understands me eventually recognizes them as nonsensical, when he has used them — as steps — to climb up beyond them. (He must, so to speak, throw away the ladder after he has climbed up it.)

He must transcend the propositions, and then he will see the world right.

What we cannot speak about we must pass over into silence (Wittgenstein, 1961).

There is either the silence of the dream or that of the Enlightened One. The silence of the Enlightened One is deciphered through the "skillful means" of the Buddha, and its analogue in our time is a hermeneutic that is able to retain silence within the structure of the common and conventional. *The Mythical Image* raises many issues and implications regarding the common, but when we inquire about these matters, we are confronted, not with common discourse, but with a silence. We still must inquire whether the professor is silent because he is asleep or because he is awake.

References

Benveniste, Emile.
    1971 ET. "Remarks on the Function of Language in Freudian Theory." In his *Problems of General Linguistics*. University of Miami Press.
Bourdieu, Pierre.
    1977 ET. *Outline of a Theory of Practice*. Cambridge Studies in Social Anthropology, 16. Cambridge University Press.
Callois, Roger. 1966.
    "Logical and Philosophical Problems of the Dream." In G. E. von Grunebaum and Roger Callois, eds., *The Dream and Human Societies*. University of California Press.
Campbell, Joseph.
    1959. *Masks of God: Primitive Mythology*. Viking Press.
    ———.
    1968a. *Masks of God: Creative Mythology*. Viking Press.
    ———.
    [2]1968b. *The Hero with a Thousand Faces*. Princeton University Press.
    ———.
    1974. *The Mythic Image*. Assisted by M. J. Abadie. Bollingen Series C. Princeton University Press.
Eliade, Mircea.
    1958 ET. *Patterns in Comparative Religion*. Sheed and Ward.
    ———.
    1967. *From Primitives to Zen: A Thematic Sourcebook of the History of Religions*. Harper & Row.
    ———.
    1978 ET. *A History of Religious Ideas*. University of Chicago Press.

Fischer, Steven R.
  1978. *The Dream in the Middle High German Epic: Introduction to the Study of Dream as a Literary Device to the Younger Contemporaries of Gottfried and Wolfram.* Berne, Frankfurt am Main, and Las Vegas: Lang.
Murti, T. R. V.
  1955. *The Central Philosophy of Buddhism.* London: Allen & Unwin.
Pye, Michael.
  1978. *Skilful Means.* London: Duckworth.
Tylor, E. B.
  1958. *Religion in Primitive Culture.* Harper Torchbooks.
Weber, Samuel.
  1978. "It." *Glyph* 4.
Wittgenstein, Ludwig.
  1961. *Tractatus Logico-Philosophicus.* London: Routledge & Kegan Paul.

12

Origins of Myth-Making Man

Wendy Doniger

The occupational hazard of mythologists is a Faustian drive to round up all the myths of the world in a single place and sprinkle scientific salt on their tales. Joseph Campbell's Historical Atlas of World Mythology, the most sumptuous and ambitious of all dictionaries and encyclopedias of mythology, raises the old question — Why do people keep trying to do this? Can it be done? And has Mr. Campbell done it at last?

Most attempts to synthesize world mythology rest on the assumption that there is an overarching pattern linking all myths. But the synthesizers disagree about what the pattern is. Structuralists like Claude Lévi-Strauss say it is the universal need to impose logical order on our cognition of the world; Freudians say it is the universal experience of sexuality within the nuclear family; Jungians say it is inherited archetypes carried in the collective unconscious of the human race.

Throughout his 50-year career Mr. Campbell has been tracking the archetypes — in his collections and interpretations of world myths (particularly the four-volume Masks of God and the magnificent *Mythic Image*), as well as in his edition of the six volumes of *Papers from the Eranos Yearbooks*, lectures on scientific and philosophical studies given by scholars at conferences in Switzerland. His

Review of Historical Atlas of World Mythology, volume 1: *The Way of the Animal Powers*, reprinted from *New York Times Book Review*, December 18, 1983. Copyright © 1983 by The New York Times Company. Reprinted by permission.

spiritual companion in this quest for the archetypes has been Mircea Eliade, a historian of religions, who, like Mr. Campbell, has been strongly influenced by Jung and who has been spending the most recent years of a long career on massive overviews of mythology and religion. One might say Jung, Mr. Eliade, and Mr. Campbell constitute the mythological troika of this century.

In his past work Mr. Campbell tended to ignore geographical and chronological variations in favor of a single, often composite version of a myth. Even when he traced a single myth through several cultures, he focused on those features that were the same in all the variants and suggested that they are similar not because the myth was diffused from one culture to another, but because the myth re-emerges out of the same human springs in all the cultures.

That approach differs sharply from the methods of anthropologists who argue that a myth can be understood only in the context of other "thick description" about a culture; structuralists who demand a context containing many other, related myths from the same culture; and historians of religion who take into account the influence of other cultures and the intellectual history of the culture in which the myth occurs. These scholars emphasize what Jung called manifestations, characteristics inherited through the culture, while Mr. Campbell emphasizes the Jungian archetypes, inborn characteristics transmitted through a kind of individual psychic DNA.

Now, in the Historical Atlas of World Mythology, he sets out to combine these two approaches. If he were to succeed, the contradictions between them would be resolved. For if one could trace the historical diffusion of myths back to the dawn of human prehistory, it would not be necessary to choose between the theory that myths are transmitted from one culture to another related culture and the idea that archetypes are inherited by people in unrelated cultures. For, in fact, at the beginning there would be no unrelated cultures.

The first volume of the atlas, *The Way of the Animal Powers*, traces the archetypes from the animal mythologies of the earliest paleolithic hunters and gatherers. Three more volumes are scheduled. Volume 2, *The Way of the Seeded Earth*, will account for the plant mythologies that accompany the origins of agriculture and the dispersal of those myths through the Americas, Asia, and Africa. Volume 3, *The Way of the Celestial Lights*, will trace the archetypes through the sky mythologies of the great ancient cities with their mathematically ordered cosmos. And Volume 4, *The Way of Man*, will follow them into the breakdown and transformation of mythological structures in our post-Renaissance world.

By the time we reach the end of his atlas, Mr. Campbell intends us to see that we all tell tales about snakes and birds because we are all descended from the first man who told tales of snakes and birds (because they were important in his life); and that those tales take on different forms as snakes and birds play different roles in the lives of primitive hunters and gatherers, early farmers and city-dwellers, and finally people in the computer age. By mapping out both historical development and the geographical occurrence of myths on a grand scale, he means to show simultaneously the endurance of the great archetypes and their infinite variety in specific cultural manifestations.

No one but Joseph Campbell could conceive of such a scheme or carry it out as boldly as he does in this extraordinary book. He has woven an intricate and beautiful web in which one can trace the threads of a number of basic religious concepts through time and space. He has reconstructed the life history of the archetypes. Of course, his reconstruction is only a hypothesis and at least two major factors prevent it from becoming a proof.

First, there is not enough data available to allow him to draw unbroken lines from one culture to another back to the paleolithic age. In order to explain the meanings of the prehistoric cave drawings at Lascaux, for instance, he is forced to rely on analogies with present-day "primitive" peoples such as Australian Bushmen to supply words for the silent pictures on the cave walls. That is an old and popular method among scholars, but it remains an artistic rather than a scientific undertaking. Mr. Campbell is well aware of the problem. "Strictly thinking," he confesses, "it is improper to make comparisons of this kind, jumping centuries and culture provinces. However... where so many extraordinary features fall so neatly into place, it is difficult not to suspect a connection."

The second major problem with constructing an atlas linking specific myths to specific stages of culture is that there is no reliable way to deduce myths from physical facts or facts from myths. We cannot tell from myths about bear-hunting how people actually hunted bears, nor can we tell from ancient images of spears and traps (let alone from actual spears and traps) how people of now silent cultures imagined the supernatural powers associated with the trapping and spearing of animals. Though Mr. Campbell sometimes assumes such connections, he is critically aware of the great gaps in our knowledge, and he usually identifies his hypotheses as no more than that. And as a substitute for nonexistent data, he often draws on his staggering knowledge of world mythology to supply striking parallels from cultures in which we know both the myths and the facts. The force of the resemblance and the sheer weight of the amassed examples suggest connections that can never be proved.

To prove the hypothesis that there has been a diffusion of myths through time, one ought to cite examples only from cultures that might have had contact with one another. But Mr. Campbell draws on examples from cultures that do not have any known links. He assumes that all hunters and gatherers share the same mythological structures since they share the same life structures, so there is no need to trace the migration of a myth from one tribe to another. He also assumes that the archetypes found among hunters and gatherers survive, in essence, among planters, early city-dwellers, and modern people.

At the outset he is determined to stick to his historical paradigm. He defines four levels of myth — metaphysical, psychological, social-historical, and exploitative. He remarks that the one which is "properly of moment for a historical atlas, of course, is the social-historical, treating of the variations in time and space of the forms through which psychological and metaphysical realizations are inspired and expressed," but he adds, "the other three cannot be dismissed."

The 50 maps scattered through the book consistently anchor the discussion to specific places, ruthlessly slicing up the territory of archetypes. For instance, a map titled "The Diffusion of Bisexual Mythic Beings and Powers" and another, "The Ritualistic Permanent Sex Change," powerfully delimit the concept of the androgyne and show it is not the universal theme scholars often assume it to be. And when he compares Bushmen and the Shamans of Tierra del Fuego, Mr. Campbell points out the similarities between them in keeping with a Jungian point of view; but then he argues, as a Jungian might not, that there are important distinctions and he suggests there might have been contacts between them which no one has yet studied.

In his pursuit of history, he often seems to ignore the whole notion of archetypes. "This philosophy," he says of the American Indians' notion that all creatures, not just humans, are made in the likeness of God, "in fact, is fundamental to archaic thought generally, and must have been carried to the Americas by the earliest paleolithic immigrants. It would have been carried also by all those other Asians who subsequently crossed the Pacific to these shores, whether from neolithic Japan, Shang, or later China, North Vietnam, or Cambodia. There has been, of course, considerable argument concerning the possibility of such crossings; but the evidences now multiplying can no longer be denied."

So, even for a concept "fundamental to archaic thought generally," the ultimate implication is a historical and geographical diffusion. On every page, Mr. Campbell gives not merely generalizations but detailed, specific accounts — long colorful excerpts from diaries of early European visitors first encountering tribal peoples, first-person descriptions of how trances feel to people who have them and brilliant photographs of people dancing for joy over the body of a newly killed animal. These surely are manifestations.

But as examples mount up, the effect is not so much a continuous history as a series of stills, frozen moments lifted abruptly out of human history that do not form even the impression of an unbroken line. For there is no development, no discussion of how one variant of a myth or image adds something to the one preceding it, or how the myth changes as it moves from one land to another. Mr. Campbell is interested not in variants but essences. He cannot see the trees for the forest.

Tied by his own willing hand to the historical-geographical mast, he nevertheless succumbs over and over again to the siren song of the archetypes as he sails among the myths. But, like an unfortunate Mafia victim, he knows too much. He cannot resist pointing out parallels in all times and places. Bone figurines of waterbirds made about 16,000 B.C., which were found in Mal'ta in Siberia, share the symbolism of the wild gander in art and ritual in India around 600 B.C. A myth of the origin of evil among the Pygmies reminds him of Genesis. A series of myths from the Northern Great Plains of America "all conform to that universal pattern of the 'Adventure of the Hero' — Departure, Initiation, Return — which in 'The Hero with a Thousand Faces,' I have termed the Monomyth." These links exist not merely between unconnected hunters and gatherers, but between primitive peoples and the builders of the first great cities, the people of the "Celestial Lights" who will be covered in Volume 3. Indeed, this is the whole point of the four-volume series — "The recognized sharing of such mythic themes by the simplest known religions with some of those we think of as the most advanced would seem, at least, to say something about the constancy of mythological archetypes."

That constancy is charted in the Historical Atlas of World Mythology. The fact that it is the central axis of the book results in part from the enormity of the project and in part from Mr. Campbell's tastes. For there is no logical way to select the most significant data from such an overwhelming collection of sources. Every fact in the material and spiritual history of humanity is relevant to Mr. Campbell's enterprise, and the vastness of his undertaking leads not so much to occasional errors of fact as to less obvious distortions created by choice — which myths, or variants of them, are told and which facts are selected to explain them. What is inevitably lost in any selection is the texture of the variants, the peculiar details that give a special character to each retelling of a myth.

But what is more arbitrarily lost in Mr. Campbell's selection is ugliness — he is a Jungian without shadows. The beauty of this volume is not merely an incidental feature. It is a clue to Mr. Campbell's world view, which is an undeclared argument in his text. Everything is beautiful. The world is beautiful, God is beautiful, what is archaic is particularly beautiful, and man's myths and rituals, however barbaric or perverse they may at first seem, express the beauty of man's awe in the presence of the sacred. When Mr. Campbell documents variations in skull types with photographs, he finds ways of lighting and positioning the skulls so they are beautiful; when he compares racial characteristics, he finds individual examples of each race who are magnificent human beings. There are a few fleeting shadows — an encounter with a particularly nasty shaman, a story that has an "ugly ending," and a harrowing photograph and description of a circumcision and subincision ritual eliciting an uncharacteristic editorial comment that "the dreadful seriousness of some of the ordeals of these rites is grimly illustrated" by a photograph of the men who died in them.

But the overwhelming impression of *The Way of the Animal Powers* is majesty and ecstasy. An extraordinary photograph of two birds fighting over a serpent, surreal double-image masks, paintings by George Catlin — all are selected for their beauty and brilliantly photographed. Beauty is the ultimate archetype for Mr. Campbell. He looks for it everywhere and finds it everywhere. The book is good because Mr. Campbell has impeccable taste, but it is good art, not good science. To see the universe of myths through Mr. Campbell's eyes is to see *la vie en rose*, perhaps, but it is an exhilarating experience.

Notes

1. Dancing to the Music of the Spheres:
The Religion in Joseph Campbell's "Non-Religious"
Mythography
William G. Doty

1. Bill Moyers, in the introduction to *Power*, xix.

2. *Unconventional* religious expectations are satisfied, however, insofar as the maverick is one of the by-forms of the mythical trickster, a powerful figure in many cultures. Not only does the trickster get involved in creating and/or shaping the natural and social environments, but he does so with great humor — and certainly, as Moyers notes, Campbell's storytelling humor is very infectious (*Power*, 220). While we were editing a volume of essays on the trickster figure, my co-editor and I found that we needed to remind followers of the Western religious traditions that many *other* traditions incorporate humor as an essential element of deity.

3. *Flight*, 73. In *Power*, 141, Campbell refers to:
the reduction of mythology to theology. Mythology is very fluid. Most of the myths are self-contradictory. You may even find four or five myths in a given culture, all giving different versions of the same mystery. Then theology comes along and says it has got to be just this way. Mythology is poetry, and the poetic language is very flexible.
See also *Historical Atlas* 1/2, 194.

4. *Inner Reaches*, 58.

5. See my review of Hans Blumenberg, *Work on Myth*, in the *Journal of the American Academy of Religion* 55, 2 (1987), 374–76, and "Myth as/or Science, Logic, and Truth: Challenges to Our Orientalizing Discourses," a discussion of Blumenberg and other German mythographers, in a special issue of *Annals of Scholarship — Studies of the Humanities and Social Sciences* 5, 1 (1988), 65–81.

6. Robert A. Segal, *Joseph Campbell: An Introduction* (New York: Garland, 1987), 146–50.

7. See the sharp criticism by Tamar Frankiel, "New Age Mythology: A Jewish Response to Joseph Campbell," *Tikkun — A Bimonthly Jewish Critique of Politics, Culture, and Society* 4, 3 (1989), 23–26, 118–20.

8. In a review essay in *Parabola: Myth and the Quest for Meaning* 1, 1 (1976), 99–103, entitled "Speaking in Images," I also criticized the general tendency behind Campbell's search for a *single* mythic image. As I re-read the book today, I am even more struck by Campbell's inflexibility; see *Mythic Image*, 278–80, 313. Again in *Inner Reaches*, 63–68, he uses discussion of the chakras of yogic philosophy as a primary means of discussing the central universal religious pilgrimage.

9. *Hero*, 4.

10. *Power*, 20.

11. Ibid., 9.

12. Campbell was dismayed repeatedly by the failure of Judaism and Christianity to adjust their cosmology to the scientific world view: he argued that interpreting the mythological world picture of the first book of the Bible as some sort of literal representation of the makeup of the earth and humankind's place upon it reflected a failure of the West to mature psychologically and spiritually. He considered such literalism spiritually misguided:

If, in a period like our own, of the greatest religious fervor and quest, you would wonder why the churches are losing their congregations, one large part of the answer surely is right here. They are inviting their flocks to enter and to find peace in a browsing-ground that never was, never will be, and in any case is surely not that of any corner of the world today. Such a mythological offering is a sure pill for at least a mild schizophrenia. (*Myths to Live By*, 215)

Campbell noted that:

The difficulty faced today by Christian thinkers... follows from their doctrine of the Nazarene as the *unique* historical incarnation of God; and in Judaism, likewise, there is the no less troublesome doctrine of a universal God whose eye is on but one Chosen People of all in his created world. The fruit of such ethnocentric historicism is poor spiritual fare today; and the increasing difficulties of our clergies in attracting gourmets to their banquets should be evidence enough to make them realize that there must be something no longer palatable about the dishes they are serving. (Ibid., 254)

In another place Campbell complains that in spite of the displacement of the earth by the sun in Copernicus's *De revolutionibus* of 1543, organized religion plays out its life in a never-never land: "the heliocentric universe has never been translated into a mythology. Science and religion have therewith gone apart" (*Inner Reaches*, 43).

And he actually calls *idolatrous* the refusal of Judaism and Christianity to disengage their god-concept from its merely-localized historical manifestations: *"any god who is not transparent to transcendence is an idol, and its worship is idolatry"* (ibid., 44).

Florence Sandler and Darrell Reeck, in "The Masks of Joseph Campbell," *Religion* 11 (1981), 1–20, note that in spite of his "hostility to the Christian church," Campbell was "not opposed to the one whom the church honors"

(10); they correctly note, however, that Campbell appeals "to Romanticism and a romantic or gnostic version of Christianity" (17).

13. *Power*, 217–18. The most concentrated collection of Campbell's opinions and pronouncements on religion and spirituality will be found in *Open Life*.

14. *Creative Mythology*, 678.

15. Daniel C. Noel, "An Analytical and Technological Culture Revels in the 'Power of Myth,'" *The Chronicle of Higher Education*, February 15, 1989, B2. In a draft of this essay Noel indicated some of the context of Campbell's appeal and refered to his reception by several of us who contribute to this volume. I am grateful to Noel for many years of conversation and stimulation, and now especially for his editorial help in revising my essay.

16. The point is Parker Palmer's, in his very broad indictment of "objectivism" in our society and schooling: *To Know As We Are Known: A Spirituality of Education* (New York: Harper & Row, 1983).

17. I've been involved in several of these, especially James Wiggins, ed., *Religion as Story* (New York: Harper & Row, 1975; repr. Lanham, Md.: University Press of America, 1985), and in a forthcoming volume edited with Robert Detweiler, in which a group of biblical scholars and religion-and-literature specialists analyze in parallel a short story by Canadian novelist Margaret Atwood and a biblical passage.

18. *Power*, xvii.

19. Strangely enough to those of us familiar with Campbell's illustrated lectures or his large-format publications, the series was primarily "talking heads," and underplayed the rich visual possibilities. In *Open Life*, 61, Campbell mentions his decision to include more visual materials in *Mythic Image* because of his "realization that mythology is basically pictorial and the language elucidates the pictures or communicates a story of pictorial transformations." They are so important to the mythographic work because "the mythological image [is] an energy-evoking sign that hits you below the thinking system" (22).

20. Ibid., 5.

21. Ibid., 22.

22. *Hero*, 3.

23. I am playing upon the assumed etymology of *religion*, from *religare*, "to bind up, to form ligatures around." In this sense I am pleased with a recent definition of religion by N.J. Girardot, *Myth and Meaning in Early Taoism: The Theme of Chaos (hun-tun)*, Hermeneutics: Studies in the History of Religions (Berkeley: University of California Press, 1983), 7; religion, "as a kind of sum of all other cultural systems," Girardot writes:

> is a system of symbols that tell a story (through myths and rituals, cosmological classification and thought, sacred biographies, exemplary histories, theological and ethnical doctrines, the theory and form of meditation and mysticism, etc.) of the "fall" (or multiple "falls" and anxieties) of ordinary human existence and, at the same time, provides

a means of periodically recovering in this lifetime a condition of original wholeness, health, or holiness — terms that are all etymologically related to the primary meaning of the word "salvation."

24. For some of the most striking examples, see *Power*, 155, 190–93, 198, 118, 210. In *Open Life*, 31, Campbell refers to the *toughness* of the bliss path — even if in the video series we saw him use "follow your bliss" as the answer to too many questions! He notes:

the real power of the lefthand path of following your bliss instead of instructions. You're following the lead of your emotion and of your vitality; but the head has to be there all the time because you're on a narrow ridge [referring to a Buddhist story just recounted] and in danger of falling off. That is to say, letting too much of the torrent of energy come through will blow it.

25. *Creative Mythology*, 677. Remember the programmatic intention expressed at the beginning of *Primitive Mythology*, to develop "the first sketch of *a natural history* of the gods and heroes" (5, my emphasis). Campbell wrote in *Flight*, 51, that:

A serious science of mythology must take its subject matter with due seriousness, survey the field as a whole, and have at least some conception of the prodigious range of functions that mythology has served in the course of human history.

One is cautioned early in *The Power of Myth* to begin by reading "other people's myths, not those of your own religion, because you tend to interpret your own religion in terms of facts — but if you read the other ones, you begin to get the message" (6).

One wonders just why Campbell irritated some of the professionals so much: in one of the secondary studies not cited by Segal, Frank Whalen cites Campbell's "unconcern for empirical history," his false "stress upon data from primal, archaic, and Indian religions," "inclination to apply prior theory to comparative religions" (?), and "indifference to the conscious religious intentions of particular persons and particular traditions" (*Contemporary Approaches to the Study of Religion in Two Volumes*, vol. 1, *The Humanities* [New York: Mouton, 1982], 223). M. C. D'Arcy, S.J., criticizes his "poor philosophy and . . . careless [use of] his evidence," "God and Mythology," *Heythrop Journal* 1 (1960), 99.

26. *Historical Atlas* 2/1, 111.

27. David Miller has been exploring such themes in Christian theology, James Hillman in psychology, Christine Downing in women's imagery, to name just three authors who are importantly shaping new aspects of our contemporary mythico-imaginal work. Some of the most relevant titles from these prolific authors include: David L. Miller, *The New Polytheism: Rebirth of the Gods and Goddesses*, 2d ed. (Dallas: Spring Publications, 1981), *Christs: Meditations on Archetypal Images in Christian Theology* (New York: Seabury, 1981), *Three Faces of God: Traces of the Trinity in Literature and Life* (Philadelphia: Fortress, 1986), and *Hells and Holy Ghosts: A Theopoetics of Christian*

Belief (Nashville: Abingdon, 1989); James Hillman, *The Dream and the Underworld* (New York: Harper & Row, 1979), *Re-visioning Psychology* (New York: Harper & Row, 1975); Christine Downing, *The Goddess: Mythological Images of the Feminine* (New York: Crossroad, 1981).

The "symbolic" approach makes some people uncomfortable when it is taken to refer exclusively to older patterns of interpretation by which a foreign structure of ideas was imposed upon texts arbitrarily. This was a sort of allegory, and the best single remedy for it is still Susan Sontag's essay, "Against Interpretation," in *Against Interpretation and Other Essays* (New York: Dell, 1966). Miller, Hillman, and Downing are operating in a much more "femininist" manner, if the other gets labeled masculinist: they seek to discern symbolic structures arising out of the mythological materials themselves.

28. *Power*, 210.
29. *Flight*, 226.

2. Living by Myth: Joseph Campbell, C. G. Jung, and the Religious Life-Journey
Richard A. Underwood

1. *Power*, 148.
2. Cf. Eric Voegelin, *Israel and Revelation* (Baton Rouge: Louisiana State University Press, 1956), and Eric Voegelin, *The World of the Polis* (Baton Rouge: Louisiana State University Press, 1957). These volumes discuss the break with the myth in both Hebrew and Greek tradition.
3. C. G. Jung, *Memories, Dreams, Reflections*, ed. A. Jaffé, trans. Richard and Clara Winston (New York: Pantheon Books, 1963), 339.
4. *Hero*, vii.
5. *Skeleton Key*, 361.
6. *Hero*, 391.
7. *The Portable Jung*, edited, with an introduction, by Joseph Campbell, trans. R. F. C. Hull (New York: The Viking Press, 1971), 3–22.
8. *Ibid.*, 17–18.
9. *Flight*, 110.
10. Jung, *Memories, Dreams, Reflections*, 171.
11. C. G. Jung, *The Symbolic Life: Miscellaneous Writings*, Collected Works: vol. XVIII, trans. R. F. C. Hall (Princeton, N.J.: Princeton University Press, 1975), 270.
12. *Flight*, 144.
13. Ibid.
14. *Myths to Live By*, chap. 11, "The Moon Walk—The Outward Journey."
15. *Flight*, 188.
16. *Myths to Live By*, 143.
17. *Skeleton Key*, 360–61.
18. *Inner Reaches*, 130.

3. The Thousand and First Face
Walter B. Gulick

1. *Power*, 41.

2. See Friedrich Schleiermacher, *On Religion: Speeches to Its Cultured Despisers*, trans. John Oman (New York: Harper Torchbooks, 1958). The introduction by Rudolf Otto explains something of the impact of the work in 1799.

3. *Hero*, 30.

4. Ibid., 246.

5. *Power*, 41. In line with Campbell's interest in numerology, it is worthy of note that in addition to *The Hero with a Thousand Faces*, Campbell dealt with another work involving a "thousand" in its title; he edited the *Thousand and One Nights*. According to an early form of the story, Shehrzad told stories to the king each night for a thousand days in order to retain her life. On the thousand and first night, when she knew she was pregnant, she revealed her story-telling ruse to the king, who spared her life (see *Primitive Mythology*, 162–63). The parallel is intriguing: the thousand faces of the hero represent a thousand stories that have "saved" the lives of many. The thousand and first face has explained the actuality behind the thousand stories; in an analogous way is Campbell's work pregnant with the possibility of new life?

6. *Power*, 130.

7. Ibid., 141.

8. Whether he is seen as a creator or a restorer, Campbell can join the ranks of a virtual army of individuals who have sought in the past two centuries to strengthen the mythical resources for people in the Western world. For example, T. S. Eliot used his considerable literary talents on behalf of a rejuvenated Christianity. In *The Reenchantment of the World* (Ithaca, N.Y.: Cornell University Press, 1981), Morris Berman relies on the thought of Gregory Bateson to counter Cartesian reductionism. A very recent attempt has been authored by Loyal Rue. In *Amythia: Crisis in the Natural History of Western Culture* (Tuscaloosa: University of Alabama Press, 1989), Rue calls for artists to use the resources of sociobiology and evolutionary theory as a basis for a mythic world vision which reconciles sciences and other modernist elements with the biblical covenantal tradition.

9. *Power*, 89.

10. Indeed, Campbell tends to treat biblical resources and Jewish and Christian conceptuality with a woodenness and even inaccuracy that is not characteristic of the respect he accords most other religious traditions. (To be sure, his interpretation of myths from any tradition can be idiosyncratic.)

11. *Power*, 141.

12. Ibid., 5. Note that Campbell and I both stress experiencing meaning *in* life. I concur with his skepticism regarding the existence of a purpose (or meaning) *for* life (*Power*, 229).

13. Joseph Campbell, "Mythological Themes in Creative Literature and Art," in Joseph Campbell, ed., *Myths, Dreams, and Religion* (New York: E. P. Dutton, 1979), 144.

14. *Power*, 15.

15. Ibid., 31.

16. Ibid., 71, 126.

17. William G. Doty does a superb job of including the many dimensions of myth in one complex definition — see *Mythography: The Study of Myths and Rituals* (University, Ala.: University of Alabama Press, 1986), 11. Because the topic of myth study is so complex, confusion is best avoided if one identifies specifically the aspect of myth one is dealing with.

18. See *Power*, 31. Mythical intentionality is an important example of the narrative mode of thought, which is identified by psychologist Jerome Bruner as one of the two primary modes of human cognition. The narrative mode "deals in human or human-like intention and action and the vicissitudes and consequences that mark their course" (*Actual Minds, Possible Worlds* [Cambridge, Mass.: Harvard University Press, 1986], 13).

19. Religious intentionality may thus take on quite different forms. Sometimes it is used to interpret events as dependent upon spiritual forces. Religious discernment, in such cases, involves reading what these forces (a storm cloud, an accidental death) might be "saying" in the events one perceives. Zen Buddhist intentionality, to take a contrasting example, involves minimizing the influence of any linguistic framework of interpretation so that one might respond spontaneously to what unfolds. Thus the framework of Zen intentionality is shaped more by practice than by theory.

20. Brendan Gill takes Joseph Campbell to task for his lack of sensitivity to ethical concerns in an article that generated a stormy reaction ("The Faces of Joseph Campbell," *New York Review of Books*, September 28, 1989, 16–19). While I would admit that there is more than a hint of ethical impropriety in the way Gill savages "his friend," the deceased Joseph Campbell, I also think Gill raises some issues that must be dealt with in any final summing up of Campbell's work and impact. In essence, Gill suggests that Campbell, in refusing to take sides on moral issues or to combat evil, has created a pleasant (but reactionary) aesthetic bastion for the comfortable. The implication is that mythical intentionality is an incomplete guide to meaningful living if it is restricted to mystical, cosmological, sociological, and psychological functions while avoiding ethical concerns. I am indebted to Roy Smith for urging me to take account of this shortcoming in Campbell's views.

21. *Power*, 40.

22. While among tribes and archaic cultures myths tended to be generally accepted, in today's world of pluralism and individualism a social myth need not speak to the whole society to have the power of myth; it need only appeal to some subculture.

23. In *Rethinking Symbolism*, trans. Alice L. Morton (Cambridge: Cambridge University Press, 1975), Dan Sperber helpfully describes the nature

of symbolic forms, which are the ancestors of what I am calling existential symbols. Campbell understands the importance of something like religious symbols, religious intentionality, and religious meaning, even though he devotes little effort to clarifying his conceptuality. The best brief indication of his views on these matters I am aware of is found in *The Inner Reaches of Outer Space:* "A hierophany [manifestation of the sacred in a specific cultural form] occurs when through some detail, whether of a local landscape, artifact, social custom, historical memory, or individual biography, a psychological archetype or elementary idea is reflected. The object so informed becomes thereby sacralized, or mythologized. Correspondingly, a religious *experience* will be realized when there is felt an immediate sense of *identification* with the revelation. The sense of a mere *relationship* is not the same" (100).

24. A. Alvarez, *The Savage God: A Study of Suicide* (New York: Random House, 1972), 121–22.

25. Simon Wiesenthal, *The Sunflower* (New York: Schocken Books, 1976), 40–41.

26. *Power*, 22.

27. In agreement with Freud, I argue for the priority of experience over innate archetypes as a shaper of our psyche (see my "Archetypal Experiences," *Soundings* 64, 3 [1981], 237–66). But Campbell is no doctrinaire Jungian; he also emphasizes the importance of experience in shaping a worldview (see *Power*, 151, for instance).

28. Paul Tillich, *Dynamics of Faith* (New York: Harper Torchbooks, 1958), 43.

29. *Mythic Image*, 490.

4. Joseph Campbell and Eastern Religions: The Influence of India
Harold G. Coward

1. *Power*, 208.

2. Ibid., xvi.

3. Ibid., 22.

4. Ibid., 10.

5. See my *Jung and Eastern Thought* (Albany: State University of New York Press, 1985), 5ff.

6. *Power*, 11.

7. All were published by Princeton University Press in the Bollingen Series between 1946 and 1955.

8. Mircea Eliade, *Yoga: Immortality and Freedom*, trans. W. R. Trask (Princeton, N.J.: Princeton University Press, 1969).

9. *Inner Reaches*, 55.

10. Ibid.

11. Campbell virtually adopts Carl Jung's notion of the collective unconscious as composed chiefly of the archetypes or the latent ancestral knowledges of the human race. When structured by individual growth these represent universal human reactions to typical human situations, e.g., birth, death, heroic behavior, relationships with the divine and between the sexes. (See J. Jacobi, *The Psychology of C. G. Jung*, trans. R. Manheim [New Haven, Conn.: Yale University Press, 1973], 39.) For Campbell these manifestations make up the myths of religions and cultures.

12. *Power*, 23.

13. *Chandogya Upanisad*, 8.3.2.

14. *Power*, 62–64. This Hindu scripture appears in virtually every one of Campbell's books or lectures.

15. *Inner Reaches*, 56.

16. *Hero*.

17. Heinrich Zimmer, *Philosophies of India*, ed. Joseph Campbell (Princeton, N.J.: Princeton University Press, 1969), 155–58.

18. Jacobi, *Psychology of C. G. Jung*, 107–52.

19. *Power*, 70.

20. See Ananda K. Coomaraswamy, *Buddha and the Gospel of Buddhism* (New York: Harper & Row, 1964), 9–89.

21. Hermann Hesse, *Siddhartha*, trans. Hilda Rosner (New York: Bantam, 1971).

22. Zimmer, *Philosophies of India*, 160.

23. *Hero*, 149, 246.

24. *The Bahagavad Gita* 2:18 and 22, trans. R. C. Zaehner (Oxford: Oxford University Press, 1969), 130, 133.

25. *Power*, 59.

26. Ibid., 70.

27. Ibid., 14. One thinks here of the *cit* or pure consciousness of Brahman in Hinduism and the pure flowing *vijñāna* consciousness of Yogacara Buddhism.

28. *Power*, 57. Moyers summarizes Campbell's position: "The images of God are many he said, calling them 'the masks of eternity' that both cover and reveal 'the Face of Glory.'" In support of this position Campbell frequently quoted from Hindu scripture: "Truth is one; the sages call it by many names" (xvii). What Campbell did not seem to know was that this passage in its original context referred only to the various names for Brahman used within the Hindu tradition, e.g., Siva, Vishnu, etc.

29. Ibid.

30. Ibid., 162.

31. See, for example, Campbell's central use of Kuṇḍalinī Yoga in *Inner Reaches*, 63–116, *Mythic Image*, chapter 4, and *Power*, 173–74.

32. See my chapter "Jung and Kuṇḍalinī" in *Jung and Eastern Thought*, 109–24.

33. C. G. Jung, "Psychological Commentary on Kuṇḍalinī Yoga," *Spring* (1976), 16–17.
34. Taken from *Mythic Image*, 335.
35. *Mythic Image*, 341.
36. Ibid.
37. Ibid., 345.
38. See, for example, *The Laws of Manu*, vol. 25 of The Sacred Books of the East, ed. F. Max Muller, trans. G. Bühler (Delhi: Motilal Banarsidass, 1984).
39. Sigmund Freud, *The Future of an Illusion*, trans. W. D. Robson-Scott (New York: Anchor Books, 1964).
40. Sigmund Freud, *Civilization and Its Discontents*, trans. J. Riviere (London: Hogarth Press, 1975).
41. *Inner Reaches*, 63–64.
42. *Mythic Image*, 356.
43. *Power*, 174.
44. Ibid., 176.
45. Dante, as quoted by Campbell in *Mythic Image*, 364.
46. Ibid., 368.
47. *The Gospel of Sri Ramakrishna*, trans. Swami Nikhilananda (New York: Ramakrishna-Vivekananda Center, 1942), 829–30.
48. Coward, *Jung and Eastern Thought*, 122–23.
49. *Inner Reaches*, 67.
50. Ibid.
51. *Mythic Image*, 380.
52. Eliade, *Yoga*, 243.
53. As quoted by Campbell in *Mythic Image*, 381.
54. Jung, "Psychological Commentary on the Kuṇḍalinī Yoga," 17.
55. Zimmer, *Philosophies of India*, 576.
56. *Power*, 57.
57. Ibid., 58.
58. Coward, *Jung and Eastern Thought*, see chapter 5, "Jung and Karma."
59. *Power*, xv.
60. *Patañjali's Yoga Sūtras*, trans. Rama Prasad (New Delhi: Oriental Books, 1978), 2:29–32, 154–59.
61. *Power*, 186ff.
62. Ibid., 186.
63. Ibid., 187.

5. Social Factors in Mythic Knowing: Joseph Campbell and Christian Gnosis
Karen L. King

1. *Power*, 59.
2. Ibid., 5.

3. See, for example, ibid., 187.

4. See, for example, ibid., xvii, 21, 24, 29, 32, 182.

5. For a short description and critique of American individualism, see Robert N. Bellah et al., *Habits of the Heart: Individualism and Commitment in American Life* (New York: Harper & Row, 1986), especially chapter 6. See also Robert A. Segal, *Joseph Campbell: An Introduction* (New York: Garland Publishing, 1987), 74–78.

6. See Segal's discussion of the difference in approaches to the comparativist study of myth in *Joseph Campbell*, chapter 8.

7. Campbell describes himself as a "generalist." See *Power*, 9.

8. See Segal, *Joseph Campbell*, 131–32.

9. These are Campbell's terms; see *Power*, 9.

10. *Occidental Mythology*, 366.

11. See, for example, *Occidental Mythology*, 362–75.

12. *Power*, 28.

13. "Excavations in the Deep-Structure of the Theological Tradition," Occasional Papers 14 (Claremont, Calif.: Institute for Antiquity and Christianity, 1989), 8 and 9.

14. "Excavations," 11.

15. See *Power*, chapter 7.

16. Ibid., 167.

17. Ibid., 190.

18. Ibid., 31.

19. See ibid., chapter 6.

20. Torjesen, "Excavations," 11.

21. *Power*, 163.

22. *Allogenes* 52.8–13.

23. See ibid., 61.1–4.

24. See ibid., 61.25–66.38.

25. *Power*, 163.

26. See ibid., 123ff., concerning Campbell's view of the hero.

27. See Karen L. King, "Ridicule and Rape, Rule and Rebellion" in *Gnosticism and the Early Christian World*, vol. 2 of Essays on Antiquity and Christianity in Honor of James M. Robinson, ed. James Sanders, James Goehring, and Charles Hedrick (Sonoma, Calif.: Polebridge Press, 1990), 1–22.

28. *Habits of the Heart*, 142.

29. *Power*, 31.

30. Ibid., 53.

31. *Creative Mythology*, 84.

32. See ibid., 86.

33. See ibid., 88–90.

34. Ibid., 84.

35. Ibid., 94.

36. Ibid., 146.

37. *Occidental Mythology*, 364.

38. Despite the fact that Campbell duplicates their descriptions of Gnostic ethics, he would have scandalized the Church Fathers since Campbell *likes* precisely what the Fathers opposed so strongly!

39. See " 'Gnosis' and 'Askesis,' " by Michael A. Williams in *Aufsteig und Niedergang der römischen Welt* 2.22, ed. Hildegard Temporini and Wolfgang Haase (Berlin-New York: Walter de Gruyter, forthcoming).

40. As an example of libertinism, Campbell quoted at length Epiphanius's account of the Phibionites (*Creative Mythology*, 159–61). There is considerable dispute among scholars about the accuracy of Epiphanius's report, but even so Phibionite practice is not an example of attempts to break every rule set down by the wicked Creator God, as Campbell portrays it in *Creative Mythology*, 156–57. See Stephen Benko, "The Libertine Gnostic Sect of the Phibionites According to Epiphanius," *Vigiliae Christianae* 21 (1967), 103–19; *Pagan Rome and the Early Christians* (Bloomington: Indiana University Press, 1986), 64–70; and James E. Goehring, "Libertine or Liberated: Women in the So-called Libertine Gnostic Communities," *Images of the Feminine in Gnosticism*, ed. Karen L. King, Studies in Antiquity and Christianity 4 (Philadelphia: Fortress Press, 1988), 329–44; and Williams, " 'Gnosis' and 'Askesis.' "

41. See Michael Williams, " 'Gnosis' and 'Askesis.' "

42. *The Book of Thomas the Contender*, in The Nag Hammadi Library in English, ed. James M. Robinson and Richard Smith, 3d ed. (San Francisco: Harper & Row, 1988), 203–4.

43. Ibid., 157–59.

44. *Gospel of Thomas*, 113.

45. For a fuller presentation of the dualism of *The Gospel of Thomas* and a short, but insightful critique, see Segal, *Joseph Campbell*, 72.

46. See Francis T. Fallon and Ron Cameron, "The Gospel of Thomas: A Forschungsbericht and Analysis," *Aufsteig* II.25.6 (1988), 4230–36, for a short summary of the debate. What is clear, however, is that the world-affirming character of the text is due to the fact that it draws heavily upon traditions of Jewish Wisdom literature. See especially Stevan L. Davies, *The Gospel of Thomas and Christian Wisdom* (New York: Seabury Press, 1983).

47. Nag Hammadi Library, 142–43 with slight modification.

48. See ibid., 188–89.

49. See ibid., 120.

50. Ibid., 189, slightly modified.

51. See Segal's discussion in *Joseph Campbell*, 136–38.

52. It is interesting to note that when Moyers raises the issue of sexual discrimination in Western culture, Campbell's response is: "One can look back and quarrel with the whole situation, but the situation of women was not that bad by any means." Yet two sentences later he affirms without criticism that: "Women are booty, they are goods. With the fall of a city, every woman in the city would be raped" (*Power*, 171).

53. See *Power*, 65.

54. See, for example, Elaine Pagels, *The Gnostic Gospels* (New York: Random House, 1979), for a consideration of the political implications of Gnostic belief in docetism; Karen L. King, "Sophia and Christ in the *Apocryphon of John*" in *Images*, 158–76, concerning criticism of gender subordination; and "Ridicule and Rape, Rule and Rebellion," for a biting Gnostic critique of totalitarian political power.

55. See Bellah, *Habits of the Heart*, chapter 6, especially 151–52.

56. This attempt at wide community formation satisfies a deep American need to express, as Bellah puts it, "an individualism that is not empty but is full of content drawn from an active identification with communities and traditions" (*Habits of the Heart*, 163).

57. *Power*, 25.

6. Joseph Campbell the Perennial Philosopher: An Analysis of His Universalism
Robert A. Segal

1. *Power*, 38.

2. In no field is the clash between universalists and particularists more endemic than in cultural anthropology. While the initial effect of immersion in an alien culture is invariably hypersensitivity to differences, the very experience of overwhelming differences frequently spurs a quest for orderly similarities. Here, too, the opposition between those who undertake the quest and those who do not is over the importance, not the fact, of the similarities found. See, for example, the universalist Melford E. Spiro, "Culture and Human Nature," in *The Making of Psychological Anthropology*, ed. George D. Spindler (Berkeley: University of California Press, 1978), especially 355, and the particularist Clifford Geertz, "The Impact of the Concept of Culture on the Concept of Man," in his *The Interpretation of Cultures* (New York: Basic Books, 1973), especially 43.

3. Huston Smith, "Is There a Perennial Philosophy?" *Journal of the American Academy of Religion* 45, 3 (1987), 561.

4. Ibid., 558.

5. I take this example from my *Joseph Campbell: An Introduction*, rev. ed. (New York: New American Library, 1990), 185–88.

6. Smith, "Is There a Perennial Philosophy?" 563.

7. Aldous Huxley, *The Perennial Philosophy* (New York: Harper & Row Perennial Library, 1970), 236.

8. Alan W. Watts, *Myth and Ritual in Christianity* (Boston: Beacon, 1968), 15.

9. Strictly, Stace partly falls here, too: he distinguishes types of mysticism but then says that the similarities between one type and the other outweigh the differences.

10. Walter T. Stace, *The Teachings of the Mystics* (New York: New American Library Mentor Books, 1960), 14–15.

11. Ibid., 14.

12. See W. T. Stace, *Mysticism and Philosophy* (London: Macmillan, 1961), 61–81, 85–111, 131–33; *The Teachings of the Mystics*, 15–18.

13. Stace, *Mysticism and Philosophy*, 62.

14. Ibid., 106.

15. Gershom G. Scholem, *Major Trends in Jewish Mysticism*, 3d ed. (New York: Schocken Books, 1961), 5–6.

16. Stace, *Mysticism and Philosophy*, 106–7. Not Scholem but fellow particularist Steven Katz responds to Stace's attempt at encompassing Judaism within perennialism. Katz rejects Stace's rigid distinction between experience and interpretation, rejects Stace's interpretation of the experiences of Hasidic mystics, and *accepts other* facts of Stace's but dismisses their *significance:* see Steven T. Katz, "Language, Epistemology, and Mysticism," in *Mysticism and Philosophical Analysis*, ed. Katz (New York: Oxford University Press, 1978), especially 26, 50–53.

17. *Power*, 59.

18. *Hero*, 245–46.

19. Ibid., 246.

20. Ibid.

21. *Mythic Image*, 11.

22. Ibid.

23. *Inner Reaches*, 11, 99.

24. *Open Life*, 60.

25. Ibid., 68.

26. *Atlas* 2/1, 111.

27. *Power*, 135.

28. Ibid., 136.

29. "Commentary" to *Where the Two Came to Their Father: A Navaho War Ceremonial*, given by Jeff King, text and paintings recorded by Maud Oakes (New York: Pantheon Books, 1943), 61–62.

30. *Power*, 104, 11.

31. *Inner Reaches*, 43–44.

32. *Myths to Live By*, 7–8.

33. Even though Campbell is often labeled a Jungian because he is an archuniversalist, Jung himself is at least as concerned with the different meanings of the same myths or of the elements within myths as with the similarities: see my *Joseph Campbell*, 261.

34. *Myths to Live By*, 264.

35. *Inner Reaches*, 110.

36. *Power*, 49.

37. See Stace, *Mysticism and Philosophy*, 61–111; *The Teachings of the Mystics*, 14–23.

38. *Power*, 31.

39. See, for example, *Open Life*, 21–22.

40. *Power*, 141–42.

41. See Huston Smith, *Forgotten Truth: The Primordial Tradition* (New York: Harper & Row, 1976), especially chapter 1.

42. See, for example, my analysis of Campbell's interpretation of *Tristan, Parzival*, and Gnosticism in my *Joseph Campbell*, 126–37.

7. Masks of the Goddess: A Feminist Reponse
Christine Downing

1. *Power*, 165.
2. *Creative Mythology*, 366.
3. *Occidental Mythology*, 70.
4. *Primitive Mythology*, 334.
5. Ibid., 67.
6. Ibid., 313.
7. Ibid., 315.
8. Ibid., 324.
9. Ibid., 389.
10. Ibid., 325.
11. Ibid., 139.
12. Ibid.
13. Ibid., 180, 181.
14. *Occidental Mythology*, 7.
15. *Primitive Mythology*, 321.
16. *Creative Mythology*, 388.
17. *Oriental Mythology*, 112.
18. Ibid., 164
19. Ibid., 320.
20. *Occidental Mythology*, 25.
21. Ibid., 17.
22. Ibid., 22.
23. Ibid., 179.
24. Ibid., 237.
25. *Creative Mythology*, 58.
26. *Primitive Mythology*, 352–53.
27. Ibid., 388–89.
28. Ibid., 6.
29. Ibid., 60.
30. Ibid., 62.
31. *Occidental Mythology*, 70.
32. Cf. Nancy Chodorow, *The Reproduction of Mothering* (Berkeley: University of California Press, 1978), 92–110.
33. *Hero*, 3.
34. *Occidental Mythology*, 42.
35. Ibid., 149.
36. Ibid., 240.

37. Ibid., 139.
38. *Hero*, 256.
39. *Creative Mythology*, 674.
40. *Occidental Mythology*, 254.
41. *Creative Mythology*, 677.

8. The Flight of the Wild Gander:
The Postmodern Meaning of "Meaning"
David L. Miller

1. *Power*, 5–6.
2. Ibid., 9.
3. Wallace Stevens, "A Mythology Reflects Its Region," *The Palm at the End of the Mind*, ed. Holly Stevens (New York: Vintage Books, 1972), 398.
4. *Flight*, 125.
5. *Historical Atlas* 2/1, 111.
6. *Flight*, 33.
7. *Power*, 26.
8. Sam Keen, *Voices and Visions* (New York: Harper & Row, Publishers, 1974), 86.
9. *Hero*, 4.
10. Ibid., 391. Campbell is quoting Nietzsche here.
11. Keen, *Voices and Visions*, 79, 81.
12. Robert Segal, in his book, *Joseph Campbell: An Introduction* (New York: Garland, 1987), has already argued that Campbell is not a "Jungian." That will be the thrust of this essay as well, but the present argument is very different from Segal's there, and is even at odds with his critique of Campbell.
13. *Flight*, 127, 157, 169.
14. Ibid., 168.
15. Ibid., 169.
16. See *Primitive Mythology*, 229–346.
17. Ibid., 351, 151–228.
18. Ibid., 229, 242, 252–54, 263, 348. Compare *Power*, 70.
19. *Primitive Mythology*, 177, 201, 242, 253, 263, 350–51.
20. *Flight*, 129–38. Compare Campbell's later (1959) Eranos lecture, *Renewal Myths and Rites of the Primitive Hunters and Planters* (Dallas: Spring Publications, 1989), and David L. Miller, "*Homo religiosus* and the Death of God," *Journal of Bible and Religion*, 34, 4 (October 1966), 305–15.
21. *Flight*, 157.
22. Ibid., 130.
23. Jacques Derrida, *Of Grammatology*, trans. G.C. Spivak (Baltimore: Johns Hopkins University Press, 1974), lix, xxix, xliii, 143; *Dissemination*, trans. Barbara Johnson (Chicago: University of Chicago Press, 1981), viii–x; *Writing and Difference*, trans. Alan Bass (Chicago: University of Chicago

Press, 1978), 198; "La différance," *Bulletin de la société française de philosophie*, 62, 3 (1968), passim.

24. *Flight*, 178.
25. Ibid.
26. Ibid., 177–78.
27. Ibid., 190.
28. See Aniela Jaffé, *The Myth of Meaning*, trans. R. F. C. Hull (Zürich: Daimon, 1983), 140. Jaffé is referring to Jung's "late thoughts" in the autobiography, *Memories, Dreams, Reflections*, ed. A. Jaffé, trans. Richard and Clara Winston (New York: Vintage Books, 1965), 338–40; compare 171.
29. Jaffé, *The Myth of Meaning*, 141.
30. Ibid., 149.
31. Ibid., 140.
32. C. G. Jung, Collected Works: vol. IX.i, The *Archetypes of the Collective Unconscious*, trans. R. F. C. Hull (Princeton, N.J.: Princeton University Press, 1971), 32–35 [paras. 67–72] and 226 [para. 413].
33. Ibid., 229 [para. 417].
34. Ibid., 31 [para. 65].
35. *Flight*, 188.
36. *Power*, 6.
37. *Flight*, 164, 183, 192.
38. Ibid., 192.
39. C. G. Jung, Collected Works: vol. XIII, *Alchemical Studies*, trans. R. F. C. Hull (Princeton, N.J.: Princeton University Press, 1967), 12 [para. 13].
40. *Flight*, 182.
41. *Power*, 108.
42. Ibid., 114.
43. Ibid., 160.
44. C. G. Jung, *The Psychology of Transference*, trans. R. F. C. Hull (Princeton, N.J.: Princeton University Press, 1969), 36 [para. 400].
45. Ibid.
46. Jung, *Memories, Dreams, Reflections*, 196.
47. *Power*, 6.
48. *Mythic Image*, 494.

9. Harney Peak Is Everywhere: The Place of Myth in a Planetary Future
Daniel C. Noel

1. *Power*, 89.
2. See my own attempt to pursue this exploration in Noel, *Approaching Earth: A Search for the Mythic Significance of the Space Age* (Warwick, N.Y.: Amity House, 1986).
3. *Myths to Live By*, 246.
4. Ibid., 243.

5. Ibid., 244.

6. Ibid., 245.

7. Keen, *Voices and Visions* (New York: Harper & Row, 1974), 84.

8. *Power*, 32.

9. *Myths to Live By*, 258–75.

10. Ibid., 274.

11. Mailer, *Of a Fire on the Moon* (Boston: Little, Brown and Company, 1969), 471.

12. The notion of the modern artist as shaman is stated with special subtlety in the 1957 lecture "The Symbol without Meaning" (collected in *Flight*, 120–92) but can be found as early as Campbell's *Skeleton Key* in 1944 and as late as the 1981 lecture "The Way of Art" in *Inner Reaches*, 117–48, as well as throughout the conversations in *Power*.

13. Barrett, *Time of Need* (New York: Harper Torchbooks, 1973), 386.

14. Ibid.

15. *Flight*, 63–64.

16. *Hero*, 388.

17. *Flight*, 76.

18. *Occidental Mythology*, 519.

19. Ibid.

20. See René Passeron, *René Magritte*, trans. Elisabeth Abbott (Chicago: J. Philip O'Hara, 1972), 26. Campbell's indebtedness to James Joyce and Thomas Mann, together with the poet Robinson Jeffers and painters Paul Klee and Wassily Kandinsky, cannot be denied. But he seldom commented on more recent fiction, poetry, or visual art, and, as we have found, he had as questionable a view of the modern artist's actual work as of the indigenous shaman's: it is only with considerable distortion that either can be called *primarily* "metaphysical" in Professor Campbell's sense.

21. See *Black Elk Speaks*, as told through John G. Neihardt (Lincoln: University of Nebraska Press, 1932/1961), and *The Sacred Pipe*, recorded and edited by Joseph Epes Brown (New York: Penguin, 1953/1971).

22. *Flight*, 80.

23. Ibid., 116.

24. *Occidental Mythology*, 522.

25. *Creative Mythology*, 677.

26. *Myths to Live By*, 243.

27. Ibid., 245.

28. Ibid., 255.

29. See Ursula King, *The Spirit of One Earth: Reflections on Teilhard de Chardin and Global Spirituality* (New York: Paragon House, 1989); Thomas Berry, *The Dream of the Earth* (San Francisco: Sierra Club Books, 1988); and Anne Lonergan and Caroline Richards, eds., *Thomas Berry and the New Cosmology* (Mystic, Conn.: Twenty-Third Publications, 1987).

30. See James Hillman, "Peaks and Vales: The Soul/Spirit Distinction as Basis for the Differences between Psychotherapy and Spiritual Discipline,"

in Hillman et al., *Puer Papers* (Dallas: Spring Publications, 1979), 54-74; also see my *Approaching Earth, passim.*

31. *Power,* 89. The passage misquoted is in *Black Elk Speaks,* 43, n. 8. In a recent conversation with a tèacher of the Lakota language of the Sioux I was told that much of Neihardt's rendering reads more like Platonic than Sioux philosophy. I have no way of knowing whether other Sioux would agree, but this seems to accord with Sam Gill's recent account of how quickly and insidiously Euro-American categories infected expressions of Native American religion. See Gill, *Mother Earth: An American Story* (Chicago: University of Chicago Press, 1987).

32. *Power,* 89.

33. See "Twentieth Anniversary Rendezvous: Jerry Mander," *Whole Earth Review,* 61 (1988), 84-85.

34. Ventura, *Shadow Dancing in the U.S.A.* (Los Angeles: Jeremy P. Tarcher, 1985), 229. Also see his article, "Dreamtime," *Whole Earth Review,* 61 (1988), 2-6.

35. Joshua Meyrowitz, *No Sense of Place: The Impact of Electronic Media on Social Behavior* (New York: Oxford University Press, 1985); and Peter Bishop, "The Shadows of the Holistic Earth," *Spring* (1986), 59-71.

36. I should like to single out for particular praise in this regard Professor Campbell's *first* significant publication, his "Commentary" to *Where the Two Came to Their Father: A Navaho War Ceremonial,* an account given by Jeff King with text and paintings recorded by Maud Oakes (New York: Pantheon Books, 1943; reissued in 1969 by Princeton University Press). This was the opening volume in the prestigious Bollingen Series, and despite a full-blown statement of Campbell's universalism at one point, the commentary is mainly a moving evocation by a non-native (inspired by Jeff King's "horizon-bound" rendition) of the wonderfully local imagery of the American Southwest and the Navaho lifeway. Here as elsewhere Joseph Campbell's narrative *language* gives us a planet whose mythic places we can reconnect with.

10. Let Talking Snakes Lie: Sacrificing Stories
Lynda Sexson

1. *Power,* 107.

2. John 20:11-17.

3. *Hero,* 19. "Dream is the personalized myth, myth the depersonalized dream: both myth and dream are symbolic in the same general way of the dynamics of the psyche."

4. *Power,* 99.

5. Ibid.

6. Marjorie Malvern, *Venus in Sackcloth: The Magdalen's Origins and Metamorphoses* (Carbondale: Southern Illinois University Press, 1975), 4.

7. *Power,* xvi, 3, 5.

8. Ibid., xiv.

9. Ibid., 13.

10. Ibid.

11. Ibid., illustration, 90.

12. Ibid., 97.

13. Sam D. Gill, *Mother Earth: An American Story* (Chicago: University of Chicago Press, 1987), 7. He states that "...though the structure of Mother Earth may be primordial and archetypal, historically this structure was not formally identified nor did it take on importance until recently, that is, within the last hundred years. However, when it did take on this importance, it soon became widespread and important for Europeans, for Americans of European ancestry, and finally for Native Americans, and pretty much in that order historically" (152).

14. Paul Reps, compiler, *Zen Flesh, Zen Bones: A Collection of Zen and Pre-Zen Writings* (Garden City, N.Y.: Doubleday & Company, Anchor Books, n. d.), 10. From *Sand and Pebbles*, the tales of Muju Ichien.

15. *Power*, 101.

16. Ibid., 125.

17. Ibid., 141.

18. Heinrich Zimmer, *Philosophies of India*, Joseph Campbell, ed. (New York: Pantheon Books, 1951), 19–20. One of Campbell's enduring contributions is his editing of Zimmer's work, particularly this one.

19. *Philosophies of India*, 460–61.

20. *Power*, 107.

21. *Historical Atlas* 1/1, 76.

22. Victor Turner, *Revelation and Divination among the Ndembu* (Ithaca, N.Y.: Cornell University Press, 1967), 31–32.

23. *Brihadaranyaka Upanishad* IV:3:30.

24. Antonio T. de Nicolas, *Avatara: The Humanization of Philosophy through the Bhagavad Gita* (New York: Nicolas Hays Ltd., 1976), 219.

25. See discussion of this story as well as significant permutations on the theme of sacrifice in Lewis Hyde, *The Gift: Imagination and the Erotic Life of Property* (New York: Vintage Books, Random House, 1983), 58–60.

26. Frederick Turner, "Life on Mars: Cultivating a Planet — and Our selves," *Harper's Magazine*, August 1989, 34. (The article is part of a forth coming book to be published by Persea Books.)

27. René Girard, trans. Patrick Gregory, *Violence and the Sacred* (Baltimore Johns Hopkins University Press, 1972).

28. It might be fruitful, in this context, to consider the fascination Camp bell's audience has with the Western fantasy of the Orient; what is it that we still want to "discover"? This is not, however, to suggest that the conquered the forgotten, and the slaughtered did not also participate in blood-exchange stories, rites of sacrifice.

29. Mieke Bal, *Death & Dissymmetry: The Politics of Coherence in the Book of Judges* (Chicago: University of Chicago Press, 1988), 101. (Bal offers a par-

ticularly valuable commentary on Girard as well as an extraordinary feminist critique of the sacrifices in the Book of Judges.)

30. Daniel C. Noel, *Chronicle of Higher Education*, February 15, 1989.

31. Again, Campbell's patriarchal sentimentality, *Power*, 125.

32. Lu Chi, *Wen Fu*, trans., afterword, Sam Hamill (Portland, Ore.: Breitenbush Books, 1987), "The Satisfaction," IV, 14. (Emphasis mine.)

33. Plato's *Phaedrus*, the interlude (XVIII: 258E–259D). R. Hackforth's commentary (Cambridge University Press, 1952) dismisses the myth of those muse-maddened insects as something "to provide a temporary relaxation of the reader's mind by means of a charming little myth" (118). Anne Carson, in *Eros: the Bittersweet* (Princeton, N.J.: Princeton University Press, 1986) rescues the cicadas and Socrates from the mytho-phobic tradition, a tradition partially conferred on us by Plato's story of the barefoot philosopher.

34. *Power*, 230.

Contributors

Harold G. Coward, Professor of Religious Studies and Director of the Calgary Institute for the Humanities at the University of Calgary, is the author of *Jung and Eastern Thought* and *Pluralism: Challenge to World Religions*, among other books.

William G. Doty, Professor and Chair of Religious Studies at the University of Alabama/Tuscaloosa, is the author of *Mythography: The Study of Myths and Rituals*, among other works in the area of myth studies.

Christine Downing, Professor and Chair of Religious Studies at San Diego State University, is the author of *The Goddess: Mythological Images of the Feminine* and *Myths and Mysteries of Same-Sex Love*, among other books.

Walter B. Gulick, Professor of Philosophy, Humanities, and Religious Studies at Eastern Montana College, has published on issues in the psychology and philosophy of religion.

Karen L. King, Associate Professor of Religious Studies at Occidental College in Los Angeles, is the author of *Nag Hammadi Codex XI.3 Allogenes* and editor of *Images of the Feminine in Gnosticism*.

David L. Miller, Watson-Ledden Professor of Religion at Syracuse University, is the author of *Hells and Holy Ghosts*, among other books.

Daniel C. Noel, Professor of Liberal Studies in Religion and Culture at Vermont College of Norwich University, is the author of *Approaching Earth: A Search for the Mythic Significance of the Space Age* and editor of *Seeing Castaneda*.

Robert A. Segal, Associate Professor of Religious Studies at Louisiana State University, is the author of *Joseph Campbell: An Introduction* and *The Poimandres as Myth*, among other books.

Lynda Sexson, Associate Professor of Humanities at Montana State University, is the author of *Margaret of the Imperfections* and *Ordinarily Sacred*.

Richard A. Underwood, Professor of Religious Studies at the University of North Carolina/Charlotte, has published in the area of religion and culture.

Index

Achievement, 60, 99–100
Agape, 66
Agriculture, 100–101, 103
Alchemy, 21–22, 117
Allogenes, 73–74
Amor, 66–67, 72, 78, 143
Animism, 39
Annihilation, 165, 167
Apotheosis, 55, 89
Archetype, 41, 49, 53, 181–184, 186
  hero, 139
  of meaning, 115
  myth as, 160
Art, 25–27, 34, 59, 62, 68, 122–123, 131
  myth as, 27
Artist, 122, 124–126, 133
  as shaman, 204
Asceticism, 69, 74, 76–77
Assumption, 32
  patriarchal, 144
Augustine, 140–141, 159, 175
Authority, 42, 107
  of king, 101

Barrett, William, 122–130
Bastian, Adolf, 6
Being, 24, 25, 28
  nature of, 101
Bellah, Robert, 74
Benveniste, Emile, 174
Berry, Thomas, 129
Bhagavad Gita, 55–56
Bible, 102
Bigotry, 11
Black Elk, 126–128, 130–131
Blake, William, 57
Bliss, 59, 105, 132, 135, 160
  see also "Follow your bliss"
Blumenberg, Hans, 5
Body, 72, 99, 153
Bourdieu, Pierre, 161
Bradbury, Ray, 149
Brahman, 50–52, 63–64, 102, 145, 195

Brown, Joseph Epes, 127
Buddha, 53–55, 61, 64–66, 145, 148, 172–173
  death of, 166–167
  enlightened, 176–177
Buddhism, ix, 25–26, 47–48, 56, 65, 166
  Mahayana, 102
  sacrifice and, 148
  Tantric, 33

Callois, Roger, 172
Campbell, Joseph, 25, 29
  C. G. Jung and, 13–28
  Eastern religions and, 47–67
  as hero, 31–35, 40
  particularism and, 88
  as perennialist, 92–94
  universalism and, 81–94
Chakras, 57–63
Chardin, Teilhard de, 129
Childbirth, 100–103, 144
Christianity, 8, 22, 33, 56, 93
  Gnostic, 138
  mysticism and, 146
  worldview of, 188
Columbus, 24–25, 150
Consciousness, 40–41, 54, 64, 93, 143
  aesthetic, 136–137
  cultural, 171
  evolution of, 122
  human, 167–169
  independence of, 116
  individual, 144
  mystical, 87
  myth of, 114
  transformation of, 16, 36, 40, 57, 67
  universal, 56
Cosmic Order, 163–164
Cosmology, 188
Coward, Harold G., ix, 47–67
Creativity, 59
  cosmic, 165

209

Culture, 18–19, 42, 68–69, 136
  contemporary, 6–7
  international, 11
  literate v. nonliterate, 163–165
  planetary, 124, 132
  primitive, 169, 176
  public nature of, 176
  stages of, 183
  transcultural, 32
Cusanus, Nicholaus, 127–131

Dance, 9–10, 97
Darwin, Charles, 17
Death, 17–18, 101, 162–163, 167
  fear of, 41
  integration with life, 103
  mystery of, 19–20
  rebirth and, 113
Demythologization, 6–7, 135, 171
Dependency, 19
Desire, 136, 141–144
Difference, 114–116
Diffusion, 106, 163, 185
Disengagement, x–xi, 107, 112–116
Diversity, 105
Dogmatism, 5
Dominance, 71–72, 79, 99
Doniger, Wendy, xii, 5, 181–186
Doty, William G., viii, 3–12, 193
Downing, Christine, x, 97–107
Dream, 27, 49, 157–159, 205
  enigmatic, 170–171
  as literary device, 171–172
  oracular, 170
  as private myth, 38
  public, 161
  recollection of, 173–174
  types of, 170
  waking, 160
  world, 161–169, 175
Dualism, 71, 78, 141, 146, 150
  Christian, 134
  Gnostic, 77
  life-death, 105, 162
  mind-body, 16
Dumezil, Georges, 170

Earth
  center of, 118, 127–128, 130
  whole, 120
Eckhart, Meister, 63–64
Ego, 53, 63, 144, 145
  cultural, 168
  extinction of, 148
  heroic, 117

Eliade, Mircea, 5, 48, 64, 169, 182
Energy, 47, 50, 72
Engagement, 112–114
Enlightenment, 55, 73, 116, 167, 169, 172
Epic, 169–170
Erdman, Jean, 97
Eros, 66
Eternity, 140
Ethics, 74–75
  Gnostic, 75–76, 198
  social, 37
Evil, 79–80
Experience, 32, 37, 41, 69, 75, 91, 140, 194
  of being alive, 108
  extrovertive v. introvertive, 86–87
  human, 10, 52, 136
  individual, 49, 76
  interpretation of, 85
  personal, 67
  spiritual, 4, 66

Feminism, x, 97–107, 141
Fertility, 101, 104, 113
Finnegan's Wake, 15–16, 97
Fischer, Steven, 171
"Follow your bliss," 11, 13, 20, 139, 190
  see also Bliss
Forgiveness, 144–145
Freedom, 116–117
Freud, Sigmund, 15–19, 21, 60–61, 140–141, 174
  meaning of dream and, 176
Frobenius, Leo, 6, 124
Future, planetary, 118–133

Galileo, 17, 24–25
Garden, 134–135, 141–145, 151, 153
Garden of Eden, 37, 109
Geertz, Clifford, 5
Gender, 140, 142–144
Gill, Brendan, 193
Gill, Sam, 142
Gnosis, ix, 68–80
Gnosticism, 70, 139
Goddess, 72, 97–107
  fertility, 104
  move away from, 101–102
  natural history of, 98–104
Goddess mother, 106
Goodenough, Erwin R., 157
Grail, 138–139
Gulick, Walter B., viii, 29–44

Harney Peak, 118–133
Harrison, Jane Ellen, 103
Heidegger, Martin, 24
Hero, ix, 29, 44, 52, 88, 136
  analysis of, 31
  sacrifice of, 146–153
  stages of life and, 53–56
  worship of, 103
Heroism, viii, 84
Hero-journey, 15–17, 21, 88, 120
Hero myth, 89
Hero with a Thousand Faces, The, 4, 159
Hesse, Hermann, 55
Hierarchy, 74, 101
Hinduism, ix, 19–20, 47–48, 56, 65
  Vedantic, 33
Horizon, 120–122
Human nature, 140
Hunting society, 99–100, 113

Identity, 63, 105, 116
Image, 34, 123
  cult, 118
  interpretive, 160
  of mother, 105
  mythic, 121, 188
Imagination, 11, 49, 104–105, 122, 125
  religious, 27
Immortality, 135
India, influence of, 47–67
Individual, 33, 67, 113
  creative, 111
  sacredness of, 74
Individualism, 69, 75, 79, 144, 199
Individuation, 16, 21, 54
Indra, 49–53
Intentionality, 161
  human, 36
  mythical, 36–38, 40, 43, 193
  religious, 36–39, 193–94
Interpretation, 87–88, 115, 191
  of dreams, 168, 171–176
  of experience, 91
Intuition, 32
Islam, 56, 93

Jainism, 65
Jesus, 61–62, 134, 140, 145, 153,
  166–167
Journey, 13, 17
  see also Hero-journey
Joyce, James, 15–16, 23, 26–27, 97–98
Judaism, 8, 56, 75, 87, 90, 93
  perennialism and, 200
  worldview of, 188

Jung, C. G., viii, xi, 6, 61–63, 159
  archetypes and, 40–41
  collective unconscious and, 195
  Kundalini Yoga and, 57
  meaning of dream and, 176
  myth of meaning and, 114–115
  rebirth and, 65
  religious life-journey and, 13–28
  story and, 140
  yoga and, 48

Katz, Steven, 200
Keen, Sam, 111, 119
King, Karen L., ix, 68–80

Language, 34, 137, 172, 174
Laws, 74–78
Legalism, 75
Levi-Strauss, Claude, 5, 169, 181
Libertinism, 69, 77, 198
Life
  integration with death, 103
  meaning in, 34, 37–38, 47, 108
  stages of, 17–19, 53–56, 66–67
Life-journey, viii, 13–28
Literacy, 163–164
Literalism, 108–111, 121, 125–126,
  131, 140, 188
Literalizing, religious, 4–11
Logic, oneiric, 162, 168
Long, Charles H., xii, 5, 157–179
Love, 66–67, 143
  see also Agape, Amor, Eros

Macrobius, 170–171
Magic, 99, 112
Magritte, Rene, 125
Mailer, Norman, 121–130
Mandala, 21–27
Manifestation, 49, 182–183, 185
Mann, Thomas, 97–98
Marriage, 72, 143
Mary Magdalene, 134, 140
Mask, 124, 130
Materialism, 59, 76, 132
Maya, 144–145, 162
Meaning, 25, 140
  archetype of, 115
  denotative, x
  of dream, 175
  existential, viii–ix, 35, 40–44
  in life, 47
  of meaning, 112
  of myth, 31, 147, 174
  myth of, 114

Meaning (cont.)
  postmodern meaning of, 108–117
  in story, 43
  universalist v. particularist, 92
Meditation, 11, 42
Metaphor, 5, 33, 43, 56, 68
  function of, 52, 122
  interpretation of, 48–49
  language of, 137
  as myth, 48, 121
  poetic, 123
  as religion, 121
  story as, 138
  vehicle of, 128
Metaphysics, 78–79
Miller, David L., x–xi, 108–117
Monomyth, ix, 16, 31, 67, 89, 185
Moore, Marianne, 125
Morality, 77
Mother, 97, 102–105, 162
Mother Earth, 98, 142, 206
Mother Goddess, 101–102, 105
Moyers, Bill, viii–ix, 3, 47
Mueller, Max, 169
Mystery, 22
Mysticism, 39, 86, 87, 145–146
  extrovertive v. introvertive, 92–94
  Hasidic, 87–88
Myth
  as cultural resource, 10
  definition of, 108
  differences v. similarities, 81–94
  dis-placed, 130–132
  functions of, 18–20, 56, 152, 184
  Homeric, 14
  meaning in, 147, 174
  migration of, 184
  misreading of, 110–111
  place in planetary future, 118–133
  of power, 115–117
  powerlessness of, 108–110
  power of, vii, 27–28, 33
  religious, 37
  sacrificing, 138
  social factors in, 68–80
  types of, 38
Mythic Image, The, 157–179
Mythography, 8, 34
Mythologizing, 97
Mythology
  adaptive aspect of, 19, 20
  animal, 182
  biblical, 102–103
  creative, 24, 26, 160

  functions of, 27, 35–36, 98, 106–107, 111
  global, 44
  interpretation of, 109–110
  mother image in, 97
  Native American, 48
  neolithic, 112
  non-religious, 3–12
  paleolithic, 114
  patriarchal, 107
  plant, 182
  as poetry, 93, 144
  science of, 190
  v. myth, 37–38
  v. theology, 137, 187
  world, 15

Narrative, 139–143, 169, 173–175
Native Americans
  eradication of, 141–142
  mythology of, 48
Nature, 18, 72, 143
Neihardt, John, 127–128, 130
Neolithic period, 100–101
"New Age," 4, 20, 135
Nietzsche, Friedrich, 6, 15, 108
Noel, Daniel C., 9, 118–133
Numerology, 192

Opposites, 92

Paleolithic period, 99
Particularism, 81–94
  v. universalism, 199
Particularists, x, 81–82
Passion, 65, 71–72, 77, 143
Patanjali, 64–65
Patriarchy, 143
Peace, 53, 69, 80
Perception, 39, 62, 122–123
Perennialism, 85–88, 91–94, 200
Perspective, 150
  male, 104–107
  multiple, 143
  planetary, 120–121, 129
Planetization, 131
Planting society, 99–100, 113
Plato, 24, 71, 146, 157, 159, 207
Poet, 124–126, 130
Poetry, 34, 73, 144
  mythology as, 187
  "underdone," 125–126, 128
Portmann, Adolf, 18
Postmodernism, x–xi

Power, 42, 60, 99
 female spiritual, 165
 of mother, 102
 myth of, 115–117
Preuss, Theodor, 169
Priest, 23, 138
Prometheus, 116–117
Provincialism, 30, 32, 42
Psychology
 analytical, 22
 depth, 16, 93, 171
 masculine, 99
 reactive, 59
 of unconscious, 15
Psycho-spirituality, viii
Purification, 26, 64

Racism, 79
Radin, Paul, 123
Ramakrishna, 63–64
Rapture, 35, 69–70, 76–77, 105, 117
Reading, 144, 146
Reality, 57, 93, 137
Realization, 91
Reason, 70–72, 103
Rebirth, 20, 47, 65, 101
 death and, 113
 in Mother Earth, 98
 see also Reincarnation
Reflection, 9, 162
Reformation, 137
Reincarnation, 65, 67
 see also Rebirth
Religion
 demystification of, 14–15
 Eastern, 47–67
 institutional, 30, 43
 in mythology, 3–12
 organized, 93
 role of, 49
 sacrificial model of, 147
 Western, 6
Religious studies, 3–4, 6, 13–14, 34
Repression, 16
Responsibility, 12, 19, 60
 social, 66, 69–70
Revelation, 13, 126, 160
Richards, I. A., 123
Ricoeur, Paul, 5
Riddle, 150–153
Ritual, 31–33, 43, 100, 113, 146, 161,
  189
 male, 103
 religious, 9
 symbolism of, 147

Romance, 143
Romanticism, 69, 79, 141

Sacred place, 127–128
Sacrifice, 101, 134–153
 of hero, xi, 44, 142–153
 as magic, 165–166
Sanctuary, 119, 146
Savage, 121–123, 126, 130
Savior Figure, 167–168
Schlegel, Friedrich von, 6
Schleiermacher, Friedrich, 30
Schmidt, Wilhelm, 169
Scholem, Gershom, 87–88
Schopenhauer, Arthur, 6, 15, 162, 168
Seer, 125–126
Segal, Robert L., ix–x, 5, 81–94
Self, 54, 70–74
Self-discovery, 55
Self-exploration, 8
Self-nihilism, 77
Self-realization, 65
Serpent, 135, 142, 151, 162
Sex, 59, 113
Sexism, 141
Sexson, Lynda, xi, 134–153
Sexuality, 71, 181
Shaman, 23–25, 100, 114, 122–126, 133
 as artist, 204
 function of, 138
Shamanism, 112, 131
Silence, 177–178
Sleep, 160–162
Smith, Huston, 5, 82–83, 85
Social duty, 53
Social institutions, 74
Social order, 101
Social responsibility, 69–70
Society, 49, 66
Socrates, 152
Sontag, Susan, 191
Space Age, xi, 118–130
Spirituality, 4, 67
 global, xi, 124, 129
 Indian, ix
 mythic, 60
 psycho-cosmic, 121
Stace, Walter, 85–87, 90–93, 200
Stevens, Wallace, 108
Stone, Merlin, 98
Story, 9–10, 33, 37, 97, 135–139,
  140–141, 148–149
 meaning in, 34, 40
 mysticism in, 145–146
 sacrificing, 134–153

Storyteller, 31, 44
Structuralism, 181–182
Struggle, heroic, 60
Suffering, 53, 116–117
Suicide, 39
Superstition, 39
Symbol, 21, 33, 68, 98, 188
  authority of, 23
  eternal as, 52
  existential, 38–40, 42–43
  function of, 160
  religious, 38–39
  in social rites, 160
  unconscious, 174
  without meaning, 23–24, 114
  of woman, 100
Symbolism, 193–94
  feminine, 165
  mandalic, 22
  mythic, 123
  vegetative, 165
System, 140–141, 143

Technology, 40, 131–132, 139
Tenor, 123–124, 129
Theology, 5, 34, 43, 93, 144
  v. mythology, 137
Theory, 57, 172–173
Therapy, 117, 144–146
Tillich, Paul, 43
Torjesen, Karen, 71, 79
Tradition, 43
  literate v. nonliterate, 163–165
  meaning of, 34
  primitive, 163
  religious, 38
  restorer of, 32
Transformation, 17, 19–20, 56, 165
  of consciousness, 67
  human, 60
  pictorial, 189
  psychological, 59
  spiritual, 54–55, 61
  yoga and, 57–64
Transmutation, 167
Truth, 49, 52, 56, 77
  of mythology, 110
Turner, Frederick, 149
Turner, Victor, 5
Tylor, E. B., 169, 175

"Unchurched," 4

Unconscious, 49, 98
  collective, 15, 21–22, 181, 195
  psychology of, 15
Underhill, Evelyn, 86
Underwood, Richard A., viii, 13–28
Unity, 86–88
Universalism, x, 79, 81–94, 140
  perennialism and, 86–88
  v. particularism, 199
Universality, 69, 105, 161

Value judgment, 32
Values, 10–11, 17–18, 69
  American, 9
  Christian, 138
Vehicle, 123–124, 128–129
Ventura, Michael, 131
Vico, Giambattista, 14–15, 159
Victim, 146, 149–150, 166
Violence, 75, 79, 146, 150–151,
  153
Virgin, 91, 109, 147–148, 162
Virgin Birth, 61
Vishnu, 50–51, 162, 167
Vision
  global, 126
  informed, 121–122
  mythic, 40
  Native American, 126–127
  prophetic, 170

Watts, Alan, 85
Weber, Samuel, 173–174
Whalen, Frank, 190
When God Was a Woman, 98
Wiesenthal, Simon, 39
Wilde, Oscar, 146
Williams, Michael, 76–77
Wonder, 24, 27, 31
Worldview, 141, 148–150, 186
  mythical, 33
  scientific, 188
Writing, 151–152, 164, 176

Yahweh, 75, 142, 147
Yoga, 55
  dream, 62
  Kundalini, 6, 57–61, 64–65
  Tantra, 62
  transformation and, 57–64

Zimmer, Heinrich, 6, 48, 53–55, 65,
  145, 157